IGNATIUS LOYOLA
THE MYSTIC

THE WAY OF THE CHRISTIAN MYSTICS

GENERAL EDITOR

Noel Dermot O'Donoghue, ODC

Volume 5

Ignatius Loyola the Mystic

by

Harvey D. Egan, S.J.

Michael Glazier
Wilmington, Delaware

First published in 1987 by Michael Glazier, Inc. 1935 West Fourth Street, Wilmington, Delaware, 19805. ©1987 by Michael Glazier, Inc. All rights reserved.

Library of Congress Catalog Card Number: 87-82353
International Standard Book Number: 0-89453-624-9
Typography by Sandy Kelly. Cover design by Brother Placid, O.S.B.
Printed in the United States of America.

For
the Members of
the Society of Jesus,
especially

Charles H. Allen, S.J.

John V. Borgo, S.J.

William J. Burke, S.J.

Joseph J. LaBran, S.J.

Lawrence C. Langguth, S.J.

Bernard J.F. Lonergan, S.J.†

Paul T. Lucey, S.J.

Thomas G. O'Callaghan, S.J.

F. Gerv O'Toole, S.J.†

Karl Rahner, S.J.†

John R. Willis, S.J.

Contents

4. A Christ-Centered Mysticism

5. A Sacramental Mysticism of Service, Reverential Love, and the Cross

6. An Ecclesial Mysticism of Discernment, Election, and Confirmation

7. A Mysticism of Extraordinary Experiences

8. A Genuine Portrait of St. Ignatius

Editor's Preface

Up to quite recently mystics were either misunderstood or simply not understood. But now we are coming to see that, in T.S. Eliot's words, the way of the mystics is "our only hope, or else despair." As the darkness deepens, and the lights go out, those ancient lights begin to appear and to show us the way forward. They are not only lights to guide us, but are each a human countenance in which we can recognise something of ourselves—each is a portrait for self-recognition.

Unfortunately, the great Christian mystics have been generally presented as models of perfection or monuments of orthodoxy—sometimes, too, as inhumanly joyless and ascetical. Yet they were, above all else, men and women of feeling, always vulnerable, at times perhaps insecure and uncertain of the way ahead. For all that, they all shine with a special divine likeness and a special human radiance.

Each of the following portraits tries to present a true likeness of its subject, a likeness that comes alive especially in the ordinary and the everyday. In each case the author has been asked to enliven scholarship with personal warmth, and to temper enthusiasm with accurate scholarship. Each portrait hopes to be in its own way a work of art, something carefully and lovingly fashioned out of genuine material.

The main focus nevertheless is on the way in which each mystic mediates the Christian Gospel, and so gives us a deeper, richer, clearer vision of the Christian mystery. This kind of exposition demands the reader's full and prayerful attention. Each book is the story of a pilgrimage, for the mystic, the writer and the reader.

Noel O'Donoghue

Preface

When I was a senior in college, I read an article in the *Saturday Evening Post* entitled, "The Jesuits. The Pope's Commandos." Beneath the full-page photo of a scowling Father John Baptist Janssens, then superior general of the Society of Jesus, was the caption: "The Black Pope. He owes obedience to no man on earth, save the Pope." Despite the sensationalism and half-truths that filled the article, the author made one fascinating observation: Ignatius and his companions were men obsessed with God, but they used the entire world as their prie-dieu. Nothing secular was foreign to them in their praise and service of God.

I entered the Society of Jesus in 1960 and was fortunate that Father Thomas G. O'Callaghan, S.J.,was my master of novices. Within two months, I completed Ignatius' thirty-day retreat and experienced firsthand the healing and transforming power of his famous *Spiritual Exercises.* Despite my enthusiasm for the *Exercises,* however, my book list of ongoing spiritual reading compiled after the retreat did not include anything by or on St. Ignatius of Loyola. Father O'Callaghan asked ironically: "What do you have against St. Ignatius?" His question was one of the great graces of my life. To be sure, I had nothing against St. Ignatius. I simply needed direction.

Undoubtedly the most important book on Ignatius-I read as a Jesuit novice was Joseph de Guibert's *The Jesuits. Their*

Spiritual Doctrine and Practice.[1] De Guibert introduced me, as no other author has, to Ignatius' extraordinary mysticism and to the incredibly fecund spiritual and humanistic tradition of the Society of Jesus. The trinitarian, christocentric, priestly, and apostolic service aspects of Ignatius' mysticism affected me the most. I have yet to read a mystic whose personal experiences with and of the Trinity were more profound. After I began reading the Ignatian corpus, books about Ignatius, and books on Jesuit spirituality, I realized how much the Church's pastoral life has suffered from its benign neglect of the enormously rich Christian mystical heritage.

In 1969 I went to Germany for doctoral studies in theology under the direction of Karl Rahner. My dissertation[2] attempted to translate the mystical wisdom of St. Ignatius of Loyola into a contemporary framework. I found it fascinating how Ignatius' *Exercises* plunge persons into the mystery of the triune God in Christ. Equally intriguing was a mysticism that claimed to enable persons to seek and find God's specific will for them.

Rahner's theological approach had long attracted me. His theology is anchored solidly to reflection upon a central, yet often hidden, mystical experience that takes place in every human heart. He was one of the few contemporary theologians with an unabashed interest in the mystics and in their writings as a theological source. In fact, Rahner contended that his own theological thinking grew out of his experiences with Ignatian mysticism and spirituality.

According to Rahner, "a person who teaches something about mysticism is doing theology, is speaking in the light of revelation, saying something to the Church as such for the edification of the faithful."[3] For Rahner, the *Spiritual Exercises* and other mystical classics are significant because they

[1]Trans. William J. Young, S. J. and ed. George E. Ganss, S.J. (St. Louis: The Institute of Jesuit Sources, 1964) Henceforth referred to as *Jesuits.*

[2]*The Spiritual Exercises and the Ignatian Mystical Horizon* (St. Louis: The Institute of Jesuit Sources, 1976). Henceforth referred to as *Ignatian Mystical Horizon.*

[3]"Teresa of Avila: Doctor of the Church," *Opportunities for Faith,* trans. Edward Quinn (New York: Seabury, 1974), p. 123.

are a "creative prototype ... [and] a subject of tomorrow's theology."[4] Because he considered the mystics and the saints to be important theological sources, his own work has done much to heal the rift between mystical experience and academic theology.

Rahner chided me for not criticizing Ignatius enough ("Egan's hero," he wrote in the final evaluation), but I find it instructive that he himself rarely did so. In fact, the "Father of Roman Catholic Theology in the Twentieth Century" (Otto Hentz) says explicitly that his well-known "Ignatius of Loyola Speaks to a Modern Jesuit,"[5] in which Rahner puts himself in the place of Ignatius to speak to contemporary Jesuits, should be considered his last will and testament.

In 1984 my book, *Christian Mysticism. The Future of a Tradition,* was published.[6] One reviewer wondered why I began the book with an exposition of St. Ignatius of Loyola instead of the author of the *Cloud of Unknowing,* who had written much earlier than Ignatius. To repeat the reasons, which also bear on the purpose of this book, Ignatius is the mystic I know best. He is the mystic who has most influenced my own life. The more I read profitably other mystics, the more fascinated I am with Ignatius. He does not make the strong ascetical/ mystical distinction found among many spiritual writers, which has many advantages for contemporary spirituality. The Ignatian tradition is able to lead persons at any level of spiritual development into ever-deeper realms of the spiritual life. Ignatius can speak both to those in the premystical and the strictly mystical stages of the mystical journey. Finally, Ignatius' richly incarnational, kataphatic (Greek: *kataphatikos*=affirmative) mysticism finds God in all things and all

[4] *The Dynamic Element in the Church,* "The Logic of Concrete Individual Knowledge in Ignatius Loyola," trans. W.J. O'Hara (New York: Herder and Herder, 1964), pp. 86-87. Henceforth referred to as "The Logic of St. Ignatius."

[5] In *Ignatius of Loyola,* with an historical introduction by Paul Imhof, S.J., color photographs by Helmuth Nils Loose, and trans. Rosaleen Ockenden (Cleveland: Collins, 1979). Henceforth referred to as "Ignatius Speaks."

[6] New York: Pueblo Publishing Company. Henceforth referred to as *Christian Mysticism.*

things in God. This mysticism never dissociates love of God, neighbor, and world. Finally, his profound trinitarian and christocentric mysticism incarnates itself in a community of love for effective apostolic service, service that includes the social and political dimensions of human existence.

My years of Jesuit, academic, pastoral, and priestly life have brought home to me that Ignatius' and the Jesuits' pragmatic successes in asceticism, spirituality, and humanistic enterprises have obscured Ignatius the *mystic*. When I present in my classes and seminars the profoundly mystical Ignatius, students tell me they never before saw him in that light. They consider him an ascetic, an effective counterreformer, a man of considerable organizational genius, but not a mystic of such depth. Recently when I told a friend who is a member of a contemplative order that I was writing a book on Ignatius as mystic, he replied: "I *guess* he was." But to miss Ignatius the *mystic* is to miss his heart and soul. Yet, it is impossible to find a book in English that treats Ignatius strictly from the viewpoint of his mysticism. My book will attempt to rectify this situation.

I wish to thank Thomas Hamel, S.J., Charles Healey, S.J., Mary Luti, and Kevin McLaughlin for their valuable suggestions. Thanks, also, to Boston College for the faculty grant that gave me both the time and the resources to complete this book.

Feast of St. Ignatius of Loyola   Harvey D. Egan, S.J.
July 31, 1987

1

Introductory Themes

A Skewed Portrait of St. Ignatius

Ignatius of Loyola. Even today, his name evokes love or hate, rarely neutrality or indifference. Ever since he appeared with full force upon the Christian scene, many have considered him either their champion or their foe. Even within the Church that canonized him, some find it difficult to mention his name and regard him with suspicion. Nonetheless, he commands awe and respect, if only grudgingly given at times, from most who know anything at all about his extraordinary accomplishments.

Ignatius of Loyola calls forth a variety of images: founder of the controversial Society of Jesus, the "Jesuits," the pope's commandos in the Counter-Reformation; father of the advance guard of the Counter-Reformation who allegedly taught that the end justifies the means; the first "Black Pope," the first general of the Society of Jesus, a man who claimed to owe obedience to no man on earth save the pope, and who taught his followers blind obedience to the pontiff. The very name "Jesuit" is for many synonymous with a casuist, a crafty person, an intriguer. Was it not Ignatius of Loyola who inspired Dostoevsky's infamous Grand Inquisitor and Camus' unsavory Jesuit in *The Plague?*

Karl Rahner sums up why Ignatius both attracts and repels when he writes that "Ignatius has something almost of the archaic and archetypal about him."[1] Moreover, Ignatius' "individualism, deliberate reflection, his almost technically regulated self-mastery, his silence and discretion, his subordination of the highly self-aware person to the objective task, the slight scepticism which pervades everything though without lyrical self-expression or self-conscious melancholy,"[2] likewise account for the love and aversion he awakens.

A not uncommon contemporary portrait depicts Ignatius in this way. He began his "worldly" career as a courtier, a gentleman, and a soldier. After a profound religious conversion, he became a wandering pilgrim for the sake of Christ and attained heroic sanctity. For apostolic purposes, "to help souls," he decided to study and to become a priest. He gathered together a group of companions in Christ, founded a renowned religious family, established colleges, universities, and charitable institutions, and always kept his hand in directly pastoral activity. He directed a vast missionary network, and undertook sensitive diplomatic appointments. Moreover, he authored the highly influential *Spiritual Exercises,* the Jesuit *Constitutions,* and thousands of letters that demonstrate his far-reaching sociopolitical involvement.

Ignatius the Mystic

Many who know of Ignatius' well-known book, the *Spiritual Exercises,* miss its real secret—its mystical foundation. They view it as a step-by-step recipe book that teaches a will asceticism, a technically attained voluntarism, a pragmatic spirituality centered almost exclusively on practical resolutions. In fact, some contend that the *Exercises* teach only highly discursive, image-bound, and somewhat mechanical methods of prayer, suitable only for beginners, and an actual barrier to

---

[1]"Logic of Ignatius," pp. 86-87, n.1.
[2]*Ibid.*

deeper, more mystical levels of prayer.[3]

Yet, as Evelyn Underhill points out, "the concrete nature of St. Ignatius' work, especially its later developments, has blinded historians to the fact that he was a *true mystic.*"[4] This book will contend that Ignatius was an incomparable mystic whose mystical and apostolic gifts are really two sides of the same coin. Ignatius was apostolic *because* he was one of the greatest mystics the Church has ever seen. His apostolic successes are the mystical expressions, the sacramental embodiment, of his radical mysticism. In the words of one Ignatian commentator, Ignatius of Loyola was a "man of the most penetrating intellect, immense strength of will and untiring energy, averse to all fanaticism and fantasy, filled with the *purest love of God and neighbor.*"[5] Ignatius' decisive influence in the world and church history flows from his *mystical* love of God and neighbor. His mystical purification by, illumination by, and union with the God who so loved the world remains the definitive horizon within which *everything* said about him must be considered.

Because Ignatius attained the fullness of Christian life, the perfection of the life of faith, hope, and love, he was a mystic,

---

[3]One example of contemporary caricatures of the so-called Ignatian method of prayer is Paul Sauve's *Petals of Prayer* (Locust Valley, N.Y., 1974), pp. 40-46. For an example of one author who severely criticizes the *Exercises* for their alleged anti-mystical orientation, see Aldous Huxley's *Grey Eminence* (New York: Harper, 1941), pp. 94-97, 101-102. Victorino Osende, *Pathways of Love* (St. Louis: Herder, 1958), pp. 83-88, is more nuanced than Huxley, but still not insightful enough into the mystical heart of the *Spiritual Exercises.*

[4]*Mysticism* (New York: E.P. Dutton, 1961), p. 468, my emphasis. For example, *The Oxford Dictionary of the Christian Church* (ed. F.L. Cross. Second revised edition by F.L. Cross and E.A. Livingston [Oxford: Oxford University Press, 1983], p. 690) says that "Ignatius' paramount endeavours had been the reform of the Church from within, principally by education and the more frequent use of the Sacraments, and the preaching of the Gospel to the newly discovered pagan world," but merely mentions in passing that he was a mystic. William James (*The Varieties of Religious Experience* [New York: The New American Library, 1958], p. 317, my emphasis), the father of American pragmatism, writes that "St. Ignatius was mystic, *but* his mysticism made him assuredly one of the most powerfully practical human engines that ever lived." Finally, the *Encyclopedia Americana* ("Loyola, Saint Ignatius of," volume 17, p. 815) comments: "but above all it is as a leader of men that Ignatius is outstanding."

[5]Alfred Feder, *Aus dem Geistlichem Tagebuch des heiligen Ignatius* (Regensburg, 1922), p. vi, my emphasis.

and vice versa. The triune God purified, illuminated, and transformed Ignatius. The Trinity bestowed upon him full participation in its life, especially through Ignatius' radical imitation of Christ's life, death, and resurrection. The triune God called Ignatius to the very depths of his spirit and beyond all narcissistic introversion to share fully in the divine life. Ignatius courageously risked everything and surrendered totally to the Trinity. And the more deeply God united Ignatius to the inner-trinitarian life, the more deeply God united him to others in loving service to the entire world. What began in his very depths compelled Ignatius to communicate it to all dimensions of human existence.

Thus, Ignatius' mysticism is first and foremost explicitly trinitarian. But it is likewise Christ-centered, eucharistic, and priestly. Mediators, such as the Virgin Mary, the angels, the entire heavenly court, and so on, were also important for his mystical life. Ignatius found God in all things and all things in God. Karl Rahner speaks of this as a "mysticism of joy in the world."[6]

The Father placed Ignatius with Christ in order to serve. The Father promised Ignatius and his companions that he would be favorable to them in Rome. Hence, Ignatius' union with the triune God in Christ fostered a mystical community of love in service to Christ's vicar on earth. In short, Ignatius' mysticism is communal, ecclesial, and in some sense "hyper-papal" (Hugo Rahner).

What Is A Mystic?

Although a brief description of mysticism was given above, contemporary controversies surrounding the use and meaning of the word require a discussion of how the term "mystic" will be predicated of Ignatius in this book.

---

[6]"The Ignatian Mysticism of Joy in the World," *Theological Investigations* III, trans. by Kark-H. and Boniface Kruger (Baltimore: Helicon, 1967), pp. 277-293. Future reference to the *Theological Investigations* will be given as *TI*, followed by the volume number.

The word "mysticism" is commonly associated with the unreal, the otherworldly, the vague, the parapsychological, the occult, the "spooky," the poetic, or with altered states of consciousness brought about by meditation techniques or psychedelic means.[7] Ignatius' mysticism has absolutely nothing in common with these.

Some scholars contend that the essence of mysticism is found in visions, locutions, the stigmata, levitations, and isolated instances of irresistible raptures and ecstasies. To be sure, one does find many of these *secondary* mystical phenomena in Ignatius' mystical life.[8] Secondary mystical phenomena, however, do not disclose what mysticism is in its primary and strict sense—in the full sense that makes Ignatius one of the greatest mystics in Christian history.

A) Mysticism in the broad sense

Owing to the influence of Karl Rahner, Hans Urs von Balthasar, Thomas Merton, William Johnston, and others, one definition of mysticism is the implicit or explicit experience of faith, hope, and love that is rooted in all authentic human experiences. That is, mysticism is simply loving knowledge, the wisdom or knowledge of "the inner eye of love."[9] Radical fidelity to the demands of daily life, even if only through implicit, hidden, or anonymous faith, hope, and love—in short, self-surrender to the Mystery that haunts one's life—grounds the mysticism of everyday life.[10]

For example, the experience of utter loneliness; forgiving without expecting reward or even feeling good about one's selflessness; selfless love of others; radical fidelity to one's

---

[7]See my *What Are They Saying About Mysticism?* (Ramsey, N.J.: Paulist, 1982), esp. pp. 1-5. Henceforth referred to as *WATSA Mysticism.* Also see my *Christian Mysticism,* esp. pp. 1-29.

[8]For a discussion of secondary mystical phenomena, see my *Christian Mysticism,* esp. pp. 303-359.

[9]See William Johnston, S.J., *The Inner Eye of Love* (San Francisco: Harper and Row, 1978).

[10]On the mysticism of everyday life, see my *Christian Mysticism,* esp. pp. 236-237, pp. 246-249.

conscience, even when one appears like a fool before others; being faithful, hopeful, and loving, even when there are no apparent reasons for so acting; the bitter experience of the wide gulf between what we truly desire and what life actually gives us; a silent hope as one faces death—these and similar experiences are the mysticism of daily life.

Even the atheist who lives moderately, selflessly, honestly, courageously, and who silently serves others experiences the mysticism of daily life. The courageous, total acceptance of life and of oneself, even when everything tangible seems to be collapsing, is perhaps the secular mystical experience. Anyone who does this accepts implicitly the holy Mystery who fills the emptiness of both oneself and life. Because Christ's grace supports this hope against hope, the experience is at least anonymously Christian, that is, Christian in fact, if not in name.

To speak of a mysticism of daily life, of mysticism in the broad sense, offers several advantages. First, it calls attention to the astonishing fact that:

> In every human being ... there is something like an anonymous, unthematic, perhaps repressed, basic experience of God, which is constitutive of man in his concrete make-up (of nature and grace), which can be repressed but not destroyed, which is "mystical" or (if you prefer a more cautious terminology) has its climax in what the older teachers called infused contemplation.[11]

This means that *everyone* experiences, even if only vaguely and implicitly, a holy, loving Mystery who communicates its very self. God's self-communication, grace, does not invade the human situation in an extrinsic way, but is intrinsic to human nature itself. One cannot talk about being human without speaking about God's loving self-communication, if only as an offer.

This means, too, that mystical experience does not differ from the ordinary life of grace. No intermediate stage exists

---

[11] Karl Rahner, S.J., "Teresa of Avila: Doctor of the Church," p. 125.

between the everyday life of Christian faith, hope, and love and the beatific vision. The extraordinary mystical experiences of the saints never surpass supernatural faith, hope, and love. Yet, this broad definition of mysticism has disadvantages. A mysticism of daily life seems to equate piety, spirituality, and mysticism.[12] More to the point, most mystics acknowledged by the Christian tradition would agree with the author of the *Cloud of Unknowing* when he writes: "For without God's grace a person would be so completely insensitive to the reality of contemplative prayer that he would be unable to desire or long for it . . . But you will never desire to possess it until that which is ineffable and unknowable moves you to desire the ineffable and unknowable."[13] In other words, mystical prayer in the strict sense is wholly God's gift in a way *extraordinarily different.*

B) Mysticism in the strict sense

There are solid theological reasons for making a distinction between "acquired contemplation," the highest level of prayer possible through *ordinary* grace, and "infused contemplation," mystical prayer in the strict sense attainable only through *extraordinary* grace.[14] According to the mystical tradition, mystical prayer in the strict sense, or infused contemplation, cannot be attained through one's own efforts aided by ordinary grace. This prayer requires God's special activity. God gives the person something new: the explicit awareness that God is present and that the person clings lovingly to him. By actual experience the person becomes directly and

[12]Many authors, however, instinctively reject this equation. For example, in an article by M.A. Fiorito ("La vida espiritual de san Ignacio según su Diario Espiritual," *Boletín de espiritualidad,* Buenos Aires, 57 [August, 1978]), the author prefers to speak of St. Ignatius' "spiritual life" rather than of his "mystical life" because the latter makes him more admirable than imitable.

[13]*The Cloud of Unknowing and The Book of Privy Counselling,* chapter 34, p. 91.

[14]For a proponent of this position, see Joseph de Guibert, S.J., *The Theology of the Spiritual Life,* trans. Paul Barrett, O.F.M.CAP. (New York: Sheed and Ward, 1953), esp. pp. 305-352. Also see A. Poulain, S.J., *The Graces of Interior Prayer,* trans. Leonora L. Yorke Smith (Westminster, Vt.: Celtic Cross Books, 1978), esp. pp. 635-637.

immediately aware of God's loving, purifying, enlightening, and unifying presence. The person realizes that something *totally* new is occurring.

Even authors who speak of a mysticism of daily life agree that the mysticism of the saints is extraordinary and qualitatively different from that of ordinary Christians. For example, Karl Rahner contends that the saints experienced in an extraordinary *psychological* way what all Christians (and many others) experience in a more hidden way.[15]

As a minimum, then, the mysticism of the saints differs from that of ordinary Christians at least in the order of psychology and parapsychology. That is, the unusual psychology of mysticism in the strict sense gives it a special ability to root faith, hope, and love more deeply. As a maximum, the difference may be supernatural, that is, God may bestow upon the great saints extraordinary graces not given to all.

One may ask whether the terminology of acquired and infused contemplation should be changed in the light of contemporary theologies of grace, yet any new terminology must still take into account that something special and unusual happened to the saints, something that does not happen to most Christians.[16]

This book contends that Ignatius experienced not only the mysticism of everyday life—courageously living out in often humdrum love the banality and grayness of daily life. He was also, and primarily, a mystic in the strictest sense. Under God's palpable initiative and direction, he fell explicitly in love with God. At times abruptly, at times gradually, through God's special activity he realized that God is in love with us, and therefore we are all at least secretly in love with God and with each other. God's seizure of the very root of his being gave rise

[15]See my *WATSA Mysticism?*, pp. 100-103. Although Rahner maintains that the difference between the mysticism of the saints and the mysticism of daily life of ordinary Christians is not a supernatural difference, but belongs to the order of psychology and parapsychology, note the difficulties he faces in his "Logic of Ignatius," pp. 125-126, n. 24.

[16]For this reason I find the discussion of acquired and infused contemplation in William Johnston's *The Inner Eye of Love*, pp. 30-31 and *The Still Point* (San Francisco: Harper and Row, 1970), pp. 29, 138-140, requires more nuance.

to an immense longing. He was allowed no peace until he was irrevocably united to God and transformed into God's very own life.

The explicit realization that he had been grasped by the source of all love haunted and dominated Ignatius' consciousness. His normal life was interrupted, and both his inner and outer world changed. In time the inner eye of truth and the silent music of love became a permanent state, a way of life, that almost totally purified, illuminated, and transformed his entire being and consciousness.[17]

When God awakens incipient mystics to holiness, they are sensitized to their own sinfulness and vileness. Like looking at a dirty pane of glass in bright sunlight, the mystics see clearly their own dirt and filth. Their past sins may arise and torture them in a purifying way. Like the physical eye, the eye of their spirit becomes extremely sensitive to the least speck of dust. They may even experience themselves as a "lump of sin" wholly undeserving of God's mercy, forgiveness, and love.[18] Undoubtedly such experiences led St. Ignatius to wonder why "the earth had not opened and swallowed me up, creating new hells that I might suffer eternal torment in them (*Ex*, no. 60).[19] Yet this holy love purified him by removing almost all traces of disorder, inauthenticity, and barriers to integrity.

Mystics also experience profoundly their own creaturehood, the incredible distance that separates them from their Creator. Steeped in their own terrifying nothingness, they wonder why they are not simply annihilated in the presence of this all-powerful and all-consuming God. Perhaps these experiences gave rise to Meister Eckhart's unorthodox statement, "All creatures are a pure nothing: I do not say they are a bit or that

---

[17]For an excellent presentation of mysticism as a way of life, see Evelyn Underhill, *Mysticism*. This book is without a doubt the best single volume in English on mysticism. Also see Rudolph Otto, *The Idea of the Holy*, trans. John W. Harvey (New York: Oxford University Press, 1958).

[18]See *The Cloud of Unknowing*, esp. chapter 40, p. 99.

[19]A. Mottola, trans., *The Spiritual Exercises of St. Ignatius of Loyola* (Garden City, N.Y.: Doubleday, 1964). Henceforth abbreviated as *Ex* when used in the main text, followed by the standard marginal numbers.

they are something, but that they are a pure nothing."[20]

Although at this stage the mystics love God to some degree, their quest is more *self*-seeking than God-seeking. Although they taste something of God's goodness and love, the experience of their own sinfulness, radical creaturehood, and seemingly unbridgeable distance from God predominates. Hence, authentic mystics feel a deep need of penance, asceticism, cleansing, stripping, mortification, discipline, and purification. In addition to long hours of prayer, therefore, one finds in the lives of the great mystics "holy follies," or great penances to atone for the sins of their past lives.

As they are purged of sensuality and self-love, mystics gain in virtue, integrity, and an ability to surrender to God's healing and transforming love. Having stilled the surface mind, they are better able to turn inward, find interior stillness, forget themselves, and attend to God's loving self-communication. A deep, joyful sense of being united to God permeates their consciousness. They now find God in all things and all things in God.

When the living flame of love moves from the purgative to the illuminative stage, the mystic receives a sacramental expansion of consciousness, that is, loving knowledge both of God's transcendence and of God's immanence. The mystic has less need to forsake the world to find God. Yet, no matter how intimate the mystic's relationship to God may seem at this stage, the concomitant experience of separation remains. The mystic may be betrothed to God, but he or she is not yet married. The mystic possesses God, but not totally.

During this illuminative phase, the mystics experience more deeply both their enhanced, transformed self and God's intimacy. Visions, locutions, and a great variety of secondary mystical phenomena often occur. Some phenomena come from projection, repression, wish fulfillment, and the like. Others, however, are God's self-communication taking sacra-

---

[20]As quoted in *The Teaching of the Catholic Church*, prepared by Josef Neuner, S.J., and Heinrich Roos, S.J., ed. Karl Rahner, S.J., trans. Geoffrey Stevens (Staten Island, N.Y.: Alba House, 1967), p. 110.

mental hold of the entire mystic, God communicating God's self mystically through the person's spirit, soul, psyche, emotions, and body.

In short, some secondary mystical phenomena enhance the mystic's life and encourage even deeper surrender to and communion with God. At critical moments in the mystic's life, they bestow energy and deepen faith, hope, and love. Because secondary mystical phenomena "exteriorize" the mystic's inner life, because they express and reflect the mystic as a whole, these phenomena reflect both his or her God-given integration and brokenness.

But the illuminative phase of God's mystical self-communication has its dark and purgative side, too. In the initial purgative stage, the living flame of love initiated a God-given "dark night of the senses." The illuminative phase plunges the mystic into the "dark night of the spirit." It cannot be overemphasized that this mystical death is God's gift to the mystic, the dark side of God's loving, transforming self-communication. Mystical purgation, especially in this radical form, is totally God's doing. Human efforts cannot bring it about.

During this phase, the mystic has an even more heightened sense of sin. The experience of God's absence predominates, that is, the experience that God has *justifiably* abandoned the contemplative. Emotional boredom, aridity, ennui, even near despair are common. Immense longings for God, incredible loneliness, an acute awareness of God's absence, the feeling of utter impotence and isolation take possession of the mystic. Exterior trials from one's social, political, and ecclesial situation often accompany great interior trials.

Finally, the mystic realizes how trite were his or her experiences in the earlier stages of mystical ascent. The haunting presence of one's past sins, of being a lump of sin, of the incredible distance between oneself and God, of being unable to love as much as one is loved, these and similar concerns almost overpower the mystic. St. John of the Cross says this purgative contemplation "so disentangles and dissolves the spiritual substance ... absorbing it in a profound darkness" that it experiences a "cruel spiritual death." "This is like going down to hell alive."[21]

Although God prepares the mystic for this mystical death through great consolations beforehand, the mystic must possess the requisite psychological makeup to endure this stage. Mysticism in the strict sense requires extraordinary moral and psychological tenacity, as well as heroic concentration. The authentic mystics are definitely the pioneers, heroes, and geniuses of the spiritual life. There may be something in common between a Bach, Beethoven, or Mozart and any lover of music, but few music aficionados are musical geniuses. This analogy likewise holds in the spiritual life.

Mystical marriage, transforming union, or simply the unitive life is the last stage of mystical ascent. Here the mystic settles for nothing less than total union with God. He or she seeks "deification," becoming God by participation. In the words of one mystic, "For just as God is one with his being because they are one in nature, so the spirit, which sees and experiences him, is one with him whom it sees and experiences, because they have become one in grace."[22]

In short, the mystic is as closely united to God by grace as God is united to his own being by nature. The mystic becomes "God by participation." Yet, two become one while remaining two—the union remains differentiated. The mystic's person does not simply dissolve into God. In fact, the more deeply united to God the mystic becomes, the more his or her own person is confirmed in its individuality.

Transforming union bestows the conscious sharing in God's own life, power, and strength. Although external trials may continue, absolutely nothing can touch the sense of authority, conviction, serenity, peace, security, joy, and freedom at the deepest core of the mystic's being. The unitive life is characterized by an almost complete self-forgetfulness. The transformed mystic desires greatly to suffer, but in no way does this

---

[21] *The Collected Works of St. John of the Cross,* trans. Kieran Kavanaugh, O.C.D. and Otilio Rodriguez, O.C.D. (Washington, D.C.: Institute of Carmelite Studies, 1973), *The Dark Night,* book II, chapter 6, nos. 1-6, pp. 337-339.

[22] *The Cloud of Unknowing and The Book of Privy Counselling,* chapter 21, p. 186.

suffering disturb the peace and joy that flow from the ever-present, explicit awareness of living God's very own life. The mystic seeks God's honor alone, God's will, and wishes to serve God totally. In fact, the only thing separating the mystic from the beatific vision is this life itself. The mystic is united to a love that communicated itself to the point of death and resurrection for the world. Therefore, the more deeply the mystic is united with God, the deeper the union with God's creation. Having become this love by participation, the mystic becomes creative, totally self-giving, radically concerned about others—in short, spiritually fecund.

Hence, the mystics are active in attempting to heal in their own persons and through apostolic service the fragmentation found in so much of human life. They become an even deeper part of the great process of life. Wholly in God, they are likewise totally in the world. Paradoxically, they experience both absolute peace and a holy anxiety to serve God and God's world.

The mystics insist, however, that the unitive life is more than heroic virtue or the apostolate. These are the outward expressions of their union with God, the sacramental expressions of their mystical lives. Because they sought God, and God alone, they became the most powerful and impressive servants of humanity the world has ever seen.

Nonetheless, "experiences," a transformed personality, or even radical service to the world are not what gives the mystical life its real value.[23] Because the mystics sought God alone and were madly in love with God, many were also given a mystical common sense and practicality. They showed compassion and mercy to all God's people.[24] They were

[23]See Evelyn Underhill, *Mysticism*, p. viii.

[24]A constant theme in Karl Rahner's interviews toward the end of his life is that "we are here to adore God, that we have to love Him for his own sake and not only for ours' ... And if we have this relationship with Him only then is He also the God of our happiness, the God of a loving, forgiving providence." In *Karl Rahner—I Remember*, trans. Harvey D. Egan, S.J. (New York: Crossroad, 1985), pp. 107-108. The contemporary tendency to use God for human means, to turn God into a means instead of the beginning, the dynamism, and the goal of human life greatly disturbed Rahner.

socially and politically active, strongly desiring to reform the world.

In speaking about the mysticism of St. Ignatius, Karl Rahner begins by asking many questions about the exact meaning of the word "mysticism." He concludes that it is not necessary to answer every question because:

> We do after all possess a vague empirical concept of Christian mysticism: the religious experience of the saints, all that they experienced of closeness to God, of higher impulses, of visions, inspirations, of consciousness of being under the special and personal guidance of the Holy Spirit, of ecstasies, etc., all this is comprised in our understanding of the word mysticism, without our having to stop here to ask what exactly it is that is of ultimate importance in all this, and in what more precisely this proper element consists. In this sense we may now state that Ignatius was really a mystic.[25]

In the light of what has been said in this section, however, we can add that Ignatius was a mystic because he passed through special God-given stages of mystical purification, illumination, and transformation. God purged nearly all traces of sin from Ignatius' being, increased his capacity to love, and both integrated and expanded every dimension of his being around God's love itself.

This deified, christified, Spirit-filled man is a paradigm and amplifier of every person's more hidden life of faith, hope, and love. His life helps us hear the interior whispers and see the faint flickers of divine truth and love in ourselves and others. Ignatius points the way to fully authentic human life. He helps us see what our final purification, illumination, and transformation will be like. Finally, Ignatius reminds us that because God is in love with us, we are all at least secretly in love with God and with each other.

Chapter Two will give the reader an overview of Ignatius' life. We shall see that Ignatius' "pilgrim journey" was both

---

[25] "The Ignatian Mysticism of Joy in the World," pp. 279-280.

exterior and interior. Hence, we will focus on the essentials of both Ignatius' journeys. We will highlight especially the unique way God purified, illuminated, transformed, and rendered Ignatius mystically fertile in vigorous apostolic service. From this examination the genuine Ignatian portrait should emerge.

2

Loyola to Rome (1491–1556)[1]

Worldly Career in a Christian Society

Iñigo López de Oñaz y Loyola was born, most likely in 1491, at the austere castle of the Loyolas in the Basque province of Guipúzcoa. His parents, Don Beltrán Yáñez de Oñaz y Loyola and Doña Maria Sáenz de Licona, baptized him Eneco (Basque=Iñigo), in honor of the eleventh-century abbot of the Benedictine monastery of Oña, near Burgos.[2] Together with five sisters and seven brothers, he grew up in a noble

[1]See Joseph de Guibert, S.J., *Jesuits,* esp. pp. 21-109; James Broderick, S.J., *The Origin of the Jesuits* (Chicago: Loyola University Press, 1940); Mary Purcell, *St. Ignatius Loyola. The First Jesuit* (Chicago: Loyola University Press, 1957); William V. Bangert, S.J., *A History of the Society of Jesus* (St. Louis: Institute of Jesuit Sources, 1962), esp. pp. 3-45; Cándido de Dalmases, S.J., *Ignatius of Loyola. Founder of the Jesuits,* trans. Jerome Aixalá, S.J. (St. Louis: Institute of Jesuit Sources, 1985), henceforth referred to as *Ignatius; A Pilgrim's Journey. The Autobiography of Ignatius of Loyola.* Introduction, translation, and commentary by Joseph N. Tylenda, S.J. (Wilmington, Del.: Michael Glazier, 1985). Fr. Tylenda's historical commentary on the *Autobiography* is excellent. I shall use his translation throughout this book. References to this work in my main text will be abbreviated as *Auto,* followed by the appropriate paragraph number. Also see André Ravier, *Ignace de Loyola fonde la Compagnie de Jésus* (Paris: Desclée de Brouwer, 1973); Paul Dudon, S.J., *Saint Ignatius of Loyola,* trans. William J. Young (Milwaukee: Bruce, 1949).

[2]During his years of study in Paris, he called himself Ignatius, perhaps out of devotion to Ignatius of Antioch, who had such reverence for the name of Jesus.

Catholic family that prided itself on its military past and its fidelity to the king.

When Ignatius was born, Ferdinand of Aragón (1451-1516) and Isabella of Castile (1451-1504) ruled Spain, a budding European superpower. In 1492 the last Moorish fortress, Granada, fell. The ideas of the "Reconquista" influenced greatly Spain's social and political fabric. Also in 1492, Columbus, in the service of Isabella, the Catholic, discovered the New World. The world's oceans were being explored and new, exotic lands beckoned. New inventions transformed customs and morals. And Spain's spiritual ruler, Cardinal Francisco Jiménez de Cisneros, was a man intent on transforming its spiritual life.

Ignatius' family may have first earmarked him for the clerical state, but Ignatius wished to become a knight. When he was fourteen years old, he was sent to Arévalo to Juan Velázquez de Cuéllar, a relative and the chief treasurer of the royal court. Here he received the basic formation of a Spanish gentleman-courtier and attained the exquisite courtesy, gracious manners, and refinement that would serve him so well in his service to Christ.

Duels, brawls, gambling, and womanizing were also part of this life. From existing court records we know that in 1515 Ignatius and his brother, Pedro López, were arrested and prosecuted for nocturnal misdemeanors that were "most outrageous."[3] Ignatius says about this period of his life: "Up to his twenty-sixth year he was a man given to worldly vanities, and having a vain and overpowering desire to gain renown, he found special delight in the exercise of arms" (*Auto,* no. 1).

In 1517 Ignatius became part of the retinue of Antonio Manrique de Lara, duke of Nájera, viceroy of Navarre. In the service of the duke, Ignatius defended Navarre's main city, Pamplona, with a force of only a few hundred men against an army of some 12,000, commanded by André de Foix, lord of Esparros. His *Autobiography* gives a vivid account of this important incident that would change his life dramatically:

[3]See Joseph de Guibert, S.J., *Jesuits,* p. 23.

Thus he was in a fortress under attack by the French, and while everyone else clearly saw that they could not defend themselves and thought that they should surrender to save their lives, he offered so many reasons to the fortress' commander that he talked him into defending it. Though this was contrary to the opinion of all the other knights, still each drew encouragement from his firmness and fearlessness. When the day of the expected assault came he made his confession to one of his comrades in arms and after the attack had lasted a good while, a cannonball hit him in a leg, shattering it completely, and since the ball passed between both legs the other one was likewise severely wounded.

As soon as he fell wounded the others in the fortress surrendered to the French who, after they had gained control, treated the wounded man very well . . . After being in Pamplona some twelve or fifteen days they transported him on a litter to his home country (*Auto,* nos. 1-2).

Character of the Preconversion Ignatius

At the beginning of June 1521, Ignatius made the difficult and torturous journey to his home at Loyola. This was the first of many journeys that would transform him into a knight of Christ, who would seek and fulfill God's will in all things. Interior journeys, that is, conversion experiences, often accompanied Ignatius' exterior journeys.

What type of person was this Ignatius who was on the brink of conversion, the soldier soon to become the Montserrat penitent, the Jerusalem pilgrim, the missionary, the mystic, "an instrument united to God"?

First, Ignatius' Basque heritage must be emphasized. The Catholic faith was his by inheritance. It was ineradicable, it coursed through his very blood. Yet while the Basques may have lived their faith with sincerity, it was so deeply ingrained that it was often taken for granted or sinned against.[4] Faith was a matter less of dogmas than of family, land, tradition, identity, honor, pride, bravery, and pious practices. The fabric of daily Catholic life was expressed in pilgrimages, piety, and devotion to patron saints.

Ignatius' own faith was mediocre before his conversions. In 1515 he and his brother were convicted of committing rather serious crimes with deliberation and perfidy. Even after an initial conversion, he chased after a Moor to "strike him with his dagger" because he felt "he had done wrong in allowing a Moor to say such things about Our Lady and that he was obliged to restore her honor" (*Auto*, no. 15). Proud, sensuous, and driven by violent and powerful impulses, Ignatius demanded adventure and glory.

Before the battle at Pamplona, however, "he made his confession to one of his companions in arms" (*Auto*, no. 1). In danger of death after his wounds, he received the Church's sacraments (*Auto*, no. 3). Without any talk of a miraculous cure, Ignatius attributed his recovery to St. Peter, for whom he had special devotion (*Auto*, no. 3). In short, he took his faith seriously when his own situation became rather serious. He also possessed the natural virtues of honesty, loyalty, and fidelity (*Auto*, no. 12).

Ignatius' first biographer, Pedro de Ribadeneira, S.J., related that Ignatius the courtier and soldier was both cheerful and a lover of the good life. Fastidious with his grooming and clothing, very proud of his thick, blond hair, he was much influenced by tales of chivalry. He also possessed delicate sensibilities, enjoyed music, and loved to gaze at the sky and the stars (*Auto*, no. 11).[5]

---

[4]For example, there were two illegitimate children among Ignatius' siblings. Sexual escapades were viewed far more sanguinely in Ignatius' world. The sincere piety of Philip II, for example, did not appear to him or to his contemporaries as susceptible of doubt merely because he had a mistress and fathered a bastard or two. He was thought of as even holier than his father because he had only *one* mistress.

[5]*Vita Ignatii Loyolae*, in *Fontes narrativi de S. Ignatio de Loyola et de Societatis Iesu initiis*, vol. IV, ed. D.F. Zapico, C. de Dalmases, P. Leturia (Rome, 1943-1960). Henceforth the *Fontes narrativi* will be abbreviated as *FN* followed by the appropriate volume number.

Many commentators correctly depict Ignatius as a natural leader. With a forceful and courageous will, he could rally others in desperate and seemingly impossible situations, as at Pamplona. Although the others knew clearly that they could not hold out, Ignatius convinced them to defend the fort. His "fearlessness" and "firmness" gave them courage. Throughout his life Ignatius showed the ability to lead, to rally people, to stir them up for a great cause. Fiercely loyal to his companions, and to himself, he helped them reach their full potential. Quickly sizing up situations, people, and the connections between facts, Ignatius got right to the heart of any matter.

These character traits show how Ignatius handled his injury. Because his leg had been poorly set at Pamplona and injured again on the road to Loyola, another "operation" was required. But this left the wounded leg shorter and also produced an ugly bone protuberance. Despite almost dying from this "butchery," as he called it, Ignatius demanded yet another operation. His determination never to be a cripple, never to be ugly—in short, a tenacious vanity—pushed him "to endure this martyrdom to satisfy his personal taste" (*Auto,* no. 4). Moreover, "he never uttered a word nor did he show any sign of pain other than clenching his fists" (*Auto,* no. 2). For the sake of vanity and career, Ignatius eschewed both suffering and death.

The preconversion Ignatius was definitely hyperactive, vital, and exceptionally resistant to fatigue, grief, and suffering. He possessed tremendous physical and emotional courage, even in the face of incredible suffering and the possibility of death. His self-mastery and powerful will thrived on opposition, contradictions, and obstacles. Where others would capitulate, Ignatius' tenacity and magnanimity drove him on. He simply could not capitulate once he had set his mind to a task.

Unlike a St. Augustine, Ignatius was neither articulate nor eloquent. His variegated writings do not exhibit literary mastery or stylistic purity. Oddly too, very little from his university education found its way into these writings.[6] But his

---

[6]Although not an intellectual, Ignatius studied hard and obtained a solid education. But it must be emphasized that his philosophical and theological studies seem *not* to

writings do disclose a unique form of mysticism, an overpowering fullness of lived and experienced faith, hope, and love. They disclose a meticulous attention to the details of the spiritual life, a power of concentration born out of an inner richness of spiritual love and vision.

Also unlike St. Augustine, Ignatius' intelligence was less comprehensive than penetrating, less cerebral than real. The firm structure of his thinking is more organic than organized. His is a temperament and vocabulary of action, a realist's intelligence, a powerful imagination, yet lacking in color and highly developed symbolism.

One of Ignatius' reveries reveals much about him. He says about himself:

> He dreamed what he would achieve in the service of a certain lady and thought of the means he would take to go to the land where she lived, the clever sayings and words he would speak to her, and the knightly deeds he would perform for her. He was so enraptured with these thoughts of his that he never considered how impossible it was for him to accomplish them, for the lady was not one of the lesser nobility, neither was she a countess, nor a duchess, but her station was much higher than any of these (*Auto*, no. 6).

In summary, Ignatius needed to achieve, to transcend himself, to do the "impossible." He feared neither suffering nor death. But he did fear meaninglessness, mediocrity, and a banal existence. Here is a man who could dominate even his fiery temperament for the sake of an ideal. He loved the embellished life, and deep down he loved himself, his glory, and his honor that he pursued relentlessly. Without destroying this powerful personality, God was about to transform it for the greater love and service of Jesus Christ.

---

have enriched his mysticism in any perceptible way. In fact, no more than the slightest traces of the philosophy and theology he studied can be found in his writings.

Loyola (August–September 1521)

During his long, boring convalescence at Loyola, Ignatius spent many hours daydreaming about the stories of courtly love found in *Amadis of Gaul* and other trashy literature of his day. Because there were no books to his liking he finally read and pondered available books: Ludolph of Saxony's four-volume *Life of Christ* and James of Voragine's *Flos Sanctorum (The Golden Legends)*, which depict the great saints as knights of God dedicated to the eternal Lord, Jesus Christ. When he read about the life of Christ and the saints, he thought: "Dominic did this, so I have to do it too. Saint Francis did this, so I have to do it too" (*Auto,* no. 7).

Ignatius' reveries were heroic; he wanted only what was "great and difficult." Even the impossible seemed "easy of performance." Ignatius spent hours at a time thinking of how he could attain the woman of his dreams or rival the saints in their great penances. "One day," however, "his eyes were partially opened" (*Auto,* no. 8). God awakened him to his sinful past and instilled in him a tremendous desire to atone for these sins by "going barefoot to Jerusalem and of eating nothing but vegetables and of imitating the saints in all the austerities they performed..." (*Auto,* no. 8).

Ignatius perceived that his enjoyment in daydreaming about "worldly matters" quickly vanished, leaving him "dry and unhappy" (*Auto,* no. 8). Yet daydreams about imitating the saints in their holy follies not only consoled him, "but even after they had left him he remained happy and joyful" (*Auto,* no. 8). The insight that some thoughts left him sad while others consoled him struck him forcefully. "Little by little he came to perceive the different spirits that were moving him; one coming from the devil, the other coming from God" (*Auto,* no. 8). In this way Ignatius came to realize that joy was a sign of God, sadness a sign of the devil. From this seed grew his famous rules for the discernment of spirits.

During this time God coaxed Ignatius to explore his interior life and sensitized him to the evils he had done. Ignatius' intense sense of sin made him fear that no penances would suffice "to give vent to the hatred that he had conceived against himself" (*Auto*, no. 12). Nonetheless, "on fire with God" (*Auto*, no. 9), he "felt within himself a strong impulse to serve Our Lord" (*Auto*, no. 11), that is, Christ the incomparable leader and eternal prince depicted in *The Golden Legends*. Yet Ignatius was still seeking himself. This conversion was a beginning, but Ignatius still loved himself far more than he loved Christ.

At Loyola Ignatius began to experience phenomena that are most important for understanding his mysticism: visions. For example, the Virgin Mary holding the child Jesus appeared to Ignatius and purified him of much from his past life. As he said, "He felt so great a loathsomeness for all his past life, especially for the deeds of the flesh, that it seemed to him that all the images that had been previously imprinted on his mind were now erased" (*Auto*, no. 10).

Ignatius knew this vision came from God because of its lasting effects. "Thus from that hour ... he never again consented, not even in the least matter, to the motions of the flesh. Because of this effect in him he concluded that this had been God's doing" (*Auto*, no. 10).[7] This vision transformed Ignatius decisively and permanently, as would his many other future visions. And because most of his visions *confirmed* his holy desires, he held them in high regard.[8]

---

[7]Antonio T. De Nicolas (*Powers of Imagining: Ignatius of Loyola. A Philosophical Hermeneutic of Imagining Through the Collected Works of Ignatius of Loyola With a Translation of These Works,* [New York: State University of New York Press, 1986], *Auto*, no. 10, p. 251) translates this section as, "Thus from that hour ... he never had the slightest inclination to the things of the flesh." Tylenda's translation, however, is closer to the original Spanish, "... nunca más tuvo ni un mínimo consenso en cosa de carne...," than de Nicolas'. Commentators are divided on the question of Ignatius' infused chastity. That is, was Ignatius spared all inclinations of the flesh or given only the strength never to consent to the least of these motions? The above suggests that God cauterized Ignatius' memory in such a way that temptations would not arise from past memories. The Spanish text does *not* say, however, that "he never had the slightest inclination to the least motions of the flesh." Nonetheless, Ignatius' writings give no indication of problems in the area of chastity. They do show, however, that temptations to *vainglory* plagued this man of such self-mastery. On this point, see Dalmases, *Ignatius,* pp. 73, 83.

[8]Ignatius relates: "With these holy desires of his, the thoughts of his former life were soon forgotten and this was *confirmed* by a vision ..." (*Auto*, no. 10, my emphasis).

Ignatius saw God's hand in the gift of infused chastity. Even Ignatius' brother and his household "interpreted his external change . . . to mean that an interior change had taken place" (*Auto*, no. 10). He no longer wanted to serve the woman of his dreams, the woman of high earthly position. Now he wanted to serve the Mother of God herself, the Mother of such a Son. This marks the beginning of Ignatius' Marian mysticism.

Still another aspect of Ignatius' mysticism budded at Loyola, spiritual conversations.[9] Because God touched Ignatius so deeply, he had to express his experiences of God in some way. At Loyola he began to speak to members of the household "about the things of God," and realized that "he thus brought much profit to their souls" (*Auto*, no. 11). Converted by God to God's service, Ignatius discovered that he could convert others to the same service through spiritual conversations.[10]

At Loyola, Ignatius continued to pray, to read, and to write. He jotted down for future reference the things that deeply impressed him about the life of Christ and of the saints. His *Spiritual Exercises* began to emerge. While the mysticism of St. John of the Cross sought sacramental expression in his lovely poems and in commentaries, Ignatius' *Spiritual Exercises* were not to be read for their literary quality, but were to be made and lived for their transforming quality.

Ignatius wrestled with the question: how could he best serve Christ, in imitation of the saints? Should he enter the Carthusian monastery in Seville? Become a poor, unknown pilgrim wandering throughout the world? The decision had to be postponed, for the thought of a penitential pilgrimage to

---

[9]For an excellent discussion of this aspect of Ignatius' mysticism, see Thomas Clancy, S.J., *The Conversational Work of God. A Commentary on the Doctrine of St. Ignatius of Loyola Concerning Spiritual Conversation, With Four Early Jesuit Texts,* (St. Louis: Institute of Jesuit Sources, 1978). Clancy, however, does not treat Ignatius' spiritual conversations as mystical in origin, that is, as the exteriorizaton or sacramentalization of his inner experience of God.

[10]Many mystical classics teach that mystical graces come to full fruition only when they have been revealed and expressed to others. Ignatius' spiritual conversations, therefore, are the sacramental expression of his inner mystical life and an attribute of his service mysticism.

the Holy Land became all-consuming. He made the pilgrimage the following year.

The Pilgrim Sets Out

With his brother, Pedro López, Ignatius set out at the end of February 1522 to spend a night vigil praying at the pilgrim shrine of the Virgin Mary in Aránzazu. Leaving his brother at Oñate, he set off alone for the famous Benedictine abbey of Montserrat. Although Ignatius was "still blind" (*Auto*, no. 14) in spiritual matters and concerned only with the externals of outdoing the saints, he nonetheless desired ardently to follow God. Also, he did not desire to imitate the saints in their great penances to atone for the sins of his past life, but "to please and appease God" (*Auto*, no. 14).

Again he entered into spiritual conversation, this time with a seemingly pious Moor. But the Moor offended Ignatius by questioning our Lady's perpetual virginity (*Auto*, no. 15). Thinking he must avenge her honor, Ignatius hastened after the Moor to give him a taste of his dagger. Coming to a fork in the road and not knowing for certain what to do, he gave his mule free rein. The mule took the highway, not the village road that would have led him to the Moor. For Ignatius it was the work of "Our Lord."

In a large town near Montserrat, Ignatius purchased a sackcloth garment and gave his good clothing to a poor man. He gave his mule to the monastery and placed his dagger and sword before the Black Madonna at the nearby shrine. Following a three-day preparation for a general confession, he spent the night of March 22, 1522, in vigil before the altar of the Madonna. Ignatius' spirituality and mysticism was often expressed in sacramental confession, as his *Spiritual Exercises* attest (*Ex*, no. 44).

Instead of staying on the royal highway to Barcelona, where he would book passage for the Holy Land, Ignatius detoured to Manresa, an out of the way place. He intended to spend a few days jotting "down a few items in the book which he guardedly carried with him and which afforded him much consolation" (*Auto,* no. 18).[11] Little did he know what was in store for him there.

Manresa (March 1522–February 1523)

Ignatius initially intended to remain in Manresa for only a few days, but he stayed almost a year, emerging a radically transformed man. He indulged his thirst for long hours of prayer and great penances and neglected his appearance. He continued to jot things down in a notebook he seemed always to carry.

Important changes took place in his soul. Periods of great depression, doubts, temptations, disgust, and scruples alternated with periods of great spiritual joys. A mysterious serpentlike vision consoled him greatly. Yet so painful were the tortures from the scruples about his past sins that he almost committed suicide. And once again ill health brought him to the brink of death.

So intense were these fluctuations of consolation and desolation that Ignatius found himself asking: "What kind of a new life is this that we are now beginning?" (*Auto,* no. 21). God himself awakened Ignatius as if "from a dream" (*Auto,* no. 25). Through mystical discernment, Ignatius discovered the root of his scruples. "Thus he decided, and with great clarity of mind, never to confess his past sins again and from that day forward he was free of his scruples, and he held it for certain that our Lord had desired to set him free because of His mercy" (*Auto,* no. 25).

Ignatius experienced the time from Pamplona to Manresa as a period of ascetical and mystical purgation, his dark night of the senses and the spirit. The physical and psychological trauma from the leg injuries, several torturous operations, enforced confinement during convalescence, bouts with

---

[11]He also left the royal highway because he feared he might "meet many who knew and respected him" (*Auto,* no. 18). His fear of vainglory made him flee "the esteem of others...."

spiritual torpor, apathy, and scruples, the serious temptation to suicide—all this was part of Ignatius' mystical purgation.

At Manresa, God treated Ignatius like a "schoolboy" and deepened his desire to serve God by stamping indelibly into Ignatius' very being indescribable and unforgettable mystical visions of the Trinity, Christ's humanity, Christ's presence in the Eucharist, and of how the world was created. These experiences contained such purity and certitude that even "if there were no Scriptures to teach us these matters of faith, he would still resolve to die for them on the basis of what he had seen" (*Auto,* no. 29).

What may well be the most important event in Ignatius' life, however, took place on the banks of the nearby river Cardoner. Ignatius describes the event in this way:

> As he sat, the eyes of his understanding began to open; not that he saw a vision, but (he came) to understand and know many things, matters spiritual and those pertaining to faith and learning. This took place with such great clarity that everything appeared to him to be something new. And it happened to enlighten his understanding in such a manner that he thought of himself as if he were another man and that he had an intellect different from the one he had before. Though there were many, he could not set down the details of all he understood then, except by saying that he experienced a great clarity in his understanding; so much so that in the whole course of his life, through sixty-two years, even if he put together all of the many gifts he had had from God and of all the many things he knew and added them all together, he does not think they would amount to as much as he had received on that one single occasion (*Auto,* no. 30).[12]

This holistic, or architectonic, experience transformed Ignatius into "another man" with a different intellect, a man who had encountered God "in such nearness and grace as is

[12]As translated by Antonio de Nicolas, *Powers of Imagining, Auto,* no. 25, pp. 260-261.

impossible to confound or mistake."[13] The Cardoner experience altered radically the way Ignatius viewed all reality. His particular mystical horizon was born. Although not a vision, the architectonic, holistic quality of this experience unified everything and put it in a new light. Moreover, it was more than a mystical vision of oneness that excluded particulars, for he also understood new things about faith *and learning.*

Along with severe penances, long hours of prayer, and the profoundest of mystical experiences, Ignatius worked at St. Lucy's hospital caring for the poor, the sick, and the dying. Ignatius' service mysticism, centered on the corporal works of mercy, remained intrinsic to his mysticism until the day he died.

He likewise continued his spiritual conversations. "He spent time in helping other souls who came there to see him about spiritual matters..." (*Auto,* no. 26). Although spiritual conversations to help others remained part of his apostolate, "after he left Barcelona, he completely lost eagerness to search out spiritual persons" (*Auto,* no. 37). Ignatius had advanced so far in the ways of God that only God could guide him now.

Cardoner transformed him in other ways. For example, he abandoned his penitential excesses and, for the sake of the apostolate, paid more attention to his appearance. He also resolved firmly "to have only God as his refuge" (*Auto,* no. 35). This meant trusting absolutely in divine providence in matters of food, clothing, shelter, financial aid, and the like.

In addition, his fear of vainglory intensified. He feared nothing more than to be thought a saint.[14] Also evident was his lifelong practice of placing himself in the hands of his confessor when he could not make up his mind because "he saw good reasons on both sides..." (*Auto,* no. 36).

[13]Karl Rahner, S.J., "Ignatius Speaks," p. 11.

[14]See *Auto,* nos. 12, 32, 36. Did this fear also have *some* basis in the fact that a "saint's fame" might attract the attention of the Inquisition?

The Holy Land (February 1523-Lent 1524)

On February 18, 1523, Ignatius left Manresa for Barcelona and then sailed to Italy. After receiving Pope Hadrian VI's blessing for his pilgrimage to the Holy Land, Ignatius walked to Venice to await passage. Although many tried to dissuade him from this trip, Ignatius "felt a firm certainty within his soul that he would find a way of going to Jerusalem, and of this he had no doubt" (*Auto*, no. 40).

He accepted money to pay his way, but soon regretted it because he thought "this showed a lack of confidence in God" (*Auto*, no. 40). The new man of Manresa no longer trusted in nor sought himself. He now sought "the greater glory of God" (*Auto*, no. 36). Hence, "he wanted to put his trust, love, and hope in God alone" (*Auto*, no. 35), even to the point of taking nothing "with him as rations except his confidence in God" (*Auto*, no. 44). Despite a serious illness and against a doctor's advice, his decision to go to Jerusalem remained unshakable.

During this period, his visions were entirely Christ-centered. They brought him intense consolations, confirmed his desire to go to the Holy Land, and granted him the unassailable certitude that he would succeed in this pilgrimage (*Auto*, no. 42). Christ undoubtedly had transformed the tenacity and courage Ignatius had shown at Pamplona for his own greater love and service. Setting sail on July 14, he arrived at Haifa on August 24 and entered Jerusalem on September 4, 1523, experiencing a "joy that did not seem natural" (*Auto*, no. 45).

He experienced this same kind of joy and consolation in visiting the holy places. So great was the Holy Land's impact on Ignatius that "he made a firm decision to remain in Jerusalem, constantly visiting the Holy Places" (*Auto*, no. 45) and "helping souls."

Because of the parlous political situation there, however, especially for Christians, the Franciscan provincial asked Ignatius to leave the Holy Land. When Ignatius brushed the danger aside, the provincial explained that he had power from the Holy See to expel and even to excommunicate anyone who disobeyed. Although Ignatius previously had been absolutely convinced that it was God's will for him to be in Jerusalem, he obeyed without hesitation.

The ecclesial dimension of Ignatius' mysticism comes to the fore on this occasion. He left, not because he was afraid of Church authority, but because he experienced God's will in and through it. As he says, "it was not our Lord's will for him to remain in the Holy Places" (*Auto,* no. 47).

Before leaving, however, an incident occurred that illustrates Ignatius' sacramental literalism. He desired to serve Christ totally and to walk where Christ himself had walked. He relates:

> On the Mount of Olives there is a stone from which our Lord ascended into heaven, and his footprints are still visible there. This was what he wanted to see again ... he slipped away from the others and went by himself to the Mount of Olives ... After he had said his prayers with heartfelt consolation he got the desire to go to Bethphage. While there he remembered that on the Mount of Olives he had not taken full notice of the direction in which the right foot was pointing and which way the left. On his return there he gave his scissors, I think, to the guards so that they would let him enter (*Auto,* no. 47).

Rich in incarnational faith and his Christ-centered mysticism, he paid strict attention to the least detail of the mysteries of salvation, especially the mysteries of Christ's life, death, and resurrection. A powerful and consoling vision of Christ immediately after this episode confirmed his sacramental attentiveness (*Auto,* no. 48). This Christ-centered attentiveness found its way into his *Spiritual Exercises.*[15]

---

[15]For example, the first or second "prelude" to each Ignatian meditation or contemplation is a "mental image of the place ... when the meditation or contemplation is on a visible object" (*Ex,* no. 47). See also nos. 65, 91, 103, 112, 138, 151, 192, 202, 220, 232. In no. 125, Ignatius would have the exercitant, in imagination, embrace or kiss the place where the persons being contemplated sit, walk, and the like. He had certainly done this in the Holy Land. See M. Olphe-Galliard, "Composition de lieu," *Dictionnaire de spiritualité ascétique et mystique* I, pp. 1321-1326.

Yet another fact of Ignatius' service mysticism emerged during this period. We read that "the pilgrim began writing letters to spiritual persons back in Barcelona" (*Auto,* no. 46). This lifelong apostolate of correspondence has left us a legacy of almost 7,000 letters.[16] Ignatius' zeal to help souls by reforming private and social abuses is shown for the first time. Not only did he courageously dress down drunken soldiers intent on rape, but he also upbraided some in the ship's crew for their lewdness, and was almost thrown overboard. In summary, Jerusalem marked Ignatius in a way second only to Manresa. He would never forget what it meant to be near Christ in his historical existence. This Christ-centeredness in all its concreteness and detail is foundational to his mysticism. Ignatius would remain the Jerusalem pilgrim even during his many years in Rome as general of the Society of Jesus. But by that time he had learned that all the world's highways lead to a spiritual Jerusalem in Christ. Jerusalem also gave the 30 year-old Ignatius something that not even Manresa did. He turned to "spending some time in studies in order to help souls" (*Auto,* no. 50).

[16]See *Letters of St. Ignatius of Loyola,* trans. William Young, S.J. (Chicago: Loyola University Press, 1959). Henceforth referred to as *Letters.* Also see, *St. Ignatius of Loyola. Letters to Women,* ed. Hugo Rahner, S.J. (New York: Herder and Herder, 1960) and *Counsel for Jesuits. Selected Letters and Instructions of St. Ignatius of Loyola,* ed. Joseph Tylenda, S.J. (Chicago: Loyola University Press, 1985). Dominique Bertrand, S.J. ("Ignatius von Loyola und die gesellschaftliche Dynamik seines Lebensprogramms," *Geist und Leben* 4 [1986], pp. 261-269) shows convincingly that Ignatius' letters never focus merely on ideas or limit themselves to ideology. They always center on a practical, immediate goal. They deal with problems in the spiritual life, in the field of education, in obtaining sufficient revenues. They also deal with issues related to the Society of Jesus, the Church, its hierarchy, and heads of state. In short, they articulate a mysticism that flows into social-political service. They are an excellent source for watching the growing Society of Jesus take on an ever-increasing number of apostolates and how this Society interacted with the wider social and political communities. They show, moreover, Ignatius' ever-widening network, how he and his men entered into relationships with all levels of the society of their day.

Student Years (1524-1535)

As Ignatius left the Holy Land in October 1523 for Barcelona, he was about to enter a distinctive period of his inner pilgrimage.[17] Both Manresa and the Holy Land had been places of incredible mystical invasion. His "primitive Church" at Manresa transformed him into a new man by gifting him with the highest mystical favors. His Christ-centered mysticism came to full bloom in Jerusalem.

For the sake of a more effective apostolate, however, Ignatius began studying in Barcelona "with great diligence" (*Auto,* no. 54). He progressed so rapidly in his studies that after two years, "his teacher told him that he was now ready to pursue the liberal arts and that he should go to Alcalá" (*Auto,* no. 56). So he went to Acalá during Lent of 1526 to study "the logic of Soto, the physics of Albert, and the Master of the Sentences" (*Auto,* no. 57).

At Alcalá, we find something new. Not only did Ignatius give his spiritual exercises but he also engaged "in explaining Christian doctrine, and by these means he brought forth fruit for the glory of God" (*Auto,* no. 57). Intrinsic to Ignatius' mysticism is his lifelong commitment to teach catechism, especially to the young. Jesuits still take a vow to show special concern for the education of youth.

During his stay at Alcalá, Ignatius used the expression "spiritual exercises" for the first time. At this stage, however, he focused on instructing people on the commandments, the virtues and vices, basic prayers, and preparing for the sacrament of confession in order to have a more fervent communion. From the latter came the "first week" of the *Spiritual Exercises* in their present form.[18] Because he was not

---

[17]See *Auto,* nos. 54-86. Especially good on this period is Joseph de Guibert, S.J., *Jesuits,* pp. 33-36, and André Ravier, *Ignace,* pp. 463-468.

[18]The *Spiritual Exercises* are organized into four "weeks," a designation based not on seven chronological days, but upon the graces granted as a result of each week's exercises. In fact, "The time should be set according to the needs of the subject matter" (*Ex,* no. 4). The "first week" corresponds to the "purgative way" (*Ex,* no. 10); the "second week" the "illuminative way" (*Ex,* no. 10); the "third week" and the "fourth

a priest, however, Ignatius denied explicitly that he "preached" (*Auto,* no. 65). During this period his mysticism of apostolic service was highly successful. He attracted crowds wherever he went, and a few listeners became his companions. Even when he was imprisoned, many came to listen to him (*Auto,* no. 60). He also continued his work with the poor, the sick, and the dying. Ignatius was never far from a hospital.

Ignatius was so successful teaching catechism and Christian doctrine and giving spiritual exerises, that "rumors began flying throughout that region .... This matter reached the Inquisition in Toledo" (*Auto,* no. 58). He and his companions were jailed by the Inquisition for almost two months under suspicion of being *Alumbrados,* members of pietistic movements who claimed the direct and constant inspiration of the Holy Spirit. These "illuminated ones" rejected not only Church hierarchy but also all Church rules and regulations. The inquisitors found no error in what Ignatius and his companions taught, however, nor anything objectionable in their manner of life. Nonetheless, they were ordered not to wear their pilgrim's robes and forbidden to speak on matters of faith and morals until they had completed their studies.

To continue their apostolic life while they studied, they departed for Salamanca in June 1527. After only two weeks in the city, they were again imprisoned for about three weeks. The collection of notes that would eventually become the *Spiritual Exercises* were examined and the companions questioned about their teachings. Once again, they were acquitted, with the stipulation that they not teach the distinction between mortal and venial sin until they had completed their course of studies.

Teaching this distinction must have been extremely important to Ignatius. He says: "He found great difficulty in staying at Salamanca *because this prohibition on determining which are mortal and which are venial sins closed the door on his helping souls"* (*Auto,* no. 70, my emphasis). For this reason,

week" are perhaps a means of deepening, in the light of Christ's passion and resurrection, the "election," or resolution made at the end of the second week.

Ignatius resolved to go to Paris to study. There he seems to have had little difficulty with religious authorities, perhaps because he spent far less time talking to people about the things of God.

His encounters with the inquisitors reveal certain facets of Ignatius' mysticism and spirituality. He rejoiced in being jailed for the sake of Christ (*Auto,* no. 61). Nonetheless, he did everything in his power to clear his name and to prove his orthodoxy for the sake of his apostolate.[19]

His straightforward, but discreet, manner with the inquisitors and his demand that they put in writing his acquittal on all counts indicate that he was neither an ecclesial sycophant nor an ecclesial iconoclast. He obeyed their commands, but moved out of their jurisdiction in order to continue his apostolate. His is a mysticism of critical reverence for Church authority; both words must be emphasized.

His mystical life developed in yet another way during his student days. He gathered companions around him in mystical friendship who had "the same desire to help souls" (*Auto,* no. 71). Ignatius strove to build a *mystical* body of men united by love of Christ and of each other. His spiritual exercises forged such a body. More attentive to persons than to structures, Ignatius appreciated strong and endowed personalities, men born to be missionaries. His companions were to have the same spirit, elan, and apostolic zeal as Ignatius.

On the Feast of the Assumption, August 15, 1534, at the chapel of St. Denis in the Montmartre section of Paris, Ignatius and his first companions—the priest Peter Faber, Francis Xavier, Simon Rodriguez, Diego Laínez, Alfonso Salmeron, and Nicolas Bobadilla—took private vows of poverty and chastity, and vowed also to make a pilgrimage to the Holy Land. If this pilgrimage proved impossible because

---

[19]For a saint who had such an intense desire to be "considered worthless and a fool for Christ" (*Ex,* no. 167) and to suffer insults for the sake of Christ, it is instructive to note how adamant Ignatius was in maintaining both his good reputation and that of his companions. On this point, see his letter to John of Avila, January 24, 1549, in *Letters,* pp. 182-184. Quoting Augustine, Ignatius says, "Our life is necessary for ourselves, *our reputation for others*" (p. 183, my emphasis).

of the wars between Venice and the Turks, they would place themselves at the Pope's disposal. As Christ's vicar, they reasoned, he was in the best position to determine Christianity's greatest needs.

When Ignatius was preparing for ordination to the priesthood in 1537 and for his first Mass in 1538, he received powerful spiritual visions and consolations almost routinely. But "it was *just the opposite when he was in Paris*" (*Auto*, no. 95, emphasis mine). Diego Laínez, one of Ignatius' first companions, spoke of this period in Ignatius' mystical life as one distracted by study.[20] Likewise, Ignatius' first biographer, Pedro de Ribadeneira, attests that during his student years, Ignatius went to Mass regularly, but spent only a short amount of time at prayer.[21]

It can be asked, therefore, if Ignatius' mysticism atrophied or simply ceased during his student days. Commentators agree that this period was not as rich in mystical favors as Manresa and the later time in Venice, Vicenza, and Rome. Nonetheless, it was still a period of intense mystical union with God, very much in continuity with Manresa. Ignatius' mystical life seems to have consolidated itself, becoming more settled and integrated throughout his student days. He still lived a mystical life of union with God, but one with far less dramatic secondary phenomena.

We have no precise information about his prayer during this time, but if Ignatius prayed for approximately seven hours a day at Manresa, what is really meant by "shorter" periods of prayer during studies? Some witnesses claim that Ignatius the student spent long hours of prayer at night and experienced raptures, mystical tears, and the like.[22] Ignatius' letters throughout this time speak convincingly of doing everything for God's greater praise and service, of imitating the suffering and humiliated Christ, and of desiring only to seek and to do

---

[20] *FN* I, p. 430.
[21] *FN* II, p. 474.
[22] See Joseph de Guibert, *Jesuits,* p. 34.

God's will.[23] His "indifference" to everything except God's will, his spiritual liberty, and his desires during this period also give definite evidence of a person united mystically with God in Christ.

Yet Ignatius' student years taught him that absolute poverty, long hours of prayer, great penances,[24] the apostolate, and studies are not easily reconciled. While later on he would teach that God can still be found in all things, even in a life of intense study,[25] the mature Ignatius forbade long hours of prayer and severe penances.

According to Laínez, Ignatius had a natural disinclination—a great repugnance—for studies. They seemed so insipid when compared with the things of God.[26] When Ignatius tried to study, great spiritual joys and insights distracted him (*Auto,* nos. 54, 82). Yet he discerned these to be temptations and promised his teachers to attend class "as long as I can find bread and water... to support myself" (*Auto,* no. 55). Because of this firm decision "he never again had those temptations" (*Auto,* nos. 55, 82). Permeated with the love of God, his powerful will had made a firm decision in Christ. Hence, mystical judgments and decisions, not only mystical affectivity, are characteristic of Ignatius' mysticism.

In order to give himself totally to his studies, Ignatius gave up something very dear to his heart: speaking with people about the things of God (*Auto,* no. 82). He even gave up speaking about God with Peter Faber, one of his first companions in Paris, because this distracted them from their studies. For a more effective apostolate, moreover, the pilgrim who had once renounced all honors opted to receive academic titles and honors. He even gave up begging daily because this

---

[23]For one example, see Ignatius' November 10, 1532, letter to Isabel Roser, *Letters,* pp. 9-11.

[24]Although Ignatius mitigated his penances during this period of study, he did not do away with them entirely. See *Auto,* nos. 55, 79.

[25]See Ignatius' letter of May 27, 1547, to the fathers and scholastics at Coimbra and his letter of June 1, 1551, to Father Anthony Brandao, in *Letters,* pp. 120-130, 237-243.

[26]See *FN* II, pp. 90-91.

practice left him little time for studies. Instead he went to Holland and England during the semester breaks to beg sufficient funds to last him the academic year.

Azpeitia—Venice—Rome (1535-1537)

Ignatius' early leg injuries, the operations to satisfy his vanity, his excessive fasts and penances, and severe gallstones destroyed the "robust health" he had once enjoyed.[27] At this stage he became so ill that a friend suggested he travel to Spain to breathe once again his native air. Leaving Peter Faber in charge of his Paris companions, Ignatius departed for Spain early in April 1535.

Against the wishes of his relatives in Azpeitia, he lived in the hospital for the poor. There he ministered to the sick and dying, worked with the local officials to set up a social-service center for the poor, preached repentance, taught catechism, exhorted people to frequent confession and holy communion, continued his apostolate of "spiritual conversations," labored at reforming the local clergy, and attended carefully to his relatives' spiritual life. Thus, Ignatius' mysticism expressed itself, in part, in a mission of reform. Convinced that his work brought people "fruit" through God's grace (*Auto,* no. 88), he vowed to continue even if only one person came to him.

After convalescing, Ignatius arrived in Venice in December 1535 to await the arrival of his companions from Paris who had been joined by Paschase Broët, Jean Codure, and Claude Jay. Here he continued studying theology, giving the spiritual exercises, engaging in spiritual conversations, and working with the poor, the sick, and the dying.

On January 8, 1537, Ignatius' companions joined him in Venice in order to travel to the Holy Land. While awaiting favorable circumstances for this trip, they worked among the poor, the sick, and the dying. During Lent Ignatius sent companions to Rome to seek Pope Paul III's (1536-1549) permission for their pilgrimage and for priestly ordination.

On June 24, 1537, Ignatius, Xavier, Laínez, Rodriguez,

---

[27]See Dalmases, *Ignatius,* pp. 287-289.

Bobadilla, and Cordure were ordained by the Dalmatian bishop of Arbe, Vincenzo Nigusanti. To prepare for their first Mass, they retired to the abandoned monastery of San Pietro in Vivarolo to spend forty days in solitude, poverty, penance, and deep prayer.[28] Ignatius' companions said their first Masses sometime in September. Ignatius put his off for almost a year, however,—perhaps hoping to celebrate it in the Holy Land.

Ignatius, Faber, and Laînez continued to live in Venice, but in an unusual degree of solitude. The other companions carried out apostolic activities in Northern Italy. Ignatius' mysticism during this period became increasingly more pronounced. Spiritual visions, tremendous supernatural visitations, deep assurances by God about certain matters, and consolations so numerous as to be called "routine" accompanied his preparations for the priesthood. In fact, Ignatius mentions Manresa in conjunction with these mystical favors: "He enjoyed great supernatural visitations of the kind that he used to have when he was in Manresa" (*Auto*, no. 95). This was Ignatius' second Manresa, and the beginnings of his priestly mysticism.

In the midst of this powerful mystical invasion, however, what was Ignatius' deepest desire? "After he had been ordained a priest, he decided to wait another year before celebrating Mass, preparing himself *and praying to Our Lady to place him with her Son*" (*Auto*, no. 96, my emphasis). This all-consuming desire to be with Christ to serve is a hallmark of Ignatian mysticism.[29]

The war between Venice and the Turks forced the cancellation of the pilgrimage to the Holy Land. In October 1537, therefore, Ignatius, Faber, and Laínez went to Rome to place

---

[28]Hugo Rahner, S.J. (*The Vision of St. Ignatius in the Chapel of La Storta*, trans. Robert O. Brennan, S.J. [Rome: Centrum Ignatianum Spiritualitatis, 1979], p. 21—henceforth abbreviated as *Vision of La Storta*) calls this period of solitude, poverty, penance, and prayer a desert idyll. Ignatius and his companions desired to use this retreat time to deepen their ordination graces for a more effective apostolate. The Jesuit period of tertianship, or "third year of probation," after studies and ordination undoubtedly has its origin here.

[29]This desire, of course, must be present or prayed for at crucial moments when making the spiritual exercises (*Ex*, no. 147).

themselves at the Pope's disposal and to identify themselves as the *Compañia de Jesús,* the companions of Jesus. When Ignatius and his companions were approximately six miles north of Rome, he went into the small chapel of La Storta on the Via Cassia to pray. Here he "felt a great change in his soul and so clearly did he see God the Father place him with Christ, His Son, that he had no doubts that God the Father did place him with His Son" (*Auto,* no. 96).

Commentators agree that La Storta illuminated, transformed, and confirmed Ignatius in ways comparable to that of Manresa and Jerusalem.[30] He saw the "Eternal Father" with his cross-bearing Son. The eternal Father spoke interiorly to Ignatius' heart: "I shall be favorable to you [plural] at Rome," and "I want you, my Son, to take this man as your servant." Then Christ said to Ignatius: "I want you [singular] to serve *us* [Father and Son]."

Hence, the Father united Ignatius to Christ for his service. Christ also confirmed the Father's wish. Moreover, the Father promised Ignatius and his companions that something significant would transpire in Rome. The graces of La Storta confirmed Ignatius' trinitatian, christocentric, service, and ecclesial mysticism.

Rome (1537-1556)

Ignatius and his companions entered the Eternal City through the "Porta del Popolo" in mid-November 1537. In Santa Maria Maggiore on Christmas 1538, Ignatius celebrated his first Mass. Since he could not say his first Mass in the Holy Land, perhaps the special créche in this church reminded him of Bethlehem. In any case, Rome was to be his home and his Holy Land until he died. In fact, one Ignatian commentator calls Ignatius the "apostle of Rome."[31]

[30]The best commentary in English is undoubtedly Hugo Rahner, S.J., *Vision of La Storta.* André Ravier (*Ignace,* p. 471) maintains that one must speak of the vision*s* at La Storta, or at least of *two* distinct experiences.

[31]See Dalmases, *Ignatius,* pp. 179-189.

In Rome Ignatius continued his service mysticism by giving the spiritual exercises, teaching children catechism, preaching, and hearing confessions. Moreover, the extreme Roman winter of 1538-1539 gave Ignatius and his companions the opportunity to care for the freezing, the sick, the poor, the hungry, and the dying. Once again, severely slandered by some, Ignatius was summoned before the authorities. As was his wont, he demanded a formal clearing of his name (*Auto,* no. 98).

Pope Paul III sent Broët and Rodriguez to Siena during March of 1539. Because this action might permanently disperse their informal group, the companions began to think: Should they form a religious order vowing obedience to one in their group and live according to formal constitutions, or should they remain a loosely knit group working to "help souls"? After about a month of prayer, deliberation, and communal discernment, they decided to form an order.[32]

Ignatius considered his ten companions to be cofounders of the Society of Jesus. He viewed them as the pillars of the order and used them for the most important projects. Once he entrusted an apostolic work to them, he left almost everything to their on-the-spot decisions. Because they brought about God's greater service and praise, he valued the great prestige and the high esteem in which they were held.[33]

By the end of June 1539, Ignatius had written the *Prima Instituti Summa,* the first sketch of the future constitutions of

---

[32]For a more detailed treatment, see below, Chapter Six, "Communal Discernment of Spirits."

[33]It is relatively well-known that Ignatius set up two classes of priests in the Society: the professed of solemn vows (whether four or three) and the spiritual coadjutors with simple vows. The professed were the spiritually mature of the Society, and with more than ordinary learning. They were often sent to the crisis spots in the Jesuit missions, especially those places where establishing the faith might mean martyrdom. The professed became provincials and rectors of important colleges. Despite their relative immobility in such positions, Ignatius considered them more as missionaries than administrators. On this matter, see *The Constitutions of the Society of Jesus,* trans., introd., and commentary George Ganss, S.J. (St. Louis: Institute of Jesuit Sources, 1970), "Note B The Diversity of Grades among the Priests," pp. 349-356. Henceforth referred to as *Constitutions* in the footnotes, but *Const,* followed by the appropriate marginal number, when cited in the main text.

the *Compañía de Jesús,* known today as the Society of Jesus. Its members were to be "companions among themselves who loved one another, but subjects of Christ as their captain for whom they had even greater love."[34] Because of his great desire that these constitutions receive papal approval, Ignatius requested that 3,000 Masses be said with this intention. After careful examination of this document by the Holy See, on September 27, 1540, Pope Paul III issued *Regimini militantis ecclesiae,* which approved the formation of the order and gave Ignatius and his companions the right to elect a general and to draw up formal constitutions. The first official papal mission was to teach catechism. The Pope also gave them the powers to be apostolic preachers, that is, they could preach in the Roman churches and in public places.

On April 2, 1541, Ignatius was elected general. He declined on the grounds that he would rather obey than command. He was elected again on April 13, but consented to his companions' decision only after submitting the matter to his confessor.

On April 22, 1541, the group pronounced their vows in the church of St. Paul Outside the Walls. The Companions of Jesus had formed a single body, had a single heart and soul, obeyed a single leader, and had Christ for their head. Through the mystical inspiration of Ignatius, they had become a mystical body, united by mystical friendship. In short, they were the church in miniature, bound together by the Holy Spirit in faith, hope, and love.

In 1544, Pope Paul III's *Iniunctum nobis* removed the sixty-member limit to the Society. It also allowed Ignatius to admit those who were not yet priests. On July 21, 1550, Pope Julius III's *Exposcit debitum* solemnly established the order.

A new, but simple, house was erected in 1544 next to the church of Sancta Maria degli Astalli, which contains the

---

[34]*Constitutions,* p. 349. Ganss also writes: "For Ignatius and his early followers, therefore, the title *Compañía de Jesús* meant an organized group of associates, cooperating through charity, who had Christ as their head and were totally at His service" (p. 349). For an excellent introduction to the genesis and meaning of the term, *Compañía de Jesús,* read Supplementary Notes, note A, pp. 345-349.

image of the Madonna della Strada. Here Ignatius became the "immobile missionary" who directed—as his almost 7,000 letters attest—his men's incredible number of national and international apostolic and missionary activities. The Pope's letter, *Pastoralis officii,* approved formally Ignatius' famous and influential *Spiritual Exercises,* published for the first time five years before his death.

Yet even as the very busy Jesuit general, Ignatius continued to mission personally. Preaching, spiritual conversations, teaching catechism, giving the spiritual exercises, hearing confessions, working with Jesuit novices and the like, remained part and parcel of Ignatius' service mysticism.

At the beginning of 1541, Ignatius' companions commissioned him to write the *Constitutions.* They approved them in 1551 after Ignatius spent years laboring over them. As one Jesuit historian writes:

> The *Constitutions,* immensely influential on newer religious congregations, especially of women, is one of the basic documents in the history of religious life in the modern era. With their apostolic bent, their departure from monastic form, their engagement with the world, their alertness to current needs of the Church, their harmonization of intense activity and habitual prayerfulness, they have given vision to many holy souls inspired to raise up other religious families.[35]

Because of Ignatius' apostolic experiences and his emphasis upon mobility, the *Constitutions* renounced monastic choir, a code of penances obligatory on all, a fixed garb, capitular government, the regular ministry of religious women, and the foundation of any women's branch. High ecclesiastical offices were to be avoided, except in the foreign missions where great sufferings and hardships were involved.

In addition to his directly apostolic activities and the organizing and directing of the Society of Jesus, Ignatius animated social works of charity in Rome by founding

---

[35] William V. Bangert, S.J. *A History of the Society of Jesus,* pp. 43-44.

confraternities of charitable persons to finance and direct such operations. In keeping with his ecclesial mysticism of service and his pragmatism, he sought formal papal approbation of these projects.

Ignatius also did everything in his power to make it easier for converts from Judaism to receive baptism. He worked for the repeal of laws that exploited Jewish catechumens and established two houses to receive them.

He also collaborated personally in the work of the House of St. Martha, founded to take care of women who renounced prostitution. He contributed as well to the *Compañia delle vergini miserabili,* a confraternity that helped young girls escape from houses of prostitution.

Ignatius' great love and compassion for the sick has already been noted. Sparing no expense when his own men were ill, he toiled for the physical and spiritual well-being of all Rome's infirm. He was greatly concerned that the sick receive the sacraments. He even lobbied for a law requiring physicians to refuse their service to the sick if the patient refused to receive the sacraments after three requests. Of course, it must be remembered that this mitigated the decretal of Innocent III, confirmed by the Fourth Lateran Council in 1215. This decretal prescribed that physicians stop treating patients who refused to receive the sacraments after only one request.

Ignatius was also affiliated with the Roman Confraternity of the Hospital of the Holy Spirit and that of the Blessed Sacrament. Moreover, he cared for the orphans of Rome, working in conjunction with the Confraternity of St. Mary of the Visitation of Orphans.

Ignatius founded the Roman College for young men entering the Society and for outside students. He also established colleges in Jerusalem, Cyprus, and Constantinople to serve Christ among the "heathens."

To check the spread of Lutheranism in Italy, he promoted the tribunal of the Inquisition in Rome. Because of a different sociopolitical situation in Germany, he opposed its establishment there. This significant Counter-Reformation figure insisted upon great charity towards the reformers. He did not believe in polemics, but instead tried to get them "to love us" by frequent spiritual conversations. His great desire for Jesuit missions to Ireland, Britain, and Poland must be understood in this context.

The "immobile missionary" worked likewise to establish the Society throughout Europe, the Americas, India, and the Far East. Dear to his heart was the mission to Ethiopia. He toiled vigorously to bring about the union of the Coptic Church of that country with the Roman Church.

Under pressure from his companions, Ignatius dictated his quasi-autobiography, *A Pilgrim's Journey,* to Father Louis Goncalves da Câmara in 1555.

On the evening of July 30, 1556, Ignatius sensed that he would soon die. He asked his secretary, Polanco, to obtain the Pope's blessing. Polanco assured him that he would not die and that he would go to the Pope the following morning. Ignatius told him: "Do as you wish. I entrust myself to you."

Ignatius died at 5:30 that morning, praying, "O my God." The Society of Jesus numbered approximately 1,000 members with 100 houses throughout the world. Pope Paul V beatified him on July 27, 1609 and Pope Gregory XV canonized him on March 12, 1622. Pope Pius IX declared him the patron of spiritual exercises and retreats.

During his Roman years, Ignatius' mystical life reached full maturity. About this period Ignatius said of himself:

> he had often offended God after he had begun to serve Him but had never consented to mortal sin; and that his devotion, that is, his ease in finding God, was always increasing, now more than ever in his entire life. At whatever time or hour he wanted to find God, he found Him. Also that he now has many visions, especially those ... of seeing Christ as the sun. This often occurred when he was speaking of important matters and those visions came to him as corroborations (*Auto,* no. 99).

This attests to Ignatius' profound union with God in his Roman days. Both Nadal and Louis Goncalves da Câmara marveled at Ignatius' intense recollection and experience of God's presence in the midst of absorbing work. Even Ignatius' radiant face attested to his rich mystical life.[36] His "devotion," or ease at finding God, likewise enabled him to find God's will easily. Ignatius was guarded with words; he despised exaggeration. Thus the following words he dared to say about himself reveal the depths of his mystical life.

> After having read the lives of many saints, unless indeed there had been in their lives more than had been written, he would not readily consent to exchange with them what he himself had known and tasted of God . . . he was coming to believe that no other man could be found in whom God had so joined these two things together as in himself: on his part to have sinned so much, and on God's part to have granted so many graces. . . . When he sinned he desired to experience some suffering either sensible or spiritual, such as the privation of graces or of consolations and the like; and this experience never came to him, but it seemed that God visited him all the more.[37]

Hence, Ignatius' ease in finding God continued to grow. As St. John of the Cross maintains in *The Living Flame of Love,* the final stage of the mystical journey involves the deepening of transforming union.[38] Faith, hope, and love—that is, union itself intensifies—albeit not necessarily their content. Yet one Ignatian commentator asks an important question about this summit period.[39] How could the Roman years be the summit

---

[36]See *FN* II, p. 123. Also see Louis Goncalves de Câmara *Mémorial,* trad. Roger Tandonnet, S.J. (Paris: Desclée de Brouwer, 1966), nos. 175 & 183. Fr. Câmara is the Jesuit to whom Ignatius related his *Autobiography.*

[37]*FN* II, pp. 339, 473-474. Quoted by Joseph de Guibert, S.J., *Jesuits,* p. 49.

[38]Father de Guibert (*Jesuits,* pp. 55-56) says about Ignatius: "Neither does his mystical union appear as a 'transforming union' which gives the life of the soul a foundation in the life of God, and in some way causes a man's own personal life to disappear within that of the Christ who lives in him." When I speak of Ignatius' transforming union, however, I mean that Ignatius was *transformed* by and *united* with the triune God in Christ—and that he experienced this as such. De Guibert's use of the term "transforming union" seems unnecessarily narrow.

[39]See Joseph de Guibert, *Jesuits,* pp. 40-41.

if Ignatius himself seems to name Cardoner as the summit? As he said, "during the course of his entire life—now having passed his sixty-second year—if he were to gather all the helps he received from God and everything he knew, and add them together, he does not think they would add up to all that he received on that one occasion" (*Auto,* no. 30). Moreover, Nadal himself supports this when he states:

> Here (we are dealing with) the vision at the Chapel of St. Paul along the river where he was so raised out of himself that the fundamental laws of all things were revealed to him. In this elevation, he seems also to have received knowledge (about the establishment) of the whole Society: for if anyone asked him why he arranged something a certain way and not another way, he was accustomed to say "I rely on Cardoner for this." And he added that this grace exceeded all other graces he had ever received.[40]

De Guibert contends that Manresa was not the culmination of Ignatius' mystical life, although Manresa was the touchstone period in his life. He never received so much in so short a time as he did at Manresa, but further progress and deeper graces did occur. The experience provided the outline and the guiding, unifying principle by which he would discern and interpret later events. But it did not give him a detailed blueprint for writing his works or for establishing the Society of Jesus. Even architectonic experiences require the enfleshment that only history can provide.

Ignatius' mysticism of divine providence, by which he was able to surrender to the God of salvation history, helps one understand what Ignatius related to Laínez and Ribadeneira, namely, that "what he had received at Manresa ... was little compared with what he was receiving then ... those matters were the first rudiments and exercises of his novitiate, but quite different was the [present] impression made by the

---

[40] *Monumenta Nadalis* (Letters and instructions of Ignatius' companion, Jerónimo Nadal), ed. M. Nicolau, vol. V, p. 782. Quoted by Hugo Rahner, *Vision of La Storta,* pp. 118-119). Henceforth abbreviated as *M Nad,* followed by the volume number.

graces in his soul. What preceded was only a sketch, and something like an initiation."[41]

Ignatius continued to receive visions that confirmed him in important matters, but his union with God eventually transcended all visions and representations. Nadal attests that Ignatius lived in union with God in a state of pure spiritual knowledge.[42] His mystical life eventually went beyond all secondary phenomena, as numerous as these had been in his life. Radical faith, hope, and love—total interior liberty brought about by the deepening of transforming union—dominated the mature years of his life.

Because Ignatius was a genuine mystic, he still had a strong sense of sin. And as we have seen above, even at the age of sixty-two, only three years before his death, he remembered the many ways in which he had offended God (*Auto*, no. 99).

He also continued until he died a practice considered only for beginners: frequent examinations of conscience. Ribadeneira tells us that "he has always kept this habit of examining his conscience every hour, and of asking himself with careful attention how he had passed the hour."[43] This inner alertness is an essential part of Ignatius' mysticism of discernment, decision, and of having this decision approved by God. To seek and to find God's will in all things required an acute sensitivity, a mystical sensitivity, to the least sign of God's will.[44]

God, by way of great mystical graces, converted Ignatius from the courageous but vain courtier and soldier to the magnanimous Manresa and Jerusalem pilgrim. Ignatius' secret, however, is not the pure evangelical mysticism of these periods—this is, the pure liberty of the road. His secret was his

[41]*FN* I, p. 140. Quoted by de Guibert, *Jesuits*, p. 40.

[42]*FN* II, p. 315.

[43]*FN* II, p. 345. Quoted by Joseph de Guibert, S.J., *Jesuits*, p. 66. It can be argued that Ignatius had discovered the ascetical foundations of mysticism and the mystical dimension of asceticism.

[44]Seeking and finding God's will in all things seems to be the heart of Ignatius' mysticism and spirituality. This is persuasively argued by Rodrigo Mejia Saldarriaga, S.J., *La Dinámica de la Integración Espiritual* (Rome: Centrum Ignatianum Spiritualitatis, 1980), aptly subtitled, *buscar y hallar a Dios en todas las cosas*, that is, seeking and finding God in all things.

mystical ability to find God's will in all circumstances—and to adjust his life accordingly.

He may have needed Manresa and Jerusalem, but his mysticism eventually forced him to undertake illustrious ministries in Paris and Rome without losing its inner evangelical spirit. The pilgrim who detached himself from family, country, clothing, grooming, and the like, became so attached to God that his only desire was to be with Christ to serve.

This meant that "the praise and glory of the Divine Majesty being equally served and in order to be more like Christ our Lord, I desire and choose poverty with Christ rather than riches, insults with Christ filled with them rather than honor, and desire to be considered worthless and a fool for Christ who was so considered rather than to be esteemed as wise and clever in this world" (*Ex*, no. 167).

Yet God's service often demanded that Ignatius seek honors and take up again what he had so radically renounced in his pilgrim years. His indifference to everything except God's greater service allowed him to re-enter the world of secular honors, power, and wealth. Because his service mysticism never lost sight of its primary goal, God's will, everything else was simply a means to be used with evangelical "compromise" to execute this will. "Loyola's Epitaph" says it all: "to suffer no restriction from anything, however great, and yet to be contained in the tiniest thing—that is divine."[45]

Plunged to the very depths of the trinitarian life, placed by the Father with Christ to serve, Ignatius knew that God's self-communication works sacramentally, that is, in ways very earthly and human. Thus because he was so deeply in love with the triune God in Christ, he was also a mystic of joy in the world.

He was, therefore, a mystic in the strictest sense of the word in that God's love dominated and possessed his innermost being. It haunted, purified, illuminated, and integrated him. It

---

[45] A maxim composed by an unknown Flemish Jesuit and quoted by Hugo Rahner, S.J., *Ignatius the Theologian*, p. 23.

united him with the very roots of the innertrinitarian life. It spurred him on to seek, find, and carry out God's will, in a community of love focused on apostolic service.

3

A Trinitarian Mysticism

Most commentators agree that Ignatius' mysticism is first and foremost trinitarian.[1] The new man of Manresa felt compelled to talk about the Trinity. To explain the Trinity, he used everyday analogies such as three musical keys, three rational persons, three animals, and the like.

One of his early companions attests that the saint received the most profound illuminations on all matters of faith, but especially on the Trinity, and spoke often with those closest to him about the Trinity and about his great desire to write a book on the Trinity.[2]

---

[1]See Adolf Haas, S.J., "The Mysticism of St. Ignatius according to his *Spiritual Diary*," *Ignatius of Loyola. His Personality and Spiritual Heritage,* ed. Friedrich Wulf, S.J. (St. Louis: Institute of Jesuit Sources, 1977), pp. 164-199; Harvey D. Egan, S.J., *Ignatian Mystical Horizon*, pp. 112-131; Simon Decloux, *Commentaries on the Letters and Spiritual Diary of St. Ignatius of Loyola* (Rome: Centrum Ignatianum Spiritualitatis, 1982), pp. 80-123, henceforth abbreviated as *Commentaries*; Hugo Rahner, S.J., *Vision of La Storta,* pp. 69-132; Joseph de Guibert, S.J., *Jesuits,* pp. 50-52. I said in my preface that I have yet to read a mystic whose personal experiences with and of the Trinity are more profound. Ignatius' trinitarian mysticism is exceptionally fertile, and the way he formulates his trinitarian experiences is often unique. Because of this and because of today's "trinitarian timidity," I have opted for a *detailed* chapter on Ignatius' trinitarian mysticism. I would urge the reader to read this chapter with these observations in mind.

[2]*FN* I, p. 82.

Extraordinary Manresa-like graces at Venice, Vicenza, and La Storta (*Auto,* nos. 95-96) confirmed his trinitarian mysticism.[3] Constantly in communication with the triune God, Ignatius received gifts from each person corresponding to that person's nature.[4] That is, he experienced not only "God" or the "Trinity," but more specifically the Father *as* Father, the Son *as* Son, and the Holy Spirit *as* Holy Spirit. Although these trinitarian mystical experiences occurred during his early conversions, they predominated in his mature years.[5] His *Autobiography* ends with references to powerful trinitarian experiences that he had while writing the *Constitutions* (*Auto,* no. 100).

The trinitarian experiences at Manresa enabled Ignatius to find the Trinity in all things and all things in the Trinity. He saw mystically how the entire world came from the Trinity and was destined for the Trinity (*Auto,* no. 29). Even if no scriptures had existed to teach him, his trinitarian mysticism rendered him willing to die for "these matters of faith" (*Auto,* no. 29). Hence creation, salvation history, God's gifts to the person, and the like—as depicted in the *Spiritual Exercises*— can only be grasped within their trinitarian perspective.

The *Trinity and The* Spiritual Diary

In 1555, only a year before Ignatius' death, Fr. Luis Goncalves da Câmara, the Jesuit to whom Ignatius narrated his *Autobiography,* stated that Ignatius had shown him a "rather large packet of writings" (*Auto,* no. 100). It contained information about Ignatius' experience of the Trinity, Christ, and Our Lady, experiences that confirmed points found in the *Constitutions.* Ignatius refused to allow Father da Câmara to see these papers, however, because of their personal nature.

---

[3]Hugo Rahner stresses the trinitarian dimension of Ignatius' La Storta experience. But Ignatius never mentions the Holy Spirit. Hence, La Storta is less explicitly trinitarian than many of his other mystical experiences.

[4]*MNad* IV, p. 645.

[5]*MNad* V, p. 162.

The *Spiritual Diary,* as it is now called, consists of only two small surviving notebooks from this "packet."[6] The first notebook is a diary covering the period from February 2 to March 12, 1544. During this time, Ignatius was deliberating on the degree of poverty to be observed by the churches of the Society.

The second notebook covers the period from March 13, 1544, to February 27, 1545. It contains much shorter entries, many algebraic symbols, abbreviations, and cryptic notations.

Interspersed among the deliberations on Jesuit poverty is an astonishing record of Ignatius' mystical intimacy with God. One finds remarks about mystical tears, trinitarian visions and illuminations, various kinds of locutions, profound mystical consolations, mystical touches, mystical repose, mystical joys, and consolations without previous cause. In fact, these two notebooks "belong together with the most beautiful and most noble pages that Christian mystics have set down on paper."[7]

The *Spiritual Diary* is perhaps the most remarkable mystical document on trinitarian mysticism ever written in any language.[8] Ignatius mentions the Trinity explicitly 170 times, and nearly every page refers to Ignatius' prayers to and experiences of the "Most Holy Trinity," the "Divine Majesty," the triune "God," the "Three Divine Persons," the "Father," the "Son," and the "Holy Spirit."

Moreover, since most entries begin by telling us which Mass Ignatius said that day, we know of the 116 Masses named, thirty Masses of the Trinity were said. Whether preparing for Mass, during Mass, after Mass, or throughout the day, Ignatius enjoyed inexpressible intimacy with the Trinity and a host of accompanying secondary mystical phenomena. Even

---

[6]It is unknown what happened to the rest of the "rather large packet of writings."

[7]Feder, *Tagebuch,* p. 1. Quoted by Haas, "The Mysticism of St. Ignatius," pp. 164-165.

[8]No less an authority than Joseph de Guibert, S.J. (*St. Ignace mystique d'aprés son Journal Spirituel* [Toulouse, 1938], p. 35, quoted by Haas, p. 169) says: "I believe it will be difficult to find a mystical development of this mystery of spirituality which is more perfect than that which is revealed in the *Spiritual Diary* we are studying here."

the thought of being unworthy to invoke the name of the
Most Holy Trinity brought Ignatius intense interior devotion
(*SD,* no. 64).[9]

A) Trinitarian Affective Phenomena

Ignatius frequently used the word "devotion" (*devoción*)
with respect to the Trinity.[10] Especially in connection with the
Mass Ignatius experienced "devotion," "much devotion," "fresh
devotion," "plenty of devotion," "warm devotion," and "greater
devotion." On occasion, this devotion was so warm and ardent
that it brought sweetness and a light "mingled with color
(bright light)" (*SD,* no. 117). Even a warm room on a cold
night moved him to devotion to the Most Holy Trinity.[11]

Moreover, his mystical devotion, or "ease in finding God"
(*Auto,* no. 99), was often directed toward and terminated in
the Trinity or a person of the Trinity. He had little difficulty
attaining devotion, although he says explicitly that he still had
to prepare for it and that it was not always given.

Ignatius spoke frequently of his intense love for the Most
Holy Trinity.[12] Deep sobbing, mystical tears, and spiritual
visitations that drew him totally into the trinitarian life (*SD,*
no. 108) often accompanied this love.[13] He likewise experienced
"very deep inner touches ... and great and excessive love"
(*SD,* no. 107) that terminated in the divine Trinity. So intense
was his mystical love for the Trinity that it produced great
pressure in his chest (*SD,* no. 51). Often Ignatius only had to

[9]I shall use *The Spiritual Diary,* as translated by Antonio T. De Nicolas, *Powers of
Imagining,* pp. 189-238, and abbreviated in the main text as *SD,* followed by the
appropriate marginal number. For clarity, I have eliminated the brackets, parentheses,
italics, and the like, found in the text.

[10]See *SD,* nos. 6, 51, 104, 106, 107, 113, 117, 118, 137, 139, 140, 144.

[11]During the "fourth week" of the *Spiritual Exercises,* that is, when the exercitant is
contemplating Christ's resurrection, Ignatius recommends taking advantage of a
winter's fire, among other things, to promote joy in the Lord (*Ex,* no. 229).

[12]See *SD,* nos. 51, 101, 105-110, 112, 115, 121, 122, 129, 130, 162.

[13]In Ignatius' letter of September 20, 1548, to Francis Borgia (*Letters,* pp. 180-181),
he forbids Borgia to shed even one drop of blood from his penances. He recommends
instead that Borgia seek especially the gift of tears that flow from a "loving
consideration of the three Divine Persons" (p. 181).

remember the Trinity to be drawn totally to its love (*SD*, no. 110). And it should be noted that physical phenomena often accompanied Ignatius' mystical experience.

The *Spiritual Exercises* speak of a "consolation without previous cause."[14] They state that "it belongs to God alone to give consolation to the soul without previous cause, for it belongs to the Creator to enter into the soul, to leave it, and to act upon it, drawing it wholly to the love of His Divine Majesty" (*Ex*, no. 330). Moreover, "there is no deception in it" (*Ex*, no. 336), because only God can give this type of consolation.

The *Spiritual Diary* attests that Ignatius frequently received trinitarian visitations, or consolations without previous cause. In this way, Ignatius experienced a God-given consolation that was irrefutable proof of God's presence and that drew him wholly to God.

B) Trinitarian Visions and Illuminations

Mystical insights, illuminations, understandings, intellectual lights, and spiritual memories about the Trinity permeate the *Diary*. For example, uncertain about how to proceed in the matter of poverty, Ignatius "felt much devotion with many intellectual lights and spiritual memories of the Most Holy Trinity ... while vesting, with lights about the Trinity" (*SD*, no. 51).

Two things should be noted. First, Ignatius possessed a mystical memory. That is, simply remembering earlier graces brought about still more. Or else these graces stayed with him throughout the day so that he could easily find the Trinity in all things (*SD*, no. 55). Second, these trinitarian intellectual lights gave him consolation and confidence in the matter of the "election," that is, the decision concerning the degree of poverty of the Society's churches.[15]

---

[14]For a discussion of this type of consolation, see my *Ignatian Mystical Horizon*, pp. 31-65, 140-141. Also see Jules J. Toner, S.J., *A Commentary on Saint Ignatius' Rules for the Discernment of Spirits* (St. Louis: Institute of Jesuit Sources, 1982), pp. 216-222, 243-256, 291-313.

[15]*The Spiritual Exercises* call the decision to be made about a way of life or about the reform of one's life the "election." See *Ex*, nos. 169-189.

These trinitarian lights, spiritual illuminations, and understandings were so profound that he knew that he "could never learn so much by hard study . . . [he] felt and understood . . . more than if I had studied all my life" (*SD,* no. 52). The lights often guided Ignatius in selecting the person to whom he would pray, "more by feeling and seeing than by understanding" (*SD,* no. 54).

On occasion, mystical graces drew Ignatius' understanding to "behold the Most Holy Trinity, as if seeing, although not as distinctly as formerly, Three Persons" (*SD,* no. 87).[16] On other occasions, the visions seem less profound, that is, he had no "distinct vision of the Three Persons, but a simple advertence to or representation of the Most Holy Trinity" (*SD,* no. 101). Finally, he experienced vision-like understandings of the Trinity that lasted for some time (*SD,* no. 140).

One must also appreciate Ignatius' visions of the divine indwelling, that is, the "circumincession" or "perichoresis" of the three persons. For example, in praying to the Father, Ignatius realized that "He was a Person of the Most Holy Trinity . . . [and] . . . was moved to love the whole Trinity all the more since the other Persons were present in Him essentially" (*SD,* no. 63). It seems that Ignatius experienced first the three divine persons individually and then moved to the unity of their mutual indwelling. From this he mystically grasped that he could rejoice in any of the divine persons, since his consolations somehow came from all three.

In this way Ignatius untied the trinitarian "knot" that had puzzled him from his days at Manresa. At Manresa he had prayed to each divine person individually and, not knowing why, added a fourth prayer to the Holy Trinity (*Auto,* no. 28). He claimed that saying four prayers to the Trinity—there being only three persons—"appeared to him to be a matter of little importance and gave him no difficulty" (*Auto,* no. 28). Yet, he clearly remembered this trinitarian difficulty some thirty years later when dictating his *Autobiography* to Father da Câmara.

---

[16]For a similar experience, see *SD,* no. 112.

Ignatius' trinitarian mysticism moved not only from the divine persons to their mutual indwelling. It also proceeded from their circumincession to the divine essence itself. For example, occasionally Ignatius could not feel or clearly see the persons, but had "visitations" that ended in the "Name and Essence of the Most Holy Trinity" (*SD*, no. 110). He also felt or saw "very clearly, the very Being or Essence of God . . . the Being of the Most Holy Trinity" (*SD*, no. 121). On one occasion, a mystical vision revealed to him how the three persons "proceeded or exited from the Divine Essence..." (*SD*, no. 123). Or, he simply saw this same being in spherical form, or had visions of the divine essence, the divine being, and the being of the Most Holy Trinity.[17]

Ignatius saw the divine persons not only as individuals, not only in the mystery of their mutual indwelling, but also in the very unity of the divine being. Furthermore, he experienced this unity as radically associated with the person of the Father.

His mysticism, therefore, fully grasped the powerful trinitarian tension that exists between the personal fullness of the three divine persons and their eternal unity in the divine essence. Ignatius could pray, therefore, in a way that recalled something of the Manresan "knot" he untied: "Eternal Father, confirm me; Eternal Son, confirm me; Eternal Holy Spirit, confirm me; Holy Trinity, confirm me; my only God, confirm me" (*SD*, n. 48).

C) The Trinity and the Election

Ignatius made these entries on the Trinity in the *Diary* when he was writing the *Constitutions* and deciding issues of Jesuit poverty. Hence, Ignatius experienced the Trinity in the context of the "election," that is, seeking and finding God's will. His ineffable trinitarian experiences are bound inextricably to his fervent desire to be *confirmed* in the matter of the election. Hence, his *Diary* reveals nothing about contemplation for its own sake. "Holy idleness" and "spousal" union are totally absent. Rather, Ignatius' trinitarian mysticism is one of

---

[17]See *SD*, nos. 123, 125, 136, 143, 153, 172, 174, 180, 183.

discernment, election, and confirmation.

Ignatius begins by listing reasons for and against total, partial, and no revenue.[18] The *Diary* itself begins with Ignatius inclined to no revenue (*SD*, no. 1) and pleading for the Trinity to accept his "oblation." He expected the three persons to confirm him in this matter in the same way "all Three Persons confirmed" the mission of the apostles at Pentecost" (*SD*, no. 15).

Note what Ignatius desired: "I wanted that point [the question of revenue] totally closed with great peace and understanding and to be able to give thanks to the Divine Persons with a feeling of great devotion" (*SD*, no. 22). Ignatius expected the Trinity to confirm mystically his inclination toward no revenue.

Yet his discernment, decision, and confirmation were plagued with numerous inconclusive endings. For example, on February 9, he seemed to have made up his mind (*SD*, no. 11). Making an oblation on February 10, he said the Mass of the Holy Spirit on February 11 so that the oblation might be received. But during that Mass he perceived that something was wrong (*SD*, no. 14).

He repeated the process by looking once more at the advantages and disadvantages of total, partial, or no revenue for the churches of the Society. With reasoning steeped in the love of Christ, he concluded that the election is "something already agreed" (*SD*, no. 15). Because he received tremendous

---

[18]The advantages and disadvantages of having no revenue are given in Antonio T. de Nicolas, *Powers of Imagining*, pp. 186-187. De Nicolas writes (p. 185): "Ignatius had been deliberating on this point of poverty for a long time. In March of 1541 his companions gathered in Rome and voted: 'that the sacristy could have revenues to take care of all the things needed for its maintenance, as long as this income is not used for the fathers of the Society' (*Constitutions* of 1541; MHSI, *Const.* I:69-77). Furthermore, this same year of 1541 ... Paul III gave the company the temple of our Lady of the Strada and granted them the income and revenues this church already possessed." We saw in Chapter Two that Ignatius desired to place his entire trust in God's divine providence. Because of his purity of intention and the ecclesiastical abuses in money matters that abounded in his day, Ignatius eschewed payment for his apostolic service. Thus he was always inclined toward the strictest poverty. He was obviously not satisfied with the decision of 1541 and gave this point much more thought, as can be seen from the *Spiritual Diary*. See footnote no. 23 below.

consolations, he assumed that the election has been made and gave thanks (*SD,* nos. 16, 19).

But noise interrupted his prayer, so he began anew. Because he humbled himself and sought the Trinity indirectly by appealing to mediators such as Christ, Mary, and the saints, he found what he was looking for during the Mass of the Trinity. On February 17, he wrote "The Trinity and End" (*SD,* no. 42), that is, he thought the matter decided through his trinitarian experiences while saying the Mass of the Trinity.

The following morning he woke up with new doubts. He began the process once more, again turning to mediators to intercede with the Trinity. Intense consolation seemed to signal the "confirmation of past offerings" (*SD.* no. 46), so he made what he thought would be a "final confirmation to the Most Holy Trinity, in the presence of the whole heavenly court, giving thanks with great and intense affection, first to the Divine Persons" (*SD,* no. 46), and then to his mediators.

Next he prayed fervently to the Father, the Son, the Holy Spirit, the Holy Trinity, and the one God to confirm him (*SD,* nos. 48, 53).[19] Sensing during Mass, however, that "there was nothing more to learn from the Most Holy Trinity in this matter" (*SD,* no. 62), he turned to Christ for confirmation (*SD,* nos. 65-72). Despite the experience of Jesus confirming him, Ignatius stated that he would have preferred the Trinity's confirmation (*SD,* no. 73).

There seem to be three reasons why Ignatius could not find the trinitarian confirmation he desired and expected. First, slight self-seeking seems to have crept into his decision-making. He was not totally and unequivocally open to the way the Trinity might confirm this election. For example, he admitted to becoming "impatient with the Trinity" because "some slight doubt still remained" (*SD,* no. 50). Thoughts "against Jesus" (*SD,* no. 145) and others also arose, seemingly because he did not have absolute certainty about his decision.

Second, he surrendered, albeit briefly, to the thought of

---

[19]One finds this same insistence upon divine confirmation in *Ex,* no. 183.

having some revenue.[20] Third, the noise in his small, cramped house distracted him, prompting him to leave his prayer to stop it (*SD,* no. 22). He realized that he had "been at fault by leaving the Divine Persons" (*SD,* no. 23). Numerous times he experienced the need to be reconciled with the Most Holy Trinity if the election were to succeed, perhaps because he had difficulty experiencing in prayer the divine presence.[21] This may account for the section entitled, "On the Persons Who Were Hiding: The Trinity" (*SD,* no. 20).

The Trinity resolved the matter in two ways. First, Ignatius was gradually led to discern that his problem was with the "evil spirit of the past, namely, the spirit who wished to make me doubt and caused me to be angry with the Holy Trinity" (*SD,* no. 57). None other than the devil, that is, "the mortal enemy of our human nature" (*Ex,* no. 136) suggested unkind thoughts against the Trinity, and prompted Ignatius to say still another three Masses of the Holy Trinity in thanksgiving, and "caused, or wanted to cause, some hesitation in this matter" (*SD,* nos. 148, 152).

Now God gave him a grace that evoked La Storta, but in a reverse way. At La Storta, the *Father* placed Ignatius with his Son. On February 27, 1544, Ignatius "felt or more properly saw ... the Most Holy Trinity and Jesus, presenting me, or placing me, or being the means of union with the Most Holy Trinity..." (*SD,* no. 83). Now it was *Jesus* who placed Ignatius with the Trinity.

Moreover, he mystically tasted that he was created to praise, reverence, and serve God the way the Trinity, not Ignatius, chose.[22] He received the gift of "reverential love," "reverential surrender," and "reverential humility." This allowed Ignatius to experience consolations in a detached way, to surrender totally to the Trinity's way of doing things, and to pray, "Where do *you* wish to take me, Lord?" (*SD,* no. 113).

On March 12 Ignatius could write "Finished" (*SD,* no.

[20]As Ignatius says, "I seemed to lean towards income" (*SD,* no. 22).

[21]See *SD,* nos. 76, 78, 81, 115, 118, 122. Perhaps no. 112 can be interpreted in this way.

[22]See *Ex,* nos. 3, 23, 38.

150).[23] By way of reverential love, surrender, and humility, he "felt the consolations and visions of the Divine Persons and mediators as bringing every firmness and confirmation of the matter" (*SD,* no. 152). Thus, even for a saint enjoying the highest mystical favors, discernment proved to be a long and difficult process.

The Trinity and the Spiritual Exercises

Although the *Spiritual Exercises* are not explicitly trinitarian, they must be understood and given in the context of Ignatius' trinitarian mysticism. For example, the pivotal Incarnation contemplation during the second week expressly mentions "Three Divine Persons."[24] Ignatius would have the exercitant make the contemplation no fewer than five times. In the Incarnation contemplation, the exercitant must ponder the three divine persons looking down on the world and decreeing that the "Second Person should become man to save the race of humans" (*Ex,* no. 102). The exercitant must also consider "the three Divine Persons seated on the royal throne of the Divine Majesty" (*Ex,* no. 106), how they view the human situation, what they are saying, how they bring about the incarnation, and the like. Finally, the exercitant concludes each exercise with a trinitarian colloquy, "thinking of what I should say to the Three Divine Persons..." (*Ex,* no. 109).

The three divine persons overshadow all the events of this important week. They form the proper backdrop for understanding the week and provide the paradigm for the remaining

---

[23]The Formula of the Institute of the *Constitutions* (no. 5, p. 69) says: "Therefore our members, one and all, should vow perpetual poverty in such a manner that neither the professed, either as individuals or in common, nor any house *or church of theirs* can acquire any civil right to any produce, fixed revenues, or possessions or to the retention of any stable goods ... but they should instead be content with whatever is given them out of charity for the necessities of life" (my emphasis). But Ignatius did make an exception, that is, "colleges should be capable of possessing fixed revenues, rights to rental, or possessions which are to be applied to the uses and needs of the students" (*Const,* no. 5, p. 70). Also see footnote no. 18 above.

[24]See *Ex,* nos. 102, 106, 107, 108, 109, 118-126, 128.

exercises of that week.[25] Hence, the exercises that focus on Jesus Christ as the eternal Word incarnate require Ignatius' trinitarian horizon to be understood properly.

Moreover, the *Spiritual Exercises* often speak of God as "His Divine Majesty,"[26] "God our Lord,"[27] "Infinite Goodness" (*Ex*, no. 52), "God,"[28] the "Divinity," "His Divine Goodness" (*Ex*, nos. 151, 157), the "Divine Justice" (*Ex*, no. 60), the "Divine Power" (*Ex*, no. 363), and the "Giver of graces" (*SD*, no. 153). For Ignatius, these titles are almost always trinitarian.[29] Traditional commentaries on Ignatius' *Spiritual Exercises* have given insufficient attention to these implicitly trinitarian titles and the profound trinitarian orientation of the *Exercises* themselves.

A Mysticism of the Eternal Father

Ignatius mystically experienced the Father *as Father*. For example, at La Storta the Father uttered the words that transformed Ignatius' heart: "I shall be favorable to you [plural] at Rome." Moreover, when the eternal Father and his cross-bearing Son appeared to Ignatius, it is again the Father who says to Christ, "I want you to take this man as your servant." And Christ replied to Ignatius, "I want you [Ignatius] to serve us [Father and Christ]." The explicitly Father-centered aspect of Ignatian mysticism cannot be denied.

---

[25]See *Ex*, nos. 159, 204.

[26]See *Ex*, nos. 5, 18, 46, 146-148, 155, 167, 168, 183, 233, 235, 240, 248, 330, 368, 370. See also *SD*, nos. 40, 53, 81, 85, 96, 105, 107, 110, 112, 142, 159, 185.

[27]See *Ex*, nos. 3, 16, 18, 23, 25, 38, 39, 43, 48, 75, 77, 89, 92, 135, 137, 150, 151, 153, 155, 165, 169, 174, 175, 177, 179, 183, 185, 189, 232, 234, 336, 338, 339, 343.

[28]Especially *Ex*, nos. 58-59. Compare with *SD*, no. 48.

[29]On the other hand, *Ex*, nos. 146-148 *probably* refer to Jesus Christ as the "Divine Majesty." And in *Ex*, nos. 38, 39, 135, 137, 155, 343, Ignatius seems to be calling Jesus Christ "God our Lord." The *Spiritual Diary*, however, clearly calls the Trinity "God our Lord." See *SD*, nos. 39, 142, 147, 156, 159, 185, 186.

A) The Father and the *Spiritual Diary*

The *Spiritual Diary* attests clearly to the importance of the eternal Father in Ignatius' mysticism. Ignatius prayed to the Father for the Spirit of the Father and the Son to discern, decide, and be confirmed on the matter of Jesuit poverty (*SD*, no. 15). When he made the oblation to the eternal Father after resolving to have no revenue, he received mystical favors of devotion, graces, tears, and sobbings (*SD*, no. 16). Yet, preparing to say Mass, he felt powerfully drawn to say, "Eternal Father, confirm me . . . Eternal Father, will You not confirm me?" (*SD*, no. 48).

Again, getting ready to say Mass, but not knowing which one to say, the thought came to him that "the Father was revealing Himself more to me and was drawing me to His mercies, feeling that He was more favorable and ready to grant what I desired" (*SD*, no. 32). This mystical grace blossomed into great confidence in the Father and mystical tears. Likewise, despite the fault he committed during prayer because of distracting noise, he experienced full confidence that the Father would restore him to his former state of devotion (*SD*, no. 24).

The eternal Father also stirred Ignatius in a variety of ways. For example, the Father drew Ignatius to himself so powerfully that the saint's hair stood on end (*SD*, no. 8). In allowing Ignatius to feel and to see him, the Father often caused Ignatius to experience delectable bodily warmth (*SD*, nos. 8, 30). Some consolations terminated decisively in the Father alone (*SD*, no. 129). Moreover, the Father often indicated to Ignatius which mediator to use to pray to him (*SD*, no. 30). The mere saying of the Father's name brought Ignatius great devotion, tears, and interior sweetness (*SD*, no. 28).

Often the Father permitted himself to be found through Christ. In fact, Ignatius mystically felt that he had access to the Father through Christ (*SD*, no. 8), who both presented and accompanied his prayers to the Father (*SD*, no. 77). It is the Father "Who set in order the affairs of the Son" (*SD*, no. 33) and bestowed delightful spiritual lights.

In one lovely passage, Ignatius states that Jesus attracted all his love and devotion. Nonetheless, "I could not apply myself to the other Persons, except to the First Person as being the Father of such a Son ... How He is the Father, how He is the Son!" (*SD*, no. 73).

The Father is prominent even in Ignatius' mystical penetration of the divine circumincession, perichoresis, and mutual indwelling. For example, by mystical vision and understanding, he grasped how the second and third persons are in the Father (*SD*, no. 89). Moreover, he experienced "an increase of intense love for the Being of the Most Holy Trinity, without seeing or distinguishing the Persons, except that *they proceed from the Father, as I said*" (*SD*, no. 121, my emphasis).

He also "felt something towards the Father, as though feeling *the other Persons in Him*" (*SD*, no. 95, my emphasis). During an experience of the Father as a person of the Most Holy Trinity, Ignatius is moved to "love the whole Trinity all the more since the other Persons were *present in Him essentially*" (*SD*, no. 63, my emphasis). When he prayed to the other persons he experienced the same thing, namely, that the two persons are present in the Father essentially (*SD*, no. 63). Thus, Ignatius mystically grasped how the Son and the Spirit are first and foremost in the Father.

Furthermore, Ignatius' mysticism discloses an intimate relationship between the Father and the divine essence. For example, he saw "in a certain way the Being of the Father, that is first the Being and then the Father—my devotion terminating first in the Essence and then in the Father..." (*SD*, nos. 142-143). He received a "partial revelation of the Being of the Father ... and likewise of the Being of the Most Holy Trinity" (*SD*, no. 153). Hence, although Ignatius experienced the distinction between the Father and the divine essence, nonetheless it is the Father who seemingly has the most intimate relationship with it. He never speaks of the Son or the Spirit in this fashion.

This intimate relationship between the Father and the Trinity's being also revealed itself in a "vision of the Divine Essence several times ending in the Father, in a circular figure..." (*SD*, no. 172). Moreover, visions of the divine essence in circular form occurred "several times," "as before," and so on (*SD,* nos. 174, 180). The Father likewise seemed to close the circle, that is, "I also had a vision at different times of the Divine Essence, sometimes terminating in the Father, in the form of a circle" (*SD,* no. 183).

Ignatius mystically experienced the emphasis by the Greek Fathers that there is one God because there is one eternal Father. But he also experienced the Augustinian Trinity, that is, he saw that "the Father on the one hand, the Son on the other, and the Holy Spirit on the other, *proceeded or exited from the Divine Essence...*" (*SD,* no. 123, my emphasis). And Ignatius "felt and saw ... very clearly, the very Being or Essence of God ... and *from this Essence the Father seemed to go forth or derive*" (*SD,* no. 121, my emphasis).

B) The Father and the *Spiritual Exercises*

Although the *Spiritual Exercises* focus for the most part on the life, death, and resurrection of Jesus Christ, nonetheless the eternal Father is still their all-embracing horizon. For Jesus Christ is essentially the one sent by the Father to accomplish his will.[30]

The exercitant must pray to be open to the call of Christ, the eternal king. Nevertheless, one is to serve Christ intimately in order to enter into the glory of the heavenly Father (*Ex,* no. 95). Furthermore, as the Father placed Ignatius under Christ's standard at La Storta, the exercitant must beg this grace from the Father and from mediators (*Ex,* nos. 147-148).

Some of the pivotal graces and consolations of the first week come only from the Father (*Ex,* no. 63), and the eternal Father is perhaps the key figure in the frequently repeated and highly important Triple Colloquy, in which the exercitant asks Mary, then Christ, and then the Father for certain graces.[31]

Individual meditations and contemplations throughout the *Spiritual Exercises* center on Christ praying to his Father (*Ex,*

[30]See *Ex,* nos. 135, 272.

[31]See *Ex,* nos. 147, 148, 156, 159, 199. One would expect a colloquy addressed to Father, Son, and Holy Spirit. The reasons for Ignatius' timidity with Spirit-language will be given below.

nos. 201, 290), being about his Father's business (*Ex*, no. 272), being called the Father's beloved Son (*Ex*, no. 273), driving the sellers from his Father's house (*Ex*, no. 277), telling his followers to give glory to his heavenly Father (*Ex*, no. 278), dying in his Father's hands (*Ex*, no. 297), and instructing his disciples to baptize in the name of the Father, Son, and Holy Spirit (*Ex*, no. 307).

The accent placed upon the Our Father prayer throughout the *Spiritual Exercises* likewise highlights their Father-centeredness. For example, the Our Father concludes most of the individual meditations, contemplations, and colloquies. It is the first prayer mentioned for use with the Second and Third Methods of Prayer, methods that consist "in contemplating the meaning of each word of a prayer" (*Ex*, no. 249) without or with "a rhythmical recitation . . . so that between one breath and another a single word is said" (*Ex*, no. 258).[32] The words, "Our Father," are specifically used as an example of words to focus on, to relish, and to think about.

Ignatius expects the exercitant to experience transient consolations in which the creator both enters and leaves the soul (*Ex*, nos. 322, 330). These consolations teach that God and his gifts are not simply at a person's beck and call (*Ex*, no. 322). Nonetheless, when remembered, they will provide strength in future trials.[33] These consolations, moreover, actually arise from a less obvious experience of God's ever-present help, that is, from the "Divine help, which is always available to him [the exercitant], even though he may not clearly perceive it" (*Ex*, no. 320).

The basic rhythm of these consolations help the exercitant to let God be God, to adore God as the ineffable, forgiving, and loving mystery who cannot be manipulated. The exercitant experiences an Origin without origin, the ever-greater God who gives himself, but always remains incomprehensible. In short, the exercitant experiences God as *Father*.[34]

---

[32]See *Ex*, nos. 249-260.

[33]See *Ex*, nos. 320, 323-324.

[34]For ways of naming and "imaging" God other than as "Father," "Son," and "Holy Spirit," see my "Mystical Crosscurrents," *Communio* 7/1 (Spring 1980), pp. 19-23.

A Mysticism of the Holy Spirit

A) The Spirit and the *Spiritual Diary*

References to the Holy Spirit abound in Ignatius' *Spiritual Diary,* attesting to the Holy Spirit's explicit presence in his mystical life. Of the 116 explicitly named Masses in the *Spiritual Diary,* for example, he said 9 of the Holy Spirit.

On numerous occasions he prayed to the Holy Spirit, whom he saw or felt in a dense brightness.[35] Mystical experiences of the Holy Spirit produced mystical tears and intense consolations. More importantly, these experiences rendered Ignatius firm and satisfied with the decision, or election, concerning the Society's poverty.[36] This is the context for understanding Ignatius' plea to the Father that he mediate with the Spirit and place the Spirit in him. For only the Father's Spirit could inspire him to discern the particular point on poverty (*SD,* no. 36). Ignatius prayed to the Spirit, "Holy Spirit confirm me . . . Holy Spirit, will you not confirm me" (*SD,* nos. 48, 53).

On several unforeseeable occasions, the Holy Spirit drew Ignatius to himself in powerful "visitations" (*SD,* nos. 99, 140, 162). He sensed mystically, in fact, when he should pray to the Spirit and when consolations and movements "terminated" in this divine person (*SD,* nos. 54, 162). From time to time, Ignatius mystically saw how the Holy Spirit proceeds from the divine essence (*SD,* nos. 123, 125), and how the Spirit is in the Father essentially (*SD,* nos. 63, 89).

Thus it is obvious why Ignatius related to Nadal and Laínez that some of the most important gifts of his life were bestowed by the Holy Spirit. Toward the end of his life, contemplating the Holy Spirit was the most frequent grace he experienced.[37]

---

[35]See *SD,* nos. 14, 18, 169.

[36]See *SD,* nos. 14, 18.

[37]See *MNad* IV, p. 645 and *FN* I, p. 138. Also see K. Truhlar, "La découverte de Dieu chez saint Ignace de Loyola pendant les derniéres années de sa vie," *RAM* 24 (1948), pp. 313-337.

B) The Spirit and the *Spiritual Exercises*

In view of this, the relative absence of references to the Holy Spirit in the *Spiritual Exercises* is striking. Yet one must remember how frequently Ignatius and his companions were jailed and interrogated for their teachings and their conspicuous way of life. Church authorities suspected Ignatius and his companions of being *Alumbrados*, members of religious movements that in their extreme forms claimed the direct and constant inspiration of the Holy Spirit.[38] For example, when his Dominican interrogators told Ignatius that he could speak as he had only through study or through the Holy Spirit, "here the pilgrim was a bit beside himself because that kind of argument did not seem correct to him" (*Auto*, no. 65).

It can be shown that Ignatius purposely paraphrased or dropped out some gospel texts or phrases used in the *Spiritual Exercises* to avoid mentioning the Holy Spirit,[39] although the context of the unaltered gospel texts practically eliminates the possibility of an *Alumbrados*-like interpretation.[40] Yet, Ignatius' more personal writings definitely link the Holy Spirit with the experience of consolation, discernment, election, and

---

[38]Karl Rahner writes ("The Logic of Ignatius," pp. 93-94, n. 8): "The question could ... be raised whether Ignatius in early days, before the serenity which he certainly attained in Paris, did not, in fact, externally very much have the look of an *alumbrado*, and whether perhaps the very reason he later added this or that to the Exercises was to prevent misunderstanding and misuse of the fundamental 'mystical' idea of a divine inspiration in the making of the Election."

[39]This is obvious if one compares the early Cologne recension (c. 1539) of the *Spiritual Exercises* with that of the *Vulgate* submitted to papal authorities for official acceptance. On this point, see my *Ignatian Mystical Horizon*, pp. 120-126. It must also be kept in mind how the first Ignatian antagonists charged that the *Spiritual Exercises* led to mystical subjectivism! See P. Dudon, *Saint Ignace de Loyola* (Paris, 1934), appendix, "Critiques et apologists des exercises."

[40]For example, the *Spiritual Exercises* present Elizabeth as being filled with the Holy Spirit (*Ex*, no. 263); the Holy Spirit comes upon Jesus at his baptism (*Ex*, no. 273); the risen Christ gives the apostles the Holy Spirit (*Ex*, no. 304); he commands them to baptize in the name of the Father, Son, and Holy Spirit (*Ex*, no. 307); and he tells them to await the coming of the Holy Spirit in Jerusalem (*Ex*, no. 307). Ignatius spoke of the one Spirit which guides both the individual and the Church (*Ex*, no. 365), but in the safe context of the "Rules for Thinking with the Church." In this way, therefore, Ignatius does not explicitly urge the exercitant to seek out the guidance of the Holy Spirit.

confirmation.[41] To do full justice to the *Spiritual Exercises,* therefore, one must understand and give them in the light of Ignatius' own Spirit mysticism. In fact, they depend more on an implicit experience of the Holy Spirit than the "safe," explicit references indicate.

For example, the *Spiritual Exercises* assume explicitly that God will communicate himself profoundly to the devout person seeking God's will.[42] They likewise state explicitly that the exercitant will come to realize just how much God wishes to communicate himself (*Ex,* no. 234). Thus God's self-communication to the person's innermost center is not only God as gift, but also God as the power to accept this gift. This gift is the Holy Spirit, the gift of the Father and the Son. The Spirit directs the exercitant for the salvation of his or her soul (*Ex,* no 365). Moved and led by this love that comes from above (*Ex,* no. 184), the exercitant may be drawn "wholly to the love of His Divine Majesty" (*Ex,* no. 330). God's self-communication as gift, the Spirit, always remains the exercitant's foundation and source of strength, although not always directly perceived as such.[43]

The Holy Spirit will also govern and direct the exercitant, just as the Spirit governs and directs the Church (*Ex,* no. 365).

---

[41]J.H.T. van den Berg (*De onderscheiding der geesten in de correspondentie van Sint Ignatius van Loyola* [Maastricht: Canisianum, 1958], esp. pp. 60-63) has shown how Ignatius makes this connection throughout his letters. For one example, see Ignatius' letter of June 13, 1551, to Father John Pelletier, *Letters,* p. 246. For an excellent treatment of the relationship between discernment of spirits and the Holy Spirit, see Ignatius' July 1549 letter to Francis Borgia, *Letters,* pp. 195-211. This letter is important for understanding Ignatius in regard to pseudomystical phenomena. Even the *Constitutions,* nos. 414, 624, 697, 700, 701, indicate a link between the Spirit, consolation, discernment, and confirmation of an election. In the *Directories,* or brief texts written or approved by Ignatius to answer specific questions that arose in giving the *Spiritual Exercises,* one likewise sees explicitly the above connection between the Holy Spirit and the election. One may find these directories in the *Directoria Ignatiana* of the *Monumenta Historica of the Society of Jesus.* For an English translation of these texts, see: *Autograph Directories of Saint Ignatius of Loyola,* published by the Program to Adapt the Spiritual Exercises (Jersey City, N.J., no date given). For the English translation of the *Official Directory of 1599,* which certainly has its root in St. Ignatius himself, see *The Spiritual Exercises of St. Ignatius of Loyola,* trans. W.H. Longridge (London, 1919).

[42]See *Ex,* nos. 5, 6, 15, 16, 20, and so on.

[43]See *Ex,* nos. 320, 322, 324.

To make the spiritual exercises correctly, therefore, the exercitant must experience the Holy Spirit *as* Holy Spirit, for this is the Spirit of consolation, of discernment, of election, and of confirmation. Ignatius expects the Holy Spirit to work with exercitants during the spiritual exercises so that through them the exercitants will find God's will. Therefore Ignatius' Spirit mysticism must be seen in conjunction with the special role that consolation, discernment, election, and confirmation played in his life, and likewise play in the *Exercises*. For these *Exercises* evoke, deepen, strengthen, and make more explicit the exercitant's ever-present experience of God as love given, as gift, as Holy Spirit. The exercitant must seek and find God's will in and through the more explicit awareness of the Holy Spirit evoked by the *Exercises*.

Of course, an expostion of Ignatius' trinitarian mysticism must also focus upon the eternal Son who became flesh. But Ignatius' especially fertile Christ-centered mysticism requires a chapter in itself.

4

A Christ-Centered Mysticism

Christ and the Autobiography

The *Autobiography* attests to the profound influence Jesus Christ had in Ignatius' conversion, mysticism, and entire life. For example, Ignatius attributed to Christ his seemingly miraculous recovery from the brink of death on the feast of Sts. Peter and Paul. Reading *The Life of Christ* during his convalescence at Loyola led to the beginnings of a conversion and implanted the great desire to imitate St. Francis and St. Dominic in their service to Christ.

Ignatius also copied down parts of books and thoughts he had, using red ink for those referring to Christ and blue ink for Our Lady. This practice resulted from and further deepened his tremendous desire to serve Christ. Moreover, a vision of Mary with the child Jesus confirmed him in chastity and produced a still deeper conversion.

At Montserrat, Ignatius put aside his worldly clothing for the "livery of Christ." He also customarily read the Passion narratives during Mass, confessed frequently, and received the Eucharist every Sunday. This latter pious practice was not customary in his day. Eventually the inquisitors questioned him about his eucharistic theology.

When scruples about his past sins drove Ignatius to the brink of suicide, his prayer to Christ, "Lord, I will do nothing that will offend you" (*Auto,* no. 24), eventually freed him. As mentioned above, he was consumed by a tremendous desire to labor in the Holy Land for the good of "souls." This desire "for the Holy Land was a longing for Jesus, the concrete Jesus and no abstract idea."[1]

At Manresa, on the ship to Jerusalem, in the Holy Land, in Venice and Vicenza, on the road to Padua, and especially at the end of his life, Ignatius received many visions and representations of Christ. He saw him, with mystical sight, as a white, undifferentiated body, or with white rays coming from above. He likewise saw how Christ was present in the Eucharist and he received special visions about Christ's humanity. These visions consoled Ignatius, pointed out a specific way of serving Christ, and confirmed him in this service.

Because Christ and his disciples used the familiar form of addressing others, Ignatius refused to use the polite and formal "you" in addressing those in authority. To help him with his studies in Paris, he viewed his teacher as Christ and gave his fellow-students the names of Christ's apostles. Because the pope is Christ's vicar, Ignatius and his companions decided to place themselves at the pope's disposal if they could not serve Christ in the Holy Land. Finally, his oft-repeated prayer to Mary to be placed with Christ was answered at La Storta, where the Father placed Ignatius with Christ to serve them.

Christ and the Spiritual Diary

A) A Mediator Mysticism

The *Spiritual Diary* indicates that Ignatius possessed a mystical sensitivity to the function of mediators between him and the eternal Father and the Trinity, especially in the

---

[1] Karl Rahner, S.J., "Ignatius Speaks," p. 20.

election matter. In fact, the *Diary* begins with Ignatius presenting his election of no revenue by "turning to Our Lady with deep affection and great confidence" (*SD*, no. 2), and "seeing Mother and Son disposed to intercede with the Father" (*SD*, no. 4). Mystical consolations, joys, tears, and illuminations usually accompanied his devotion to mediators.

The most frequently mentioned mediators are Jesus and his Mother. Ignatius expected them to intercede with the Father and the Trinity to have his election accepted. For example, "wishing them to present this to the Father through the mediation and prayers of the Mother and the Son, I prayed first to Her to help me with Her Son and the Father, and then prayed to the Son to help me with His Father in company with the Mother" (*SD*, no. 8).[2]

Especially in the early stages of the election, however, Ignatius used other mediators. For example, he prayed to the Father "in the presence of our Lady and the Angels, etc...." (*SD*, no. 38). This "etc." became more explicit later in the election process. "Then I made the final confirmation to the Most Holy Trinity, in the presence of the whole heavenly court, giving thanks with great and intense affection, first to the Divine Persons, then to our Lady and to her Son, then to the angels, the holy fathers, the apostles and disciples, all the saints, and to all persons for the help they had given me in this matter" (*SD*, no. 47).[3]

Ignatius' mediator mysticism had a marked trinitarian orientation. He pleaded with all his mediators to aid him in finally confirming his decision, so "that my thanks may rise before the throne of the Most Holy Trinity" (*SD*, no. 46).

Especially striking is Ignatius' mystical sensitivity about when and which mediator he should call upon to intercede with the Father.[4] On many occasions Ignatius felt drawn by

[2]Also see *SD*, no. 15.

[3]Also see *SD*, nos. 38, 46. The *Spiritual Exercises* likewise emphasize the importance of mediators, especially for the exercises and colloquies that take place in the presence of the entire heavenly court. See *Ex*, nos. 53, 63, 74, 98, 147-148, 151, 157, 199, 232, and the like.

[4]See *SD*, nos. 6, 27, 30, 31, 84. Only on one occasion was Ignatius not drawn directly to the Eternal Father (*SD*, no. 32).

ineffable visions, representations, great clarity of insights to a specific mediator or mediators to present his oblation.[5] Once after Mass, for example, he "could not help feeling and seeing Her [Mary], as someone who is a part, or the doorway, of so much grace that I felt in my soul" (*SD,* no. 31).

Jesus and his Mother mediated for Ignatius in yet another way. Distracted by noise during prayer to the Trinity, he abandoned his prayer to find the cause of the noise. As a penance for giving in to this distraction and temptation, Ignatius refrained from saying the Mass of the Trinity for a week (*SD,* no. 23). Then he took Christ and his Mother as his intercessors, feeling "fully confident that the eternal Father would restore me to my former state" (*SD,* no. 24).[6] Twice Ignatius "felt or saw a likeness of our Lady" (*SD,* nos. 29, 35). This experience made him feel both the gravity of his fault and his great shame. In fact, he "thought he was putting the Blessed Virgin to shame at praying for me so often after so much failing, to such a degree that our Lady hid herself from me..." (*SD,* no. 29).

Nevertheless, throughout the *Diary,* Ignatius remained convinced that Jesus and Mary would be the means through which he would attain both confirmation and forgiveness. In fact, when the election was finally made and confirmed, Ignatius "felt the consolations and visions of the Divine Persons and mediators as bringing every firmness and confirmation of the matter" (*SD,* no. 152).

Even after Ignatius had enjoyed numerous mystical experiences of each divine person, penetrated to the Trinity's unity, and received trinitarian confirmation of his decision, mediators continued to be decisive in his relationship with the Trinity and in the discernment process.

B) *The* Mediator, Jesus Christ

The Ignatian mediator par excellence, of course, is Jesus Christ. Often referring to Jesus Christ as the Son who

---

[5]See *SD,* nos. 6, 12, 27.

[6]Also see *SD,* nos. 23, 31, 73, 74.

intercedes with the Father,[7] or the Son whose affairs the Father sets in order (*SD*, no. 33), Ignatius said twenty Masses of the Name of Jesus during the relatively brief election period. During this time, he mystically "felt or saw" that "Jesus Christ Himself presented the orations that were addressed to the Father, or that he accompanied those I was saying to the Father" (*SD*, no. 77). In fact, prayer to the Father seemed to be Jesus' "duty" (*SD*, no. 84).

Around February 23, Jesus' function changed in the discernment, election, and confirmation process. Because Jesus had sent "the Apostles to preach in poverty..." (*SD*, no. 15) and was now the Society's head, Ignatius grasped mystically that this Jesus was the "greater argument to proceed in total poverty than all the other reasons" (*SD*, no. 65). These thoughts consoled him so deeply that he expected his decision to remain firm even in times of temptation and trial.

A La Storta-like experience also occurred: "I thought, in some way, that the appearance or the felt presence of Jesus was the work of the Most Holy Trinity" (*SD*, no. 67). The trinitarian gift of the felt presence of Jesus poor seemed to confirm his decision and ended the election process. All that mattered now for Ignatius was "to carry so deeply the name of Jesus" (*SD*, no. 68).[8]

The Father had engraved Jesus' name on Ignatius' heart at La Storta. This experience now emerged as a mystical "representation" of Jesus' name that brought "much love," "confirmation," and an "increased will to follow Him" (*SD*, no. 71). Again, the Ignatian mystical connection between visions, confirmation, and transformation showed itself.

Ignatius had desired initially that the Trinity confirm him. Now he "felt that it was given to me through Jesus, when He showed Himself to me and gave me such interior strength and certainty of such confirmation, without any fear of the future" (*SD*, no. 73). This is nothing less than a mysticism of the name of Jesus.

---

[7]See *SD*, nos. 4, 8, 23, 27, 46, 47.
[8]See *Const*, no. 3.

Ignatius' felt visions of Jesus continued, bringing with them love, devotion, and tears. So strong was this love that he thought nothing could separate him from Christ, nor cause any doubt about the confirmation he had received. The experience of Jesus communicating himself gave Ignatius the courage to go on with the election.[9]

Ignatius' trinitarian and Jesus-centered mysticism now took yet another turn. By continued prayer to Jesus and a variety of Jesus-directed mystical experiences, Ignatius eventually began to pray to Jesus with the sole purpose of having Jesus make him "conform to the will of the Most Holy Trinity, in the way He thought best" (*SD*, no. 80). Ignatius also realized that self-seeking had crept into his approach to the Trinity, especially in the matter of the election. He learned not to ask Jesus for confirmation, but only that Jesus "do His best service in the presence of the Most Holy Trinity, etc., and by the most suitable manner..." (*SD*, no. 82). Thus Ignatius indirectly received infused "indifference." His passionate love for Christ led him to the mystical realization that only God's will matters, that everything else must be grasped only in relation to it. This became Ignatius' true consolation and confirmation.

At the end of February 1544, Ignatius began receiving three types of visions that show still other aspects of his trinitarian and Jesus-centered mysticism. In the first kind, both the Trinity and Jesus appeared to Ignatius. They mystically taught him that it is Jesus who presents Ignatius to the Trinity and who is the means of union with the Trinity, "in order that this intellectual vision [of the Trinity] be communicated..." (*SD*, no. 83).[10] Thus Jesus became, explicitly and mystically, Ignatius' means of loving union with the Trinity. At La Storta, Ignatius mystically experienced Jesus from a trinitarian perspective. Now he experienced the Trinity from Jesus' perspective.

These visions infused Ignatius with respectful surrender

[9]See *SD*, nos. 75-76.
[10]See also *SD*, nos. 85-87.

and loving reverence. Through Jesus, the Trinity brought Ignatius to grasp mystically the mystery of the ever-greater God who must be worshipped for his own sake. And "the same loving humility should be directed later to all creatures, for this is to the honor of God our Lord" (*SD*, no. 179). This means that God can be found in all things, when all things are used only insofar as they fulfill the purpose of life: the praise, reverence, and service of God (*Ex*, no. 23). Ignatius' mysticism of respectful surrender and loving reverence moved his focal point from himself to God. He saw the trinitarian God and all God's creatures from a trinitarian perspective, not from his own.[11]

The second type of vision revealed "Jesus at the feet of the Most Holy Trinity" (*SD*, no. 88) and brought Ignatius tears, devotion, consolations, and confirmation. Now he experienced himself continuing the election process under Jesus' "shadow" and guidance,[12] which increased, rather than decreased, his trinitarian graces, especially graces of loving reverence.[13] In addition, consolations and visions that terminated in Jesus and in the Trinity intensified notably.[14]

Ignatius likewise realized mystically that Jesus was life itself, and he proclaimed that he would rather "die with Him than live with another. . ." (*SD*, no. 95).[15] These mystical experiences also sensitized Ignatius to the devil's power to stymie the election process. This realization enabled Ignatius to conclude it successfully.

In the third kind of vision, Ignatius grasped Jesus' divinity by way of his humanity. Both the *Autobiography* and the *Diary* attest that Ignatius often saw Jesus as white light with an undifferentiated body. In one entry, however, Ignatius

[11]See *Ex*, nos. 3, 38.

[12]See *SD*, nos. 95, 98, 101, 113.

[13]See *SD*, nos. 138, 103, 112, 162.

[14]See *SD*, nos. 98. 103, 137, 138, 140.

[15]The *Constitutions* also echo this Ignatian sentiment. See *Const*, nos. 61, 62, 66, 595, 602, 728. No. 728 states that the general should be "altogether ready to receive death, if necessary, for the good of the Society in the service of Jesus Christ, God and our Lord."

states; "I thought in spirit I had just seen Jesus, that is, white; i.e., His humanity, and at this other time I felt it in my soul in another way, namely, not His humanity alone, but *being all my God*, etc...." (*SD*, no. 87, my emphasis). Ignatius had mystically experienced, grasped, and explicated the mystery of Jesus' twofold sonship. The Ignatian Christ is always the Son of the Virgin Mary according to the flesh and the Son of the eternal Father.[16]

C) A Mysticism of the Eternal Son

The *Diary* witnesses clearly to Ignatius' mystical experiences of the eternal Son, the second person of the Trinity. He prayed to the eternal Son to confirm him, "Eternal Son, confirm me ... Eternal Son, will you not confirm me?" (*SD*, nos. 48, 53). In his prayer to the Son, Ignatius experienced how the Son is present essentially in the Father (*SD*, no. 63). In fact, even his Father-centered mysticism contains a Son-directed aspect because the Father, for Ignatius, is the *Father of such a Son* (*SD*, no. 72).

Not only did Ignatius mystically see the Son proceeding from the Father (*SD*, no. 121); he also saw the Son proceeding from or exiting the divine essence (*SD*, no. 123). These Son-centered experiences brought him mystical understanding, certitude, consolations terminating in the Son in a "detached way," tears of reverent surrender and loving humility terminating in the Son, and an ever greater love of the Trinity.[17]

In summary, we have seen how Ignatius penetrated to the very heart of the innertrinitarian life. He experienced each of the three divine persons, their mutual indwelling, the Father's proximity to the divine essence, and the Trinity's very being. In short, he untied the trinitarian "knot" that mystified him for years. We have likewise seen that Ignatius' mystical experiences moved easily from Jesus in his humanity to Jesus as Son, the

---

[16]When the *Diary* speaks of "Jesus," this usually refers to the God-*man* and *incarnate* Savior. The designation "Son" refers to the second person of the Trinity. On this point, see Joseph de Guibert, S.J., "Mystique ignatienne," *Revue d'ascétique et de mystique* 19 (1938), p. 114, n. 3.

[17]See *SD*, nos. 122, 125, 129, 156, 159, 162.

second person in the Trinity. By penetrating to Christ's very heart, he mystically grasped in and through Christ's humanity that Jesus was totally his God.

But Ignatius could also begin with experiences of the eternal Son and proceed to experiencing Jesus "at the foot of the Trinity." Ignatius thereby untied the christological perichoresis of the human and divine natures in the person of Jesus Christ.[18]

Ignatius gives a lovely summary of his trinitarian and christocentric mysticism in his short explanation of the sign of the cross. He writes:

> When we make the holy Sign of the Cross, we place our fingers first on the head; and this is to signify God our Father, who proceeds from no one. When we touch our breast, this signifies the Son, our Lord, who proceeds from the Father and who descended into the womb of the Blessed Virgin Mary. When we place our fingers on both shoulders, this signifies the Holy Spirit, who proceeds from the Father and the Son. And when we fold our hands together again, this symbolizes that the Three Persons are one single substance. And finally, when we seal our lips with the Sign of the Cross, this means that in Jesus, our Saviour and Redeemer, dwells the Father, the Son, and Holy Spirit, one single God, our Creator and Lord—and that the divinity was never separated from the body of Jesus, not even at His death.[19]

---

[18]Hugo Rahner, S.J. (*Ignatius the Theologian*, p. 15) speaks of a mystically experienced *communicatio idiomatum,* or "communication of properties." Because of the hypostatic union, the properties of both the human and the divine nature must be predicated of the one person Jesus Christ. For an excellent introduction to Ignatius' christology, see his *Ignatius the Theologian*, pp. 53-135.

[19]*Monumenta Historica Societatis Jesu. S. Ignatii Epistolae* XII, p. 667. Quoted by Adolf Haas, "The Mysticism of St. Ignatius," pp. 185-186.

Christ and the Spiritual Exercises

The more subjective mystical horizon explicated above provides an excellent instrument for understanding the Christ-centered mysticism of the *Spiritual Exercises*.[20] This section will show that Ignatius proceeded not only by way of an ascent christology, that is, from the man Jesus to the divine Son, but also via descent, that is, from the divine Son to the man Jesus. Also, because the *Exercises* center mainly on the mysteries of the life, death, and resurrection of Jesus Christ, one must never forget who Jesus is for Ignatius— mediator par excellence, the one who sits at the Trinity's feet, the eternal Word incarnate, and the eternal Son. According to St. Ignatius:

> this expression "Spiritual Exercises" embraces every method of examination of conscience, of meditation, of contemplation, of vocal and mental prayer, and of other spiritual activity that will be mentioned later . . . spiritual exercises are methods of preparing and disposing the soul to free itself of all inordinate attachments, and after accomplishing this, of seeking and discovering the Divine Will regarding the disposition of one's life (*Ex*, no. 1).

Hence his *Exercises* aim at removing "inordinate attachments," that is, disordered loves in order to restore a person's right relationship with God, and "seeking and discovering the Divine Will" (*Ex*, no. 15), a unique claim in the history of spirituality. In order to accomplish this double goal, the exercitant must meditate on and contemplate the mysteries of the life, death, and resurrection of Jesus Christ, and also make other exercises composed by Ignatius. In short, meditating on and contemplating the trinitarian Christ is the principal ambience and context in which Ignatius' twofold goals are to be sought.

---

[20]Again, it must be emphasized that the *Exercises* were written by a mystic. Their deepest dynamism, therefore, flows from Ignatius' own mysticism, in the strictest possible sense. For what follows and for bibliographical references, see my *Ignatian Mystical Horizon*, pp. 86-111.

A) The Principle and Foundation

The Ignatian retreat usually begins with the "Principle and Foundation" (*Ex,* no. 23), a meditation designed to impart to the exercitant a vivid sense of life's meaning, goal, and the means to obtain this goal. For Ignatius, "Man is created to praise, reverence, and serve God our Lord." To do this, one must either "use" or "rid" oneself of "all other things on the face of the earth" insofar as they promote or hinder this goal.

From the outset, therefore, Ignatius strives to awaken exercitants to Christian wisdom, that is, to a holistic, total vision wherein everything is seen in its proper place. For Ignatius, all things hold together in the trinitarian Christ. The Ignatian person must desire only Christ and him crucified,[21] because Jesus Christ is the beginning, middle, and end of all good.[22] "All our wickedness," according to Ignatius, "shall be entirely consumed, when our souls shall be completely penetrated and possessed by Him and our wills ... transformed into His will...."[23]

Moreover, we should see all creatures as "bathed in the blood of Christ...."[24] In short, the Ignatian formula, "finding God in all things," can mean finding the trinitarian Christ in all things, or even finding all things in the trinitarian Christ.[25]

---

[21]See Ignatius' letter of April 15, 1543, to Asconius Colonna, *Letters,* p. 69.

[22]See Ignatius' letter to Francis Borgia at the end of 1545, *Letters,* p. 83.

[23]In Ignatius' letter of October 1547, to Teresa Rajadell, *Letters,* p. 153.

[24]See Ignatius' letter of October 8, 1552, to those sent to the missions, *Letters,* p. 268.

[25]A. Haas and P. Knauer (*Ignatius von Loyola. Das geistliche Tagebuch,* [Freiburg i.Br.: Herder, 1961] pp. 66-67, henceforth abbreviated as *Tagebuch.*) maintain that the phrase, "finding God in all things," often means "finding *Jesus Christ* in all things." I prefer the expression, "finding the *trinitarian Christ* in all things," because the *Diary* indicates that on some days Ignatius explicitly found the Trinity in all things; on other days, Christ in all things. Because Ignatius experienced Jesus at the foot of the Trinity, Jesus to be totally his God, Jesus as his Creator and Lord, and the second and third person in the Father, the expression "trinitarian Christ" attempts to summarize Ignatius' *explicitly* trinitarian and christocentric mysticisms. Also see Haas, "The Mysticism of St. Ignatius," pp. 196-199 and Josef Stierli, S.J., "Ignatian Prayer: Seeking God in All Things," *Ignatius of Loyola,* ed. Friedrich Wulf, pp. 135-163.

At Manresa, Ignatius grasped mystically how God had made the world (*SD*, no. 29). For him, Jesus Christ is the Creator who became man (*Ex*, no. 53), the "Eternal Lord" (*Ex*, no. 65), the "Eternal Lord of all things" (*Ex*, no. 98), the "Creator and Lord" who works in his creatures (*Ex*, no 16), "the Eternal Word Incarnate" (*Ex*, nos. 109, 130), the divinity who allows his sacred humanity to suffer (*Ex*, no. 196), the divinity who has risen from the dead and now acts as consoler (*Ex*, nos. 223-224), and the exercitant's Creator and Lord. Hence, Ignatius grasped mystically that all things hold together in Christ because he had mystically experienced him as his "Creator and Lord" and "Eternal Lord of all things."[26] Reasonably, then, Ignatius expected exercitants to experience deeply the person of Jesus Christ as their Creator and Lord.[27]

Furthermore, Ignatius' *Catechism* says that "after God our Lord had created heaven, earth, and all things, and when the first man was in paradise, it was revealed to him that the Son of God had resolved to become Man. And *after* Adam and Eve had sinned they recognized that God had resolved to become man in order to redeem their sins."[28]

Ignatius presupposed tacitly, therefore, the position of the theologian Duns Scotus on creation and the incarnation. God creates in, through, and for Christ because creation and incarnation are two "moments" of his self-communication. Divinization, or the very gift of God's self to the creature, is creation's purpose. Even if Adam and Eve had not sinned, the incarnation would still have taken place for the sake of God's self-communication, love, and divinization. Given the fact of sin, however, one aspect of God's self-communication had to be creation's redemption. But

---

[26]See *Ex*, nos. 23, 50-54, 60, 71, 93, 95, 102, 103, 106-108, 235-237.

[27]Ignatius often referred to the Society of Jesus as the "Society of Jesus the Creator," *Societas Jesu Creatoris*. On this point, see O. Vercruysse, "Our Creator and Lord," *Ignatiana* (Ranchi, 1956), pp. 245-249. Also see H. Rahner, *Ignatius the Theologian*, pp. 63-69.

[28]*Monumenta Ignatiana* I, 12, p. 668. Quoted by Hugo Rahner, *Ignatius the Theologian*, p. 78.

God does not need sin to give himself in love.

Hence, the "indifference to all created things" (*Ex*, no. 23) sought in this exercise must be seen in the light of a passionate love and service of Jesus Christ, the Creator and Lord of all. The proper horizon and context for grasping the "Principle and Foundation" exercise must be Jesus Christ, the Creator from whom everything comes and to whom it will all return. "Indifference to all created things" is actually an Ignatian mysticism of joy in the world because it was created in, through, and for Christ.

Ignatius experienced, moreover, that the same loving humility he exercised toward God should also be directed toward all creatures (*SD*, no. 179). God mystically shifted his egoistic perspective to a theocentric one. The Ignatian "use" of creatures, therefore, must be understood in this context of reverential love. This is neither "using" in Machiavelli's sense nor in the sense of American pragmatism and contemporary technology. It is certainly not "using" in the sense that the end justifies the means. In short, Ignatius' use of creatures is not "utilitarian." Rather his mysticism of reverential love "uses" everything only in its right relationship to God.

Ignatius derived great consolation from contemplating the stars and the heavens. His mystical graces also led him to see the Trinity and Christ in the humblest things of daily life. Hence, Ignatius urged his exercitants to contemplate God's gifts to them in creation (*Ex*, no. 234), to contemplate how God is present in creatures (*Ex*, no. 235), and to contemplate "how God works and labors for me in all created things on the face of the earth" (*Ex*, no. 236).

B) The First Week

The "first week" really begins after the Principle and Foundation exercise. It focuses upon the cosmic and historical unity of the mystery of evil. The exercitant must consider the cosmic origin of sin in the fall of the angels (*Ex*, no. 50), the beginnings of sin in human history through the fall of Adam and Eve (*Ex*, no. 51), "the particular sin of any person who went to hell because of one mortal sin" (*Ex*. no.

52), the history of one's personal sins (*Ex,* nos. 55-61), and finally sin's ultimate consequence: hell (*Ex,* nos. 65-71).

By situating the exercitant's sinfulness in this cosmic-historical drama, Ignatius offers an architectonic view of the mystery of iniquity. A sense of the unity of sin, knowledge of one's disorder and sinfulness, detestation of and sorrow for sin, a deep insight into the pains of hell, and a knowledge and "horror" of the world should arise during this week.

The "colloquies," or conversations, made with Christ crucified, Mary, and the Father disclose the heart of the first week.[29] Hence, Ignatius presents the mystery of sin in its relationship to the crucified Christ. When he asks, "What have I done for Christ?" (*Ex,* no. 53), he links the exercitant's sinfulness to the unity of evil that culminates in Christ's crucifixion—hardly an abstract view of evil.

The first week leads, therefore, to the profound experience of being a *redeemed* sinner, of amazement (*Ex,* no. 60) at God's mercy, of having been spared, and of "the great kindness and mercy He [Christ] has always shown me until this present moment" (*Ex,* no. 71). The first week, then, is clearly Christ-centered.

One Ignatian commentator emphasizes that the first week is Christ-directed because sin is essentially a rejection of Jesus Christ.[30] This commentator underscores the Christian tradition that depicts the first sin, the sin of the angels, as their rejection of the revealed mystery of the incarnation. The angels' emphatic, total "No" and humanity's implicit, confirming "No," especially the exercitant's, to the Creator become man is the root of all sin.

In the first week, therefore, both sin and salvation must be grasped in relation to Jesus Christ. In so doing, one links the first week with the contemplation on the incarnation, the key exercise of the second week (*Ex,* nos. 101-109). The exercitant must answer the questions, "What am I now doing for Christ? What ought I do for Christ?" (*Ex,* no. 53), in personal terms. As discussed below, the exercitant resolves these questions in

---

[29]See *Ex,* nos. 46, 48, 50, 52, 53, 58-61, 63, 71.

[30]Hugo Rahner, *Ignatius the Theologian,* pp. 69-80.

an election that answers Christ's call in the "Kingdom" meditation (*Ex,* nos. 91-100) and lives the "third degree of humility" (*Ex,* no. 167) in an explicit, personal, and specific way.[31]

C) The Second Week

During the second week, the exercitant must focus upon the biblical mysteries of the incarnation, Christ's birth, his early childhood, or "the life of our Lord Jesus Christ up to and including Palm Sunday" (*Ex,* no. 4). This week also contains the key for understanding the *Spiritual Exercises* in their entirety, for it contains several specifically Ignatian exercises.

For example, the first exercise of this week centers on "the Kingdom of Christ" (*Ex,* nos. 91-98). Ignatius depicts Christ as the "Eternal King" who "calls" each person to distinguished service in conquering "the whole world and all My enemies" (*Ex,* no. 95). As loyal, generous soldiers share in both the sufferings and glory of their leader, so too does the exercitant in the service of Christ, the "Eternal King and Universal Lord." The exercitant, therefore, must not be "deaf to His call, but prompt and diligent to accomplish His most holy will" (*Ex,* no. 91).[32]

This exercise is really the spiritual exercises in miniature, and hence a paradigm of Ignatius' radically christocentric service mysticism. "To be with Christ to serve," that is, in a

---

[31]Ignatius did not expect everyone making the *Exercises* to go beyond the material of the first week. For example, see *Ex,* no. 18. In his July 18, 1556, letter to Father Fulvius Androzzi (*Letters,* p. 434), he writes: "The first week could be given to many so as to include some method of prayer. But to give them exactly as they are, one should have retreatants capable and suitable for helping others after they themselves have been helped. Where this is not the case, they should not go beyond the first week.' Ignatius and the early Jesuits definitely limited giving the spiritual exercises in their entirety only to those who could and would be elite in God's service. Even for those who do not go beyond the first week, however, the goal is still explicitly Christ-centered: frequent confession and Holy Communion (*Ex,* no. 18).

[32]This sentiment found its way into the *Constitutions.* See nos. 50, 51, 53, 54, 101, 193, 254, 511.

redemptive mission, is a summary of Ignatius' mysticism and spirituality.[33]

The "Kingdom of Christ" exercise makes explicit the implicit christocentrism of the Principle and Foundation. Actually, it is a second Principle and Foundation because this exercise "helps us to contemplate the life of the Eternal King" (*Ex*, no. 91) and sets the entire christocentric tone for the second, third, and fourth weeks.

The "Two Standards" exercise (*Ex*, nos. 136-148) continues, expands, and forms a tight unity with the Kingdom meditation. Once again, the exercitant must focus upon Christ's call to participate in the worldwide work of redemption. The poverty, scorn, and humiliation expected under Christ's "standard" are contrasted with the riches, worldly honors, and pride of Satan's "standard." Ignatius' militant spirituality, set in the context of the courtly tradition and the Christian spiritual combat tradition, views life as a battleground between the forces of good and evil. Moreover, the Two Standards exercise is a dramatic presentation of Ignatius' well-known "Rules for the Discernment of Spirits" (*Ex*, nos. 313-336). Here the exercitant asks for basic discernment, "a knowledge of the deceits of the evil chieftain . . . and a knowledge of the true life" (*Ex*, no. 139).

The Two Standards exercise contains the important "triple colloquy" (*Ex*, no. 147), a colloquy to be made often during the second week. The exercitant addresses Mary, Christ, and the Father, begging for the grace to be placed under Christ's standard in perfect spiritual poverty, physical poverty, and humiliations. This colloquy echoes Ignatius' La Storta vision, wherein he experienced mystically the Father placing him with the Son. It also summarizes many elements in Ignatius' trinitarian and mediator mysticisms.

---

[33]G. Ganss (*Constitutions*, p. 3) writes that Ignatius had a "world view which led him to an intense desire to be associated intimately with Christ and to cooperate with Him in achieving God's slowly unfolding plan of creation and redemption." Also see pp. 7, 16-17, 20, 22, 25, 33, 76, 80, 102, 247, 332, 346-349.

The internal logic of the colloquy leads into the "Three Classes of Men" (*Ex*, nos. 149-155) and the "Three Modes of Humility" (*Ex*, nos. 165-168) exercises. The first class of men are attached to money, want to be rid of the attachment, but do nothing to rid themselves of the attachment. The second class "want to free themselves of the attachment, but they wish to do so in such a way as to retain what they have acquired. They thus want God to come to what they desire..." (*Ex*, no. 154). The third class of men "wish to free themselves of the attachment, but in such a way that their inclination will be neither to retain the thing acquired [money] nor not to retain it, desiring to act only as God our Lord shall inspire them and as it shall seem better for the service and praise of His divine Majesty" (*Ex*, no. 155). Thus, the "Three Classes of Men" exercise tests the exercitant's readiness to give up inordinate attachments and "to choose what is for the greatest glory of His Divine Majesty and the salvation of my soul" (*Ex*, no. 152). Exercitants of this caliber make decisions with the total "desire of being able to serve God our Lord *better*" (*Ex*, no. 155, my emphasis). This is the famous Ignatius *magis*, the "more" his mysticism and spirituality wished in God's service, praise, and reverence.

The exercitant of the first mode of humility will never commit mortal sin, no matter how great the reward. The exercitant of the second mode is in a state of Ignatian "indifference," that is, disposed to choose only what is for God's greater praise, reverence, and service. Also, the exercitant of this mode of humility will never commit venial sin for any reason.

Those possessing the third mode of humility "choose poverty with Christ poor ... reproaches with Christ ... and [are] willing to be considered as worthless and a fool for Christ" (*Ex*, no. 167). Note, however, that the Ignatian condition for so deciding is "the praise and glory of the Divine Majesty being equally served" (*Ex*, no. 167). There were occasions in Ignatius' life when God's greater service demanded a line of action that prevented a literal following of

Christ poor, suffering, and humiliated.[34]

The most important grace of this week is to receive an "intimate knowledge of our Lord ... that I may love and follow Him better" (*Ex,* no. 103). For all its pragmatic and "worldly" concerns for God's greater glory on earth, Ignatius' mysticism of service finds in Christ poor, suffering, and humiliated the best means to serve the eternal Father. Unless the exercitant has chosen Christ poor, suffering, and humiliated and been placed under Christ's standard in some way, the Ignatian election concerning a way of life or a reformation of life (*Ex,* nos. 169-189) is in jeopardy. The specific, concrete decision to be made during the *Exercises* results from an ever-deeper decision for Christ poor, suffering, and humiliated.

Ignatius gives detailed instructions during the second week for choosing a way of life or reforming life. These instructions focus upon the well-known Ignatian "election," or choice, that many commentators consider the primary goal of the *Spiritual Exercises.*[35] Ignatius speaks of three times during the *Spiritual Exercises* when one can make a prudent and good choice. The paradigm of the "first time" (*Ex,* no. 175) is Christ's direct, compelling call of St. Matthew and of St. Paul. They followed "without question and without desire to question...." The "second time" (*Ex,* no. 176) centers on the clarity and knowledge obtained through discerning consolations and desolations. The "third time" is a "time of tranquillity ... when the soul is not agitated by diverse spirits and is freely and calmly making use of its natural powers" (*Ex,* no. 177).[36] These three times occur while meditating and contemplating the life, death, and resurrection of Jesus Christ.

---

[34]Donatian Mollat ("Le Christ dans l'expérience spirituelle de saint Ignace," *Christus* 1 [1954], pp. 23-47) shows that Ignatius' life shortly after his Manresa conversion in many aspects literally resembled Christ's.

[35]For a nuanced discussion of the primary goal of the *Spiritual Exercises,* see de Guibert, *Jesuits,* pp. 122-132.

[36]For a detailed exposition of the three times to make the election, see my *Ignatian Mystical Horizon,* Chapter Six, pp. 132-156.

D) The Third and Fourth Weeks

In their classical form, the exercises of the third and fourth weeks deepen, stabilize, and confirm the election of the second week. The third week centers on the Last Supper and the details of Jesus' passion, crucifixion, death, and entombment. The exercitant should give special attention to "what Christ our Lord suffers in His humanity or wills to suffer (*Ex*, no. 195), asking for "sorrow, affliction, and confusion because the Lord is going to His passion on account of [the exercitant's] sins" (*Ex*, no. 177). Special consideration must also be given to "how the Divinity hides Itself ... how It leaves the most Sacred Humanity to suffer so cruelly" (*Ex*, no. 196). Again the exercitant should ask: "What ought I do for Christ?"

The fourth week deals with the mysteries of the risen Christ. The exercitant asks to "feel intense joy and gladness for the great glory and joy of Christ our Lord" (*Ex*, no. 221). Special attention should be given to how Christ's "Divinity" manifests itself now that the passion is over. For Ignatius, the risen Christ primarily consoles.

The third and fourth weeks are a time for the most intense empathy, or couvade, with Christ suffering and joyful. The exercitant must enter into the very psychosomatic rhythm of Christ suffering and risen. Perhaps because of the richness of the material, Ignatius allows considerable latitude in how these weeks are carried out. Once again, the colloquies addressed to Mary, Christ, and the Father take on greater importance. These colloquies seem aimed at maintaining a serious seeking of one's needs and the utmost spontaneity in deep prayer.

E) The Contemplation to Obtain Divine Love

The *Spiritual Exercises* end with Ignatius' "Contemplation to Obtain Divine Love" (*Ex*, nos. 230-237). For him, love must show itself in deeds, not words, and consists in the mutual sharing between lover and beloved.

During this contemplation, the exercitant must ask for a "deep knowledge of the many benefits I have received, that I may be filled with gratitude for them, and in all things love and serve the Divine Majesty" (*Ex*, no. 233). The exercitant must contemplate the gifts received from creation, redemption, his or her own personal uniqueness, and the way God exists and works in all things for the exercitant's sake. Experiencing everything as gift and reflecting upon oneself, one then offers oneself totally to the "Lord" in loving service (*Ex*, no. 234).

In this exercise, moreover, exercitants focus upon "God our Lord," the "Divine Majesty," and "God," offering themselves totally to the "Lord." Of course, these titles have a profoundly trinitarian and christocentric connotation. Thus the Contemplation to Obtain Divine Love presents a way of finding the trinitarian God in all things, the trinitarian Christ in all things, and all things in the trinitarian Christ. Therefore, this exercise summarizes Ignatius' mysticism of loving union and reverent service.

F) A Felt Knowledge of Jesus Christ

Neither a compendium of the spiritual life nor a manual in ascetical-mystical theology, the *Spiritual Exercises* must be made, undergone, and experienced. In fact, they should not even be read in advance by anyone planning to make them.[37]

But neither are they simply meditations and contemplations on the life, death, and resurrection of Jesus Christ. First and foremost, they are a method of freeing exercitants of inordinate attachments so that they may more easily find God's specific will for them. Hence, Ignatius plunges the exercitant into the mysteries of Christ's life, death, and resurrection, but within the context of specifically Ignatian exercises: the Principle and Foundation, the Kingdom of Christ, and so on. The Ignatian "method" initiates the exercitant in the inner logic and dynamism of the *Spiritual Exercises,* that is, into christocentric consolations and desolations that lead to discernment, decision, and confirmation.

---

[37]Ignatius' own *Directory* (nos. 15-16) advises the retreat director not to read the text to the exercitant. Studying beforehand the points he is to give, the director may bring in written notes and leave them with the exercitant, but only if he does not have time to dictate them. In any case, only summary notes should be left behind.

For most individual exercises in the section of the *Spiritual Exercises* called "Mysteries of the Life of Christ" (nos. 261-312), Ignatius offers only key phrases from the gospels, not complete verses. It would seem that Ignatius selected these phrases on the basis of his felt knowledge that had mystically grasped the connection between christocentric consolations and desolations, the election, and confirmation. The *Spiritual Diary* also attests to this mystical felt knowledge, albeit in a more explicitly trinitarian context.

In the preparatory prayer for each exercise, the exercitant asks for "the grace that all my intentions, actions, and works may be directed purely to the service and praise of His Divine Majesty" (*Ex*, no. 46). The preparatory prayer, therefore, orients the exercitant immediately in a simple, yet general, way to the Trinity's service and praise. The second or third Ignatian "prelude" (*Ex*, no. 48), however, makes the preparatory prayer specific. That is, one must request a specific grace that varies with each exercise. Hence, the exercitant must pray for "what I want and desire" (*Ex*, no. 48). In almost every case, the exercitant must request explicitly christocentric graces.[38]

Ignatius instructs the exercitant to seek an "interior understanding and savoring of things" (*Ex*, no. 2). In the meditations and contemplations themselves, the exercitant must see, hear, touch, taste, and smell what is going on as if present (for example, *Ex*, no. 114). But the exercitant should linger over aspects of the exercise that are "satisfying" (*Ex*, no. 76). One must never rush from point to point, but follow the consolations and the spiritual nourishment. In the "repetitions," the

---

[38]For example, one must ask for "joy with Christ rejoicing" (*Ex*, no. 48), "tears, pain, and suffering with Christ suffering" (*Ex*, no. 48), "an ever increasing and intense sorrow and tears for my sins" (*Ex*, no. 56), "that I may not be deaf to His call, but prompt and diligent to accomplish His most holy will' (*Ex*, nos. 104, 113), "a knowledge of the true life . . . the grace to imitate [Christ]" (*Ex*, no. 139), "the grace that I may be received under His standard" (*Ex*, no. 147), "the grace to choose what is for the greatest glory of His Divine Majesty" (*Ex*, no. 152), "sorrow, affliction, and confusion because the Lord is going to His passion on account of my sins" (*Ex*, no. 193), "that I may feel intense joy and gladness for the great glory and joy of Christ our Lord (*Ex*, no. 221), and "a deep knowledge of the many blessings I have received, that I may be filled with gratitude for them, and in all things love and serve the Divine Majesty" (*Ex*, no. 233).

exercitant returns to a previous exercise to "dwell upon the points in which I have felt the greatest consolation or desolation or the greatest spiritual relish" (*Ex*, nos. 62, 118). The exercitant takes mystical "soundings" of his or her being to find the nodal points particularly open or resistant to God's grace.

During the "résumé" exercise, the "intellect, without digression, is to recall and review thoroughly the matters contemplated in the previous exercises" (*Ex*, no. 64).

The "Application of the Senses" exercise (*Ex*, nos. 123-126) also directs the exercitant to see, hear, touch, taste, and smell *in imagination* certain aspects of a contemplated mystery. Usually made daily before the evening meal,[39] this exercise greatly condenses, intensifies, and transforms the prayer begun in the preparatory prayer, the preludes, the contemplation itself, the résumés, and the repetitions. In fact, some link the Ignatian application of the senses to the deeply mystical way of prayer found in the tradition concerning the "spiritual senses."[40]

Mystical writers speak of the spiritual senses as analogous to the bodily senses. During deep prayer, the mystic may see, hear, touch, taste, or smell God through the *soul's* senses, that is, the spiritual or mystical senses. Origen (+254) gave a paradigm of praying with the spiritual senses when he wrote:

---

[39]The fifth exercise of the first week is an application of the senses to the mystery of hell (*Ex*, nos. 65-71). One should note the *christocentric* basis of this exercise. *Ex*. nos. 209, 226 suggest that the application of the senses *may* be omitted in the third and fourth weeks. All the exercises of the third and fourth weeks, however, are contemplations on the passion, death, and resurrection of Jesus Christ. Furthermore, contemplations *are* application of the senses to the mysteries of Christ's life.

[40]For an excellent discussion of the "spiritual senses," see H. Rahner, *Ignatius the Theologian*, chap. 5; K. Rahner, *TI* 16, chaps. 6, 7; F. Marxer, *Die inneren geistlichen Sinne. Ein Beitrag zur Deutung ignatianischer Mystik* (Freiburg i. Br.: Herder, 1963). One finds in the *Spiritual Exercises* three explicit levels of the application of the senses. First, exercitants may reflect upon how Jesus and Mary used their five bodily senses in order to imitate them (*Ex*, nos. 247-248). Second, they must use a more interior application of the senses in imagination to the mystery of hell, to the soul, its virtues, the Divinity, and all else (*Ex*, nos. 65-71, 121-124). Third, they ought to contemplate a Christian mystery "as if I were present there" (*Ex*, nos. 102-116). I would contend that all three have the potential to become the mystical prayer of the spiritual, or mystical, senses.

Christ is the source, and streams of living water flow out of him. He is bread and gives life. And thus he is also spikenard and gives forth fragrance, ointment which turns us into the anointed (*christoi*). He is something for each particular sense of the soul. He is Light so that the soul may have eyes. Word, so that it may have ears to hear. Bread, so that it may savour him. Oil of anointing, so that it may breathe in the fragrance of the Word. And he has become flesh, so that the inward hand of the soul may be able to touch something of the Word of life, which fashions itself to correspond with the various manifestations of prayer and which leaves no sense of the soul untouched by his grace.[41]

Finally, each exercise ends with a colloquy that carries forward, strengthens, and unifies the movement initiated in the preparatory prayer, the preludes, the "what I want and desire," the meditations and contemplations, the résumés, and the repetitions.

It should be obvious that the *Spiritual Exercises* are an unusually powerful method of simplifying and deepening prayer by way of a gradual interiorization of the mysteries of the life, death, and resurrection of Jesus Christ. This method initiates a twofold process. First, the exercitant becomes connatural with the mysteries of Christ's life, death, and resurrection by assimilating them in much the same way that a student assimilates a book or a great work of art, that is, by internalizing something external. Second, the *Exercises* initiate a movement from the inside to the outside, that is, from the exercitant's core to more exterior levels of his or her being.

Contemporary theology stresses that God communicates himself as the mystery who haunts, illuminates, and loves us at the very roots of our being, even before we begin to seek him. In fact, God's loving word of wisdom at the center of our being sets in motion any genuine search for him. This inner christocentric word, the "weight" of this inner love, the inner light of faith, forces us to turn to salvation history to see if and

---

[41]Commentary on the Canticle, 2 (GCS, Origen, VIII, p. 167f.). Quoted by H. Rahner, *Ignatius the Theologian*, p. 200.

where God's self-communication has reached its irreversible high point. One lives a "seeking christology" that promotes an outward movement toward the mysteries of Christ's life, death, and resurrection.

Ignatius uses the outer word of salvation history to awaken, deepen, and set in motion the inner word of God's universal self-communication. Only the inspired outer word of revelation correctly interprets the inner word, but only in the light of the inner word can the genuine salvific meaning and significance of the outer word be found.[42]

The awakening of the inner christocentric word through the outer christocentric word, as well as the illuminating of the outer through the inner, grounds Ignatius' christocentric logic. The "inner understanding and savoring" (*Ex,* no. 2) focus primarily on the "intimate knowledge of our Lord, who has become man for me, that I may love and follow Him better" (*Ex,* no. 104). The exercitant must get to know Christ, fall in love with him, and serve him.

In other words, christocentric consolations lead to a felt knowledge of Jesus Christ. In the context of this felt knowledge, this couvade or connaturality with Christ, one experiences God's specific will. In short, Ignatius' supernatural logic links christocentric consolations and desolations, discernment, election, and confirmation.

Only when the exercitant has "elected" to be under Christ's standard and attained a passionate loving knowledge of Christ poor, suffering, and humiliated, can the specific election be attained. The exercitant's particular election, then, is nothing more than the sacrament of having elected Christ poor, suffering, and humiliated. It makes this deeper, more general election specific and concrete.[43]

For the exercitant's election to be "pure and clean without

[42]For the theology behind this position, see Karl Rahner, S.J., "Revelation," *Encyclopedia of Theology. The Concise Sacramentum Mundi* (New York: Seabury, 1975), pp. 1460-1466.

[43]In fact, the early *Directories* view the first two weeks of the *Spiritual Exercises* as leading up to a decision that would be *confirmed* during the third and fourth weeks, weeks saturated with the presence of Christ crucified and risen.

any admixture of flesh or other inordinate attachments" (*Ex,* no. 172) and in order for the exercitant to discern the way God is truly leading, the exercitant must attain incarnational or "hypostatic tact."[44] In essence one must judge an issue, decide a matter, and experience confirmation through one's experience of Jesus Christ.[45] By rendering the exercitant connatural with Christ, the *Spiritual Exercises* force the exercitant to ask the questions, "What have I done for Christ, what am I now doing for Christ, what ought I do for Christ?" (*Ex,* no. 53). The courageous, generous exercitant (*Ex,* no. 5) will be able to answer these questions and to act upon them.

We mentioned above that the second or third prelude always has the exercitant pray for a specifically christocentric grace.[46] Ignatius expected the exercitant to receive many consolations *with previous cause* (*Ex,* no. 331), that is, consolations expected on the basis of the exercise being made. The exercitant, however, may also receive consolation without previous cause. God alone can give these consolations, which contain no deception because they come from God and draw the person totally to the love of the divine majesty (*Ex,* nos. 330, 336). Moreover, the *Spiritual Diary* attests to Ignatius' experience of Jesus at the feet of the Trinity and of himself in Jesus' shadow. These consolations drew him totally to the Trinity and terminated in either one of the three persons or simply the Most Holy Trinity.

Hence, the dialectical relationship between the christocentric consolations with previous cause and those without previous cause mirrors the dialectical relationship in the *Spiritual Diary*

---

[44]Hugo Rahner, *Ignatius the Theologian,* p. 214.

[45]F. Marxer (*Die inneren geistlichen Sinne,* pp. 132-135, 152-163) has shown that the phrase *sentir en nuestro Señor* permeates Ignatius' writings. Ignatius judged and made decisions according to what he "felt in the Lord." From his writings, however, it is clear that *sentir* also means what he "reasoned in the Lord." As will be shown later, religious experience alone is never sufficient for Ignatian discernment. For a brief summary of Marxer's position, see my *Ignatian Mystical Horizon,* pp. 19-21. For an excellent presentation of Ignatius' use of the word "sentir," see: John C. Futrell, S.J., *Making an Apostolic Community of Love. The Role of the Superior according to St. Ignatius of Loyola* (St. Louis: Institute of Jesuit Sources, 1970), pp. 111-116.

[46]See footnote no. 38 above.

between "Jesus" and the "Most Holy Trinity." The exercitant must experience Jesus' full humanity, Jesus as totally his or her God, that the Father is the Father of such a Son, and that the experience of Jesus Christ takes a person into the deepest depths of the innertrinitarian life and reveals its will to the exercitant.

A Eucharistic and Priestly Mysticism

Indirectly but inextricably associated with Ignatius' christocentrism are his priestly and eucharistic mysticism.[47] During Mass at Manresa, for example, he received many mystical illuminations concerning Jesus' humanity, especially Jesus' presence in the Eucharist (*Auto,* no. 29). While preparing for and after ordination, especially in Venice and Vicenza, Ignatius again began to receive Manresa-like mystical favors, which he contrasted with the relative calm of his Paris years of study (*Auto,* no. 95). Hence, his priesthood brought on a second Manresa of extraordinary mystical gifts.

After ordination, moreover, Ignatius postponed saying Mass for a year, begging Mary to place him with Christ. He received this grace while saying Mass at La Storta, a grace that confirmed and gave full content to his eucharistic and priestly mysticism.[48]

As we saw above, in his early pilgrim years, Ignatius attended Mass daily, but confessed and went to communion each Sunday (*Auto,* no. 21), an uncommon practice in his

---

[47]See de Guibert, *Jesuits,* pp. 53-54; Decloux, *Commentaries on the* Letters *and* Spiritual Diary *of St. Ignatius of Loyola,* pp. 114-116; Haas, "The Mysticism of St. Ignatius," p. 195; H. Rahner, *Vision of La Storta,* pp. 34-37, 96. For a full treatment of this topic, see Angel Suquía Goicoechea, *La sancta misa en espiritualidad de san Ignacio* (Madrid, 1950). For a theological analysis, see Karl Rahner, S.J., *Spiritual Exercises,* trans. Kenneth Baker, S.J. (New York: Herder and Herder. 1965), pp. 203-216.

[48]In his letter of May 27 [?], 1547, to the fathers and scholastics at Coimbra (*Letters,* p. 125), he wrote of Christ: "He has made Himself our wage, becoming a brother in our own flesh, as the price of our salvation on the cross and in the Eucharist—to be with us as support and company."

day.[49] At Alcalá in 1526, for example, he and his companions encountered a priest who refused them the Eucharist because of their practice of frequent communion (*Auto,* no. 59). The inquisitors at Salamanca likewise questioned him about his eucharistic theology, indicating that he was one of many who encouraged frequent communion (*Auto,* no. 68).

Ignatius recommended frequent confession and communion even for exercitants unable to go beyond the first week of the *Spiritual Exercises* (*Ex,* no. 18). He even advised Sister Teresa Rajedell, a nun he guided spiritually, to receive communion daily.[50]

Ignatius had great respect for the efficacy of the Mass. He often said Mass for discernment, special graces, benefactors, and the like. For example, he requested of his brother Jesuits that 3,000 Masses be said with the intention that the *Constitutions* be approved by the Holy See.

The *Spiritual Diary* reveals that Ignatius received numerous explicitly eucharistic and priestly graces, although less in number than trinitarian and Christ-centered mystical experiences.[51] For example, during the consecration, Ignatius saw how Mary's "flesh was in that of her Son" (*SD,* no. 31). A mystically given "thought" or "judgement" illuminated him that he "ought to live or be like an angel for the privilege of saying Mass" (*SD,* no. 141).

Another mystical thought came to him about pronouncing the name of God during Mass with profound respect, sur-

---

[49]Ignatius' *Constitutions* recommend the frequent reception of the sacraments of confession and communion. See nos. 80, 98, 200, 261, 342, 343, 406, 530, 531, 540, 642, 644, 697. Ignatius and the Society of Jesus definitely prepared the ground for the contemporary practice of frequent, even daily, communion. See de Guibert, *Jesuits* pp. 374-386 and *passim.*

[50]See his letter of November 15, 1543, *Letters,* pp. 71-72. This letter offers a good summary of Ignatius' thinking on frequent communion.

[51]For this reason, de Guibert (*Jesuits,* p. 53) says: "While the mystical life of Ignatius is trinitarian, it is also at the same time highly eucharistic—although not in the sense that we find in it lights on this mystery as numerous as those we have found concerning the Trinity."

render, and loving reverence (*SD,* no. 156).[52] Furthermore, Ignatius realized that if he made good use of the experience of loving reverence "throughout the day without distraction" (*SD,* no. 182), he would experience it even more deeply during Mass. His mysticism of loving reverence, therefore, is related intrinsically to his eucharistic and priestly mysticism.

The *Spiritual Diary* attests that Ignatius' trinitarian and christocentric mysticism developed almost exclusively in the atmosphere of the Mass. This is also true of his mysticism of loving reverence, of discernment, of election, of confirmation, and of extraordinary mystical experiences. Ignatius focused his entire day on the Mass. The multifarious daily mystical graces occurred while thinking about which Mass to say, while preparing for Mass both interiorly and exteriorly, while saying Mass, and during his thanksgiving after Mass. In fact, many of the mystical favors he received throughout the day extended or complemented his eucharistic graces. The *Spiritual Diary* notes and associates almost every mystical grace he received with the Mass said that day.[53]

It must be emphasized that for Ignatius the Mass was the milieu in which he decided important matters for himself and for the Society. One commentator hits the mark when he writes that "the infused favors showered upon Ignatius were graces centered about Christ's sacrifice of the Mass, and dominated by the Most Holy Trinity to whom this sacrifice gives us access."[54]

[52]Ignatius' reverence for the divine names appears in *Ex,* no. 38: "By reverence I mean that one will reflect on the honor and reverence due his Creator and Lord when he uses His name." In his letter to the fathers and scholastics at Coimbra dated May 27 [?], 1547, he writes: "Behold rather, with deep grief, how His holy name is everywhere ignored, despised, blasphemed" (*Letters,* p. 125). *Ex,* nos. 67, 107 indicate that Ignatius had a special horror of ever hearing the divine names blasphemed. This is a mysticism of the divine names.

[53]Some of the algebraic notation found in the shorter entries from March 13 on mean "before," "during" or "after" Mass.

[54]De Guibert, *Jesuits,* p. 54. Nonetheless, Ignatius eventually had to give up saying Mass. The mystical graces he received during Mass were often so powerful that they left him weak or ill for a long time.

This shows up in the *Spiritual Exercises.* For example, the Last Supper contemplation (*Ex,* nos. 190-198, 289) introduces the third and fourth weeks, weeks that will confirm, strengthen, and stabilize the election. The Christ who "instituted the most Holy Eucharist, as the greatest proof of His love..." (*Ex,* no. 289) dominates these important weeks. The exercitant must experience in Christ, the eternal high priest, the incarnation of Ignatius' famous prayer, "Take, O Lord, and receive all my liberty, my memory, my understanding, and my entire will, all that I have and possess. Thou hast given all to me, to Thee O Lord, I return it. All is Thine; dispose of it according to Thy will. Give me Thy love and Thy grace, for this is enough for me" (*Ex,* no. 234). Only in and through the eucharistic, priestly Christ, therefore, can exercitants offer themselves completely and totally to God in loving service.

In addition, an attitude of gratitude and thanksgiving, *eucharist,* permeates the *Constitutions.*[55] The *Exercises* breathe this same atmosphere. For example, they counsel the exercitant to thank God for all the favors he or she has received, to be filled with gratitude for them, and to live a eucharistic life by a total love and service of the triune God in all things.[56] Ignatius experienced mystically that gratitude and thanksgiving flowed from his authentic mystical life. To experience the mystery of the triune God in Christ rendered him gracefilled, grateful. He responded appropriately with thanksgiving, a Eucharist that flowed into radical apostolic service of the Trinity.

A Marian Mysticism

Intimately and inextricably associated with Ignatius' Christ-centered mysticism is his Marian mysticism.[57] One must focus upon Mary's place in his mysticism to understand his Christ-centered mysticism, especially his mediator mysticism.

[55]See A. Haas, "The Mysticism of St. Ignatius," p. 195. See *Const,* nos. 309-319.

[56]See *Ex,* nos. 43, 61, 77, 230-237.

[57]See de Guibert, *Jesuits,* pp. 26, 37, 52-53, 137, 386-389. For one theological interpretation, see K. Rahner, *Spiritual Exercises,* pp. 262-270.

Ignatius' writings indicate that "Our Lady" had a quiet, unobtrusive, but decisive and fundamental influence in his piety, spirituality, and mysticism. For example, during his convalescence, he experienced a vision of "Our Lady with the holy child Jesus" (*Auto,* no. 10) that brought mystically-infused chastity, conversion, and lasting transformation. Again at Manresa, "he also saw Our Lady in similar form, without distinguishing the members" (*Auto,* no. 29). These Marian visions formed part of the cluster of experiences that both consoled, deepened, and confirmed him in the faith. Toward the end of the *Autobiography,* Ignatius spoke of visions of the "Virgin, at times interceding, other times confirming" (*Auto,* no. 100). It is likely that this also occurred during his second-Manresa period in Venice and Vicenza (*Auto,* no. 95). And because Ignatius begged "our Lady to place him with her Son" (*Auto,* no. 96), he received at La Storta through her intercession his second most important mystical grace.

From the very beginning, therefore, the Virgin Mary helped bring about Ignatius' conversions. Already at Loyola he began to write down her words in the gospel in blue ink. Because he spent part of the day there writing and "part in prayer," one can assume that if he wrote about Mary, he also prayed to her. He was so fond of reciting the Hours of Our Lady that he recommended them as part of the required prayer during a Jesuit's years of formation.

During the "pilgrim's journey," moreover, he had kept vigils both at the shrine of Our Lady of Aránzazu and at the altar of Our Lady of Montserrat (*Auto,* nos. 13, 17). As we have already noted, Ignatius' misguided zeal during a conversation about Mary almost led him to stab a Moor "to restore her honor" (*Auto,* nos. 15-16).

The *Spiritual Diary* reveals other aspects of his Marian piety, spirituality, and mysticism. To appreciate their profundity, it must be recalled that the *Diary* speaks about her in an ambience filled with a trinitarian-christocentric mysticism of discernment, decision, and confirmation.

Sixteen of the 116 Masses mentioned in the *Spiritual Diary* are Masses of Our Lady. In fact, the first entry in the work speaks of a Mass of Our Lady. Throughout the *Diary*, moreover, Ignatius prayed to her as mediator and intercessor with Christ, the Father, and the Most Holy Trinity—especially in conjunction with the election.[58]

Ignatius also turned to her intercession to obtain pardon and forgiveness for his faults during the election process.[59] On occasion, her presence seemed to awaken him to the gravity of his faults (*SD*, no. 29). His mystical sensitivity to which mediator ought to carry his prayer to the Father or to the Most Holy Trinity, in short, his mediator mysticism, often prompted him to choose Mary for his intercessor.[60] Mary is also part of the entire heavenly court around the Trinity's throne (*SD*, nos. 38, 46, 47), interceding with the Most Holy Trinity for Ignatius. He even used the entire heavenly court to intercede with Mary for him (*SD*, no. 46).

Ignatius experienced "clarities," "realizations," "seeing or feeling," visions, "confidence," and "consolations" with respect to Mary.[61] Perhaps the most profound experience of Marian mysticism occurred on February 15. During the consecration at Mass, he "could not help feeling and seeing Her, as someone who is a part, or the doorway of so much grace that I felt in my soul. At the Consecration she showed that *her flesh was in that of her Son,* with such great clarity that I could never write about it" (*SD*, no. 31, my emphasis).

Ignatius' incarnational, or sacramental, mysticism grounded his Marian piety, spirituality, and mysticism.[62] He experienced

---

[58]See, for example, *SD*, nos. 1, 3, 4, 8, 15, and so on.

[59]See, for example, SD, nos. 23, 29. In Ignatius' letter of December 6, 1524, to Agnes Pascal (*Letters*, p. 4) ,we find the emphasis upon Mary's intercessory powers and her ability to give courage. He writes: "May it please our Lady to intercede with her Son for us poor sinners and obtain this grace for us, that with the cooperation of our own toil and effort she may change our weak and sorry spirits and make them strong and joyful to praise God."

[60]In *SD*, no. 4, he knows that Mary wants to intercede for him. In no. 30, the Father gives Ignatius a sign that He wants to be asked via Our Lady.

[61]See *SD*, nos. 4, 12, 24, 29, 31, 129, 152.

[62]Ribadeneira recounts an episode in Ignatius' life that highlights the radical nature of his mysticism of Jesus' "flesh." He says: "One day when we were eating with many present, because of a remark dropped by another he stated about himself that he

the Blessed Virgin as a special mediator in his mystical life because she was first and foremost the mother of Jesus Christ, who comes from her flesh. This is perhaps one of the most profound mystical experiences of Mary as *theotokos,* the "God-bearing one," ever recorded.[63]

Ignatius had perceived mystically not only Christ's eternal "conception" by the eternal Father, but also Christ's earthly conception in Mary's womb. And if Ignatius praised the Father because he was the Father of such a Son (*SD,* no. 72), he could extol Mary as the mother of such a Son: "How She is the Mother, How he is the Son!"

The Blessed Mother is also to be found in the *Spiritual Exercises.* During the first week, the exercitant prays to her to obtain from her Son many of that week's key graces.[64] Her presence permeates the important second week, in the matter contemplated; in the important oblation the exercitant makes "in the presence of Thy infinite goodness and in the presence of Thy glorious Mother and of all the Saints of Thy heavenly court . . ." (*Ex,* no. 98)[65]; and in the pivotal "triple colloquy." [66] During the third week, the exercitant must also contemplate

would consider it as a special grace from our Lord to come from a line of Jewish ancestors. He gave the reason by stating: 'Why!—to be able to be a person related, *according to the flesh,* to Christ our Lord and to our Lady, the glorious Virgin Mary!' These words he uttered with such a countenance and such feeling that tears flowed from his eyes, and this was something which was extensively noticed." *FN,* II, p. 476, my emphasis. Quoted by Dalmases, *Ignatius,* p. 180. For an excellent overview of Ignatius' attitude toward the Jews, see James Reites, S.J., "St. Ignatius and the Jews," *Studies in the Spirituality of Jesuits* XIII/4 (September 1981).

[63]In his November 10, 1532, letter to Isabel Roser (*Letters,* p. 11, my emphasis), Ignatius writes: "May it please the *Mother of God* to hear my prayer for you. . . ."

[64]See *Ex,* nos. 63-64.

[65]In this oblation the exercitant prays that it is his or her "wish and desire, and . . . deliberate choice . . . to imitate Thee in bearing all injuries, all evils, and all *poverty both physical and spiritual,* if Thy most Sacred Majesty should will to choose me for such a life and state" (my emphasis). Ignatius' love of poverty in imitation of Christ *and Mary* is expressed in his August 7, 1547, letter to the members of the Society in Padua (*Letters,* p. 147) when he writes: "Christ likewise showed us the high esteem He had of poverty in the choice and employment of His friends, who lived in poverty, especially in the New Testament, beginning with *His most holy Mother.* . . ." Jesuits, of course, take their vows "in the presence of His Virgin Mother, the whole heavenly court. . . ." See *Const,* nos. 527, 532, 535, 540.

[66]See *Ex,* nos. 98, 102-118, 132, 147, 148, 157, 159, 262-273, 276.

"the desolation of our Lady, her great grief and weariness..." (*Ex*, no. 208).[67] The first contemplation of the fourth week focuses upon Jesus' appearance to his Mother (*Ex*, nos. 218-225). She is also quietly present in some of the other contemplations of this week.[68]

There is also a Marian dimension to the application of the senses exercises and to the contemplations. For example, one must construct a mental image of the place where Jesus or Mary are (*Ex*, no. 47), or see and hear Mary or kiss the place where she has been (*Ex*, nos. 121-126). In addition, the time it takes to say one or more "Hail Mary" prayers often sets the time frame for certain Ignatian instructions.[69] Exercitants may compare the way they use their five bodily senses with the way Mary used hers (*Ex*, no. 248). The "Hail Mary" and the "Hail Holy Queen" prayers may be used in Ignatius' second and third methods of prayer, that is, pondering each word or phrase of a prayer" as long as he finds meanings, comparisons, relish, and consolation..." (*Ex*, no. 252).[70]

Finally, although Ignatius did not wear a rosary around his cincture, he did keep one in his room and wore it when he went to bed. One can assume that he prayed on this rosary (a series of beads strung on a cord with no medal) the Hail Marys that substituted for the recitation of the Divine Office, from which the pope dispensed him for reasons of health.[71]

---

[67]Explicitly in *Ex*, nos. 297, 298, but implicitly throughout the entire passion.

[68]See *Ex*, nos. 300-302.

[69]See *Ex*, nos. 73, 241.

[70]See *Ex*, nos. 249-260.

[71]See Dalmases, *Ignatius*, p. 290.

5

A Sacramental Mysticism of Service, Reverential Love, and the Cross

A Service Mysticism

Ignatius experienced a purification by, illumination of, and eventual union with the triune God in Christ and was, therefore, a mystic in the strictest sense of this word. Moreover, his mysticism focused explicitly on the Trinity, Jesus Christ, and mediators—often within a eucharistic context. Ignatius' mystical illuminations and God-given impulses of love, however, oriented his mysticism to apostolic service, a distinctive characteristic of his mysticism.[1]

Apostolic service informed by God's light and love dominates all Ignatius' writings. He was impelled by the idea of serving God, of promoting God's glory, of learning God's will and carrying it out. Ignatius wanted nothing less than to reform the entire world.

For one commentator, Ignatius was as great a realist as Machiavelli, but as haunted by the ever-greater God as

[1]See de Guibert, *Jesuits,* pp. 55-57, 83-96; Decloux, *Commentaries,* p. 117; Egan, *Christian Mysticism,* pp. 41, 199-200.

Savonarola. Decidedly anti-utopian, he was nonetheless driven to seek and find God, not in ideals, but in all things, including the political and social realms.[2] For Ignatius, the ideal of the ever-greater God and the realities of political and social power never conflicted.

Of course, evaluating means, human relationships, and social and political power becomes more acute as one strives for the only goal that counts: the greater praise and service of God. It is in this sense that the Ignatian prayer at the end of most of his letters must be understood: "May it please Him to give us His bountiful grace always to know His most holy will and perfectly to fulfill it."[3]

The *Autobiography* shows that after his conversion, the firm will to advance in God's service haunted him. He sought mystical experiences, not for their own sake, but for what they disclosed about God's will. And from both his interior life and the situations of his external life, he learned to discern and carry out God's will. One of his key desires was "to help souls" so that they would "surrender completely to the service of God" (*Auto,* no. 79).

Even a cursory reading of the *Spiritual Diary* reveals that Ignatius never sought mystical experiences as such, but inasmuch as they helped or hindered him in seeking, finding, and executing God's will. The question that runs through the first part of the *Diary* is whether to exclude all fixed income, not merely for the support of the professed members of the Society of Jesus, but also for the expenses of divine worship in the churches of these professed houses.

Hence, a relatively minor point about poverty is the real focal point of the *Diary,* not mystical experiences for their own sake. "Where do you want to take me Lord?" is his prayer during this period (*Auto,* no. 113). He looked to mystical experiences to reveal the divine will, to confirm him with certitude about it, to conform him to it, and to strengthen him in carrying it out.

[2]Dominique Bertrand, S.J., "Ignatius von Loyola und die gesellschaftliche Dynamik seines Lebensprogramms," p. 266.

[3]Letter of August 29, 1555, to Peter Camps. *Letters,* p. 400.

This service mysticism permeates his *Spiritual Exercises*. One makes them to seek and find God's will "regarding the disposition of one's life..." (*Ex*, no. 1).[4] The Principle and Foundation exercise states immediately why the exercitant has been created: "to praise, reverence, and serve God our Lord..." (*Ex*, no. 23). The exercitant frequently must request the grace "to know more thoroughly the eternal Word Incarnate, so that I may better serve and follow Him" (*Ex*, nos. 130, 104).

The exercitant contemplates Christ's life, death, and resurrection in order to serve the Father as totally as Christ himself did (*Ex*, no. 135). Ignatius demands of his exercitants nothing less than distinction "in every service of their Eternal King and Universal Lord..." (*Ex*, no. 97), an attitude that "only the service of God our Lord ... prompts their action. Thus, the desire of being able to serve God our Lord better will move them either to accept things or to give them up" (*Ex*, no. 155).[5]

The exercitant must pray the Triple Colloquy for the grace Ignatius received at La Storta. The Father placed Ignatius under Christ's banner at La Storta and Christ engraved in Ignatius' heart the words, "I want you to serve us." The exercitant also must partake of these graces. In fact, exercitants must come forth from the retreat "to be with Christ to serve," to manifest their love in deeds, not merely in words (*Ex*, no. 230).

Even Ignatius' famous Contemplation to Obtain Divine Love (*Ex*, no. 230-237) does not focus upon contemplation for its own sake. The exercitant must "ask for a deep knowledge of the many blessings I have received, that I may be filled with gratitude for them, and in all things love and serve the Divine Majesty" (*Ex*, no. 233).

Ignatius' *Constitutions* also underscore the service orientation of his spirituality and mysticism. One finds in the *Constitutions* the expression, "the service of God," or its equivalent over 140 times; "the glory of God," some 105 times; "the service and praise of God," 28 times. Hence, expressions

---

[4]On this important point, see de Guibert, *Jesuits*, pp. 527-534.

[5]Also see *Ex*, no. 169.

dealing with God's greater glory through service can be found on almost every page of the *Constitutions.* "These expressions come again and again like a refrain and conclusion to highly delicate prescriptions."[6]

Ignatian spirituality and mysticism, then, find God in all things in order to love and serve God in all things. It is a mysticism of joy in the world because it serves God in and through this world. This meticulous search to find God's will and to carry it out perfectly accounts for Ignatius' frequent examinations of conscience and for his sensitivity to his least fault. All his mystical gifts converge upon being with the triune God in Christ to serve. Illuminated by God and filled with ardent love for God, Ignatius served with humility, magnanimity, and the loving attitude of a servant.

A) Not a Bridal Mysticism

As noted above, Ignatius' service mysticism focused explicitly on seeking, finding, and doing God's will. Never does it depict the triune persons or Christ as the love or spouse of the soul united in mystical marriage. Reading Ignatius' works, one is struck by the complete absence of the nuptial aspect that predominates in other mystical classics.

Although Ignatius was mystically united to the Trinity and Christ in the deepest manner possible, he never calls this union a "spiritual marriage." St. John of the Cross, for example, described the mystical journey as moving increasingly closer to the beloved, who is seen through ever thinner veils of love until death rips through the final veil and fully discloses the beloved in the beatific vision.

If the bridal mystics tend to describe their experiences in honeymoon language, Ignatius speaks more like a man who has been happily married for a number of years.[7] Passionately

---

[6]De Guibert, *Jesuits,* p. 84.

[7]Some commentators have suggested that because of Ignatius' sinful womanizing and the time he wasted reading romantic literature in his preconversion period, he was psychologically adverse to using erotic and romantic imagery to express his unitive experiences with God. I would maintain, however, that Ignatius experienced his union with God so powerfully in terms of service that one ought to allow *his* images, language, and emphases to speak for themselves. Ignatus' person, life, spirituality, and

in love with God, Ignatius emphasized generous, respectful, courageous, loving service by seeking, finding, and accomplishing God's will. Nowhere does he speak about the mystical "sleep" of bridal love, or the dalliance and playfulness of contemplative love.

Ignatian mysticism, then, is not a mysticism of introversion, absorbed in God's activity at the center of the soul. His mystical union with the Trinity and Christ did not force him away from the senses and the world.[8]

B) An "Angelic" Mysticism

Mystical theologians commonly have made a distinction between "seraphic" mystics and "cherubic" mystics.[9] The former experience their mystical gifts predominantly in the will; the latter, predominantly in the intellect. The seraphic mystics emphasize the inner attraction of God's love; the cherubic mystics, the inner attraction of God-given illuminations.

Although St. Ignatius indeed experienced mystical love and illumination, his mystical union with the Trinity and Christ did not affect merely his spiritual faculties. Hence, one important Ignatian commentator places Ignatius in the category of the "angelic" mystics. That is:

> in them the infused gifts do not concentrate in such a manner as to unite only and exclusively the spiritual faculties of the mystic to God. Instead, they affect both the spiritual and the bodily faculties, thereby including such powers as the memory and imagination which serve for

mysticism explicitly revolve around service. Hence, I find the above hypothesis pure conjecture. There is *nothing* in Ignatius' writings or in the testimony of his first companions to support such a hypothesis.

[8]For a treatment of the importance and value of *bridal* mysticism, see my *WATSA Mysticism,* pp. 118-120 and my *Christian Mysticism,* pp. 95-96, 137-138, 144-146, 175-176, 193-203.

[9]On this point, see A. Saudreau, *The Degrees of the Spiritual Life,* trans. Bede Camm, O.S.B. (London, 1926), II, nos. 45-46, pp. 48-50. Also see Joseph de Guibert, *Jesuits,* p. 55.

execution. Thus the infused gifts themselves impel the mystic both toward union with God and toward service.[10]

Ignatius was an "angelic" mystic because his mystical union with God sacramentalized, or incarnated, itself in apostolic service. This union remained incomplete until it was expressed in all dimensions of life. As the human spirit must have a bodily component in order to be spirit, so Ignatius' mysticism had to flow from the soul's deepest interiority and express itself in every human dimension.

Service, therefore, was not merely an adjunct to Ignatius' mystical life. It was its fully mystical, sacramental, and incarnational flowering. For these reasons, one commentator compares Ignatius to St. Paul, the paradigm of angelic mystics, whose full union with God impels them to apostolic service.[11]

C) Long Hours of Prayer?

One must not overlook that Ignatius spent very long hours at prayer. As Louis Goncalves da Câmara attests, even when Ignatius was burdened with the almost crushing office of superior general, after Mass he customarily spent two hours in mental prayer.[12] The *Spiritual Diary* witnesses that Ignatius made even the most minute decisions before and in God. In the decision on fixed income, we have seen how long Ignatius could take on this procedure. As general, moreover, he could find God at any time, so powerful were the inner attractions of God's love. In fact, he often had to resist the inner attraction forcibly in order to concentrate on the task at hand.[13]

---

[10] De Guibert, p. 55.

[11] De Guibert, *Jesuits,* p. 55. I would agree, therefore, with those commentators who refuse to reduce Christian mysticism to only one kind, namely, bridal mysticism. But neither would I denigrate bridal mysticism. This type of mysticism is essential for the Church's very life and mission. There are manifold ways in which a mystic can be purified by, illuminated by, and united to God. On this point, see Joseph Veale, S.J., "Ignatian Prayer or Jesuit Spirituality," *The Way. Supplement* (27/1976), p. 11.

[12] *Mémorial,* no. 179, p. 149.

[13] *Mémorial,* nos. 175, 177, p. 148.

Ignatius prayed daily for the Pope and for the sick.[14] He likewise prayed daily for the reform of the Church, for Jesuits in temptation, for those leaving the Society, for those reentering, for captives, and for benefactors. He mobilized the prayers of the entire Society for specific apostolic tasks. Indirectly, of course, this prayer united the companions of Jesus. Besides, as general Ignatius experienced that somehow his prayer actually held the Society together and maintained its unity. To be sure, Ignatius was also concerned about the prayer of the entire Society. He chided those who neglected prayer for the sake of studies and apostolic action.[15]

Yet Ignatius never gave in to the demand from some of his men for long hours of prayer. Ignatius' handling of this crisis in the early Society indicates that he did not see mystical prayer as the summit of earthly life, nor as an end in itself, but only as a means to service. For example, he branded the opinion that "prayer of one or two hours is no prayer, and that more hours of prayer are necessary" as "bad doctrine."[16] Ignatius insisted that the majority of those who gave themselves to long hours of prayer and severe penances did themselves great harm. He was convinced that a person using mortification and self-denial could make more progress in fifteen minutes of prayer than an unmortified person could make in two hours.[17] In what has become almost a classic statement of his attitude toward prayer, we read:

[14] *Mémorial*, no. 301, p. 215.

[15] Ignatius' letter of September 20, 1548 (*Letters*, pp. 179-182) to Francis Borgia is instructive. Ignatius speaks about *increasing* prayer and penances "when our thoughts arise from ourselves, or are suggested by our enemy, and lead us to fix our attention on objects that are distracting, frivolous, or forbidden, if we wish to prevent the will from taking any satisfaction in them or yielding any consent. I say that, as a rule, we ought to *increase* these exercises, both interior and exterior, the more these thoughts are multiplied, in order to conquer them..." (p. 179, my emphasis). Because of Borgia's state of soul, however, Ignatius counseled him to reduce prayer time by half and to give some of that time to study and to managing his practical affairs. "Try to keep your soul always in peace and quiet," Ignatius wrote, "always ready for whatever our Lord may wish to work in you. It is certainly a more lofty virtue of the soul, and a *greater grace, to be able to enjoy the Lord in different duties and places than in one only*" (p. 180, my emphasis).

[16] Letter of July 1549 to Francis Borgia, *Letters*, p. 210.

[17] *Mémorial*, no. 256, pp. 188-189.

> When the Father [Ignatius] speaks about prayer, he always seems to presuppose the passions as being subdued and mortified, and he esteems this fact more than anything else. I recall that once when we were speaking about a good religious whom he knew, I said that he was a man of great prayer. The Father corrected me and said: "He is a man of much mortification."[18]

Ignatius spent long hours in prayer and enjoyed extraordinary mystical experiences. Nonetheless, he still emphasized the "pure intention of the divine service" (*Const*, no. 813) and sincere zeal for "souls" for God's glory as the primary means of union with God. Thus, to be with Christ to serve means to embrace the poor, humble, reviled Christ of the Kingdom, the Two Standards, and the Third Degree of Humility. As Ignatius says, "each one must realize that he will make progress in all spiritual matters in proportion to this flight from self-love, self-will, and self-interest" (*Ex*, no. 189).

For Ignatius, therefore, to be a genuine contemplative in action, to find God above all and in all things and to love all things, to seek only the praise, reverence, and service of God Our Lord, required the readiness to renounce one's ease, honor, and especially one's judgment and will. This is the proper context for understanding Ignatius' emphasis upon obedience.[19]

In short, Ignatius' service mysticism focused upon the attitude of indifference demanded in the Principle and Foundation and the Second Degree of Humility, as well as the attitude of conforming oneself to Christ poor, humble, and reviled. Not only mystical prayer unites a person to God. For Ignatius, self-emptying service for God's honor alone and forgetting oneself for the sake of others are also significant means of uniting a person with God.[20]

---

[18]*Ibid;* no. 195, p. 157. Quoted in de Guibert, *Jesuits,* p. 89, n. 50.

[19]The classic locus for Ignatius' ideas on obedience can be found in his March 26, 1553, letter to the members of the Society of Jesus in Portugal. See *Letters,* pp. 287-295.

[20]The question may be raised, however, if the abnegation, mortification, and selflessness Ignatius demanded as the presupposition of a service that unites a person

A Mysticism of Reverential Love[21]

Ignatius' *Diary* reveals that he received many extraordinary trinitarian, christocentric, and mediator-centered mystical graces as he discerned and sought confirmation of a poverty-related issue in the *Constitutions*. The principal mystical grace bestowed during the final stages of this discernment, however, was the experience of "respectful surrender," "reverential love," "interior reverence," "humility," "loving humility," and "loving reverence."[22] This significant mystical grace not only gave Ignatius a new attitude toward discernment and confirmation; it also became the all-pervading atmosphere wherein he received other mystical graces. Respectful surrender, reverential love, interior reverence, humility, and loving reverence set a new tone for his mysticism of discernment, decision, and confirmation.

We have already seen how tenaciously Ignatius sought God's will and God's confirmation regarding his decision on poverty. But his discernment, election, and confirmation may have been tainted initially by occasional impatience with God. It would seem that Ignatius was looking for far too many signs (*SD,* no. 146), that he wanted God to condescend to his way of doing things (*SD,* no. 147). To surrender to God's powerful confirmation (*SD,* nos. 151-152), moreover, he also struggled against the devil's temptations, which weakened his certitude.

The hierarchical, or descending, movement of graces during critical periods in this discernment must be underscored. Ignatius received such powerful mystical graces that "it was obvious to me that I saw with greater clarity what lay *beyond the heavens* than what I sought to consider here or see united with my understanding" (*SD,* no. 122, my emphasis). Yet very

with God is possible without mystical prayer in the strict sense. On this point see my *Christian Mysticism,* pp. 360-374.

[21]See de Guibert, *Jesuits,* pp. 57-59; Decloux, *Commentaries,* pp. 118-119; Haas, "The Mysticism of St. Ignatius," pp. 172-175.

[22]These terms are synonyms only in the broad sense. Strictly speaking, respectful surrender, interior reverence, and humility may be either "fearful" or "loving." Ignatius, however, experienced predominantly the loving version.

soon Ignatius could find nothing with his upward gaze (*SD,* no. 126). By humbling himself and lowering his gaze, however, he discovered even greater God-given gifts (*SD,* nos. 127-128). A descending movement of experiences related to the Trinity, the Father, the Son, Our Lady, and the saints terminated in one of hell that purified him (*SD,* nos. 129, 132).

Ignatius attributed great importance to this grace of loving surrender and reverential love. Despite trinitarian, christocentric, mediator-centered, and a host of extraordinary mystical experiences, Ignatius nonetheless wrote about respectful surrender and loving reverence in these significant terms: "Thus, while saying Mass, I was persuaded that a *higher* value was placed on this grace and knowledge or the spiritual advantage of my soul, than on all those that went before" (*SD,* no. 157, my emphasis). Hence, the most important grace in the *Diary's* final period may well be mystical reverence.

Often Ignatius realized that this grace "did not seem to be anything of my own or coming from me" (*SD,* no. 157). He desired to have this grace, but said on occasion that he "was completely unable to find it..." (*SD,* no. 163). He complained that "in the Mass I was not only unable to feel any interior surrender, but not even able to find a disposition for helping me. From this I inferred and saw that I could do nothing to find surrender" (*SD,* no. 173). In short, "at times I thought that neither love nor reverence was in my power" (*SD,* no. 181). Even in these cases Ignatius realized: "But even if I did not find it, I thought to search for it was good" (*SD,* no. 164).

Although he came to experience that "humility, reverence, and surrender should not be *fearful* but *loving...*" (*SD,* no. 178, my emphasis), this grace was so important that he sought another form of it that was somewhat under his power. He says: "Not finding loving reverence or surrender, I must seek *fearful* surrender by examining my own faults so as to reach Him who is love" (*SD,* no. 187, my emphasis). He valued this grace so highly that he prayed, "Give me a loving humility, and thus reverence and surrender" (*SD,* no. 178), instead of praying for other graces that had formerly captured his attention, namely, tears and visitations.

Often a variety of Ignatius' mystical experiences terminated in respectful surrender and reverential love. For example, when Ignatius "felt or saw" Jesus as the means of his union with the Trinity, he relates: "With this feeling and seeing, I was covered with tears and love, ending in Jesus; and to the Most Holy Trinity I felt respectful surrender which was more on the side of a reverential love than anything else" (*SD,* no. 83). This experience sometimes terminated in or was directed toward the persons of the Trinity (*SD,* no. 127) or occurred merely in conjunction with recalling or naming them (*SD,* nos. 156, 160, 164).[23]

Ignatius likewise experienced the need for respectful surrender and loving reverence "for the altar and other things having to do with the sacrifice of Mass" (*SD,* no. 159).[24] The realization that "the same loving humility should be directed later to all creatures, for this is to the honor of God our Lord..." (*SD,* no. 179) may have grounded his finding God in all things and his mysticism of joy in the world. In order to find loving humility during Mass, Ignatius experienced that "it was necessary for me to use [loving humility] throughout the day without distraction" (*SD,* no. 182).[25] Finally, God-given

[23]*Ex,* no. 38 states: "By reverence I mean that one will reflect on the honor and reverence due his Creator and Lord when he uses His name." On other occasions, this experience terminates in a specific person of the Trinity or the divine essence (*SD,* nos. 169, 172, 174). Moreover, the *Spiritual Exercises* attempt to inculcate this attitude. For example, *Ex,* no. 3 says: "We should realize that in acts of the will, when we are speaking vocally or mentally with God our Lord or His saints, more reverence is required than when the intellect is used in reasoning."

[24]In his letter of May 24, 1541, to Magdelene Loyola, Ignatius writes: "Confident that you will receive them with the reverence and affection (*reverencia y acatamiento*) due to the things of our Creator and Lord, I am sending you a dozen blessed rosaries which have many graces attached to them...," in *Letters,* p. 50. *Acatamiento* is better translated as "surrender," "homage," or even as "worship." Also, in the Application of the Senses exercise, the exercitant is "to use in imagination the sense of touch, for example, by embracing and kissing the place where the persons walk or sit, always endeavoring to draw some spiritual fruit from this" (*Ex,* no. 125). We saw this reverential enthusiasm for holy places during Ignatius' pilgrimage in the Holy Land.

[25]The attitude of loving reverence is essential if one is to make the *Spiritual Exercises* successfully. Before each specific exercise, Ignatius instructs the exercitant: "A step or two from the place where I am going to meditate or contemplate, I will stand for the space of an 'Our Father,' and with my mind raised on high, I will consider that God our Lord sees me, etc. And I will make an act of reverence or humility."

tears often ended with respectful love and loving reverence.[26]

This God-given reverential surrender and love almost immediately intensified Ignatius' prayer, "Where do *you* wish to take me, Lord?" (*SD*, no. 113). This mystical grace removed the slight disorder in his mysticism of discernment and confirmation. Now Ignatius surrendered completely to God's ways, even in the matter of confirmation. He became indifferent to all mystical favors and realized about reverential love "that it was by this way that I was to go directly to the service of God our Lord, valuing this more than anything else" (*SD*, no. 159). Thus, interior surrender and reverential love perfected his mysticism of discernment and service.

But exactly what comprised Ignatius' respectful surrender and reverential love? Essentially, it was a mystical experience of God as the tremendous and fascinating mystery, as the ever-greater God.[27] God's infinite majesty and transcendent holiness seized Ignatius in his deepest interior and illuminated his least sin and imperfection, his radical creaturehood, and God as his greatest and total good. Fearful surrender likewise resulted from the painful experience of his own unholiness in contrast to God's, of the infinite distance that separated him from God, and of the gap that only God could bridge. Nonetheless, he still continued to experience God as loving (*SD*, no. 187), for God had bestowed upon him the supreme grace of tasting that reverence and surrender should be loving and not fearful (*SD*, no. 178). Hence, the attitude of loving reverence predominates in the *Spiritual Diary.*

The mystical attitude of reverential love worships God for God's sake alone. Experiencing God precisely as God and creatures precisely as creatures now prevented Ignatius from using God. He likewise apprehended mystically that the all-transcendent, ever-greater God, who cannot be manipulated, had given his very own self to him in love. Genuine Christian mysticism must impart the attitude of reverential love because God is love who unites the mystic with himself, but never

---

[26]For a few examples, see *SD*, nos. 166, 167, 168, 170, 171, 182.

[27]See Rudolf Otto, *The Idea of the Holy.*

dissolves the difference between them, as in some forms of Eastern mysticisms. To say *reverential* love is to emphasize *differentiated* unity, that the mystic becomes God *by participation.* To say reverential *love* is to emphasize differentiated *unity,* that the mystic *does in fact become God,* by participation.

Moreover, Ignatius experienced reverential love toward all creation. He found all things in God, understanding mystically how all things are in God. Reverential love of creatures is a theocentric view of creation that grasps them in their proper essence as traces of God, and as ordered to God. Reverential love, in short, is a deeply mystical view of creation and its proper relationship to God.

One must likewise comprehend Ignatius' Principle and Foundation exercise from this point of view. Only with an attitude of reverential love can one fathom the seeming platitude that "man is created to praise, reverence, and serve God," that "all other things on the face of the earth are created for man to help him fulfill the end for which he is created. From this it follows that man is to use these things to the extent that they will help him to attain his end" (*Ex,* no. 23).

The goal of life is full union with the God of love. For Ignatius, therefore, one "uses" or refrains from using creatures in order to attain this goal. Only reverential love for creatures, however, discloses the meaning of this "use." Ignatius' use of creatures is not an end-justifies-the-means philosophy, or an early form of American pragmatism. A person with the contemplative view of loving reverence uses creatures as God meant them to be used. Reverential love of creatures is actually their fulfillment.

The contemplative in action finds God in all things and all things in God. Hence, a mysticism of joy in the world fulfills this world through reverential love, so that God may be all in all. Reverential love is also the attitude sought in the Contemplation to Attain Divine Love, that is, "a deep knowledge of the many blessings I have received, that I may be filled with gratitude for them, and in all things love and serve the Divine Majesty" (*Ex,* no. 233).

A Mysticism of the Cross

Any genuine Christian mysticism must embrace the cross of Jesus Christ and participate in St. Paul's desire to know only Christ and him crucified.[28] Ignatius' mysticism is undeniably a mysticism of "Jesus and the Cross," revealing its "inner continuity with the universal stream of Christian piety before it and so its Christian character."[29]

When Ignatius was recuperating from the cannonball injury to his leg, he read *The Life of Christ* and another book on the lives of the saints (*Auto*, no. 5). His desire to imitate St. Dominic and St. Francis flowed from a penchant for great deeds, but he wished to imitate their deep devotion to Christ suffering and crucified. In fact, Ignatius' great desire for almost constant penance can be traced to this devotion (*Auto*, nos. 12, 14).

The cross of Christ was likewise instrumental in teaching Ignatius discernment. For example, at Manresa, he received much consolation from a serpent-like form that "had many things that shone like eyes..." (*Auto*, no. 19). When this serpent form disappeared, it left him disconsolate. But while giving thanks for his Cardoner enlightenment, this insight occurred: "Kneeling before the cross he noticed that the object [the serpent form] was without the beautiful color it usually had, and he distinctly understood, and felt the firm agreement of his will, that that was the evil spirit" (*Auto*, no. 31). In the light of the cross, Ignatius discerned the difference between demonic and divine consolations.

We have mentioned already that Ignatius attempted a literal imitation of Christ during his early pilgrim years. In part, this imitation focused on following Christ in his passion (*Auto*, no. 52). Also, Ignatius usually read the passion when he attended daily Mass (*Auto*, no. 20). In fact, one must understand his

---

[28]See Karl Rahner. "The Ignatian Mysticism of Joy in the World," pp. 280-283, 288; Karl Rahner, "Ignatius Speaks," pp. 19-22; Hugo Rahner, "The Christology of the *Spiritual Exercises*," in *Ignatius the Theologian*, pp. 53-135.

[29]Karl Rahner, "The Ignatian Mysticism of Joy in the World," p. 280-281. Rahner contends that mysticism is a piety of "special depth and power" (pp. 280-281).

priestly mysticism in the context of his cross mysticism, and vice versa.

It would seem that the real source of Ignatius' mysticism of the cross, however, was his La Storta experience. The eternal Father placed Ignatius with his cross-bearing Son, saying, "I want you, my Son, to take this man as your servant." And the cross-bearing Christ said to Ignatius, "I want you to serve us." Ignatius was now a mystically-confirmed son of the cross. Furthermore, it was this Christ who was to become the means for his union with the Most Holy Trinity (*SD*, no. 83).

The *Spiritual Exercises* also contain this mysticism of the cross. For example, the colloquy with Christ crucified dominates the entire first week. Exercitants must ask themselves in the presence of Christ on the cross: " 'What have I done for Christ? What am I now doing for Christ? What ought I do for Christ?' And as I see Him in this condition hanging upon the cross I shall meditate on the thoughts that come to my mind" (*Ex*, no. 53).

The contemplations on Christ's life in the second week—as well as the important exercises of the Kingdom, Two Standards, Three Classes of Men, Three Degrees of Humility, and Triple Colloquy—have only one important purpose: to help the exercitant to choose Christ poor, suffering, and reviled.[30] The entire second week attempts to mediate to the exercitant Ignatius' experience at La Storta of being placed under the standard of the cross-bearing Christ.

[30]Of course, the *Constitutions* remind aspiring Jesuits of Christ poor, suffering, and reviled. One well-known section states: "It is likewise highly important to bring this to the mind of those who are being examined [for entrance into the Society] ... to how great a degree it helps and profits one in the spiritual life to abhor in its totality and not in part whatever the world loves and embraces, and to accept and desire with all possible energy whatever Christ our Lord has loved and embraced ... because of the love and reverence which He deserves, to such an extent that where there would be no offense to His Divine Majesty and no imputation of sin to the neighbor, they would wish to suffer injuries, false accusation, and affronts, and to be held and esteemed as fools (but without their giving any occasion for this), because of their desire to resemble and imitate in some manner our Creator and Lord Jesus Christ..." (*Const*, no. 101). One should note, however, that one should not give "any occasion for this," that is, for being treated like a fool. That some in the Society, under the inspiration of Simon Rodriguez, so acted occasioned Ignatius to write his letter of May 27, 1547 to the Fathers and Scholastics at Coimbra (*Letters*, pp. 120-130) to put an end to these "holy follies."

Furthermore, one should recall that the *Spiritual Diary* attests to the poor, suffering, and reviled Christ as the main reason Ignatius decided as he did on the poverty issue. As he said, "it seemed to me interiorly, since He was the Head of the Society, to be a greater argument to proceed in total poverty than all the other reasons..." (*SD,* no. 66).

Of course, the third week focuses upon Christ's passion, death, and entombment. Ignatius also ties the fourth week tightly to the third week. The first prelude to each exercise of the third week has the exercitant ponder "how after Christ expired on the cross, and His body remained separated from the soul, yet always united with the Divinity" (*Ex,* no. 219). The fourth prelude asks the exercitant to "consider that the Divinity which seemed to hide itself during the Passion, now appears and manifests itself so miraculously in the most holy Resurrection by its true and most holy effects" (*Ex,* no. 223). For Ignatius, the crucified Christ who was raised from the dead dominates the fourth week, that is, the Christ who had to suffer before entering his glory (*Ex,* no. 303).

The medieval prayer, the "Soul of Christ" (*Anima Christi*), provides an excellent summary of Ignatius' mysticism of the cross.[31] It reads:

> Soul of Christ, sanctify me. Body of Christ, save me. Blood of Christ, inebriate me. Water from the side of Christ, wash me. Passion of Christ, strengthen me. O good Jesu, hear me. Within Thy wounds hide me. Suffer me not to be separated from Thee. From the malignant enemy defend me. In the hour of my death call me. And bid me come to Thee, that with Thy saints I may praise Thee for ever and ever. Amen.

One finds in Ignatius' letters that "the enlightened soul ... when it suffers contradictions ... desires nothing but Christ

---

[31]Although not found in the autograph Spanish or the two oldest Latin versions of the text of the *Spiritual Exercises,* this prayer, so dear to Ignatius, has been printed at the beginning of the *Exercises* since the end of the sixteenth century. The Triple Colloquy of the Two Standards (*Ex,* no. 147) and the Second Method of Prayer (*Ex,* no. 253) explicitly mention this prayer.

and Him crucified, so that, if it is crucified in this life, it will rise in the next."[32] He also offered advice on predisposing oneself to accept the cross and to bear one's cross with gratitude and even with gladness.[33]

All genuine Christian mystics plumb the redemptive, healing, and transformative effects of suffering in imitation of and in union with Christ's suffering. This is true of St. Ignatius. As a genuine companion and servant of the cross-bearing Christ, he experienced mystically the necessity, place, meaning, and value of suffering in the service of Christ, and under the banner of his cross.

A) Not a Victim-soul Mysticism

Ignatius' mysticism is one of apostolic service in the shadow of Christ's cross that participates fully in Christ's redemptive mission. Nonetheless, it is not a victim-soul or a suffering-servant mysticism.[34] Victim-soul or suffering-servant mystics incarnate in their lives the absurdity of Christ's rejection, terrible passion, cruel crucifixion, and lonely entombment. The attractive, personal integration and successful apostolic service that characterize many of the service mystics is absent from the lives of victim souls, or else is overshadowed by their lives of seemingly futile sufferings. Victim souls explicitly reveal God's hand even in life's apparent absurdities: natural failings, physical and mental defects and illnesses, accidents, old age, death, and the like.

Because of Ignatius' strength of character and apostolic effectiveness, for example, William James, the father of American pragmatism, praised him. He said, "Saint Ignatius was a mystic, but his mysticism made him assuredly one of the most powerfully practical human engines that ever lived."[35]

---

[32]In the letter of April 15, 1543, to Asconius Colonna, *Letters*, p. 69.

[33]See the letter of March 13, 1554, to Mary Frassona del Gesso and the letter of August 25, 1554, to Michael de Nobrega, *Letters*, pp. 331, 351.

[34]See my *Christian Mysticism*, pp. 101-106, 275-277; *WATSA Mysticism?*, pp. 9, 119-120.

[35]*The Varieties of Religious Experience*, p. 317. Note the significant "but" in this quotation.

James, however, underscored the apparent uselessness of St. Margaret Mary Alacoque's life, labeling her "pathological" and a prisoner of "stupefaction."[36] For some commentators, then, mysticism takes on value when it transforms mystics with strong personalities. For these same commentators, the long-term psychosomatic illnesses permeating the lives of the "weak," "feeble," and "passive" mystics call into question the entire mystical enterprise.

Yet, one must be slow to evaluate the lives of great saints in terms of American pragmatism, apostolic service alone, self-actualization, holistic health, and the prevalent "beautiful and successful person" syndrome. The Christian tradition has long valued the lives of victim-soul and suffering-servant mystics as a reminder that salvation came to the world through Christ's loneliness, isolation, and shameful death on the cross, not only through his apostolic service and glorious transformation on Easter Sunday. God has indeed called some to live a victim-soul mysticism, as difficult as it may be to discern in individual cases that special and uncommon vocation. For example, if read with the eyes of faith, the lives of St. Margaret Mary Alacoque, St. Catherine of Genoa, and Marie of the Incarnation, to name but a few, reveal the fruits of the Holy Spirit.[37] Their lives highlight, moreover, that divine power often manifests itself in weakness.

Ignatius, for one, never would have rejected suffering-servant mysticism because he knew the redemptive value of the cross. Like the Roman centurion at the end of Mark's gospel who recognized the Son of God in the lonely, abandoned, dead man on the cross, Ignatius would have easily discerned the divine presence in authentic victim souls and suffering servants.

But God did not lead Ignatius along the path of victim-soul or suffering-servant mysticism. To understand his mysticism

---

[36] *Ibid.*, pp. 244, 268-269, 317.

[37] See Catherine of Genoa, *Purgation and Purgatory* and *The Spiritual Dialogue*, trans. Benedict J. Groeschel, O.F.M. Cap. (Ramsey, N.J.: Paulist, 1979); Fernand Jetté, O.M.I., *The Spiritual Teaching of Mary of the Incarnation*, trans. Mother Herman, O.S.U. (New York: Sheed and Ward, 1963), esp. pp. 152-156.

of the cross, one must appreciate fully that the Father placed Ignatius with his cross-bearing Son to *serve* them in direct apostolic service.

B) The Cross of Daily Life

After Manresa, Ignatius' poverty was as radical as that of St. Francis. For the sake of apostolic service, however, Ignatius discerned the need to study and to modify his radical life of poverty.[38]

For Ignatius, the third degree of humility exists "when I choose reproaches with Christ thus suffering rather than honor, and when I am willing to be considered as worthless and a fool for Christ Who suffered such treatment before me, rather than to be esteemed as wise and prudent in this world" (*Ex*, no. 167). But this, too, must be understood in the context of Ignatius' life and his service mysticism.

For example, the *Spiritual Diary* indicates that Ignatius was jailed and interrogated frequently by inquisitors over his manner of life and doctrine. He, his companions, and the Society of Jesus were often subjected to persecutions, calumnies, detractions, and the like. But Ignatius always worked unrelentingly to have his name, that of his companions, and that of the Society cleared of all taint of suspicion and scandal—for the sake of the apostolate. He regarded a good reputation as absolutely essential for his and the Society's apostolic service, and he labored boldly to restore the least damage done to it, always demanding from his inquisitors a formal, written declaration of his innocence and orthodoxy.[39]

---

[38]Still, André Ravier (*Ignace de Loyola*, pp. 268-284, 416-429, and *passim*) gives a graphic account of the life of penury and destitution lived by Ignatius and early members of the Society of Jesus, even when he was general. Ignatius' invitation, "Do stay with us, your honour, if you wish to do some penance" (*Mémoriale*, no. 185, quoted by Dalmases, p. 290), implied much more than the poor meals at Our Lady of the Way house. One should also remember that this radically poor Ignatius begged alms from a great variety of people and often handled relatively large sums of money, but always for matters dealing with apostolic service.

[39]In his letter of March 15, 1545, to John III, king of Portugal (*Letters*, pp. 79-80), Ignatius went to great lengths to set the record straight concerning the false accusations made against him and his companions. In his letter of September 10, 1546, to Michael de Torres (*Letters*, pp. 100-101), we read that Ignatius had Isabel

In one case, the theology faculty of the University of Paris issued a highly critical statement on the Society of Jesus. Ignatius did not let the matter stand. But instead of going directly to the Pope to secure his help Ignatius gathered testimony from bishops, cardinals, princes, and the like, attesting to the good works the Society had done for them. Thus, instead of directly attacking detraction and calumny, Ignatius created a good atmosphere.[40]

One must understand, therefore, the significant qualifier in his description of the third degree of humility, namely, that when "the first and second forms are already possessed and the praise and glory of the Divine Majesty being *equally* served, in order to be more like Christ . . . I choose reproaches . . . am willing to be considered as worthless and a fool for Christ. . ." (*Ex,* no. 167, my emphasis). The praise, glory, and service of the divine majesty is the key to Ignatius' mysticism of the cross. His service mysticism qualifies that of the cross.

When the Principle and Foundation exercise speaks of indifference, it says that one should not "prefer health to sickness" (*Ex,* no. 23). But again, in order to understand this properly, one must look at Ignatius' own life.[41] Jesuits who knew Ignatius well recounted that until Pamplona and Manresa he enjoyed good health and possessed a robust constitution. The leg injuries sustained at Pamplona and the excessive fasts and severe penances at Manresa, however, produced a dramatic physical change. For the rest of his life, Ignatius suffered discomfort and pain in his right leg and stomach.

The *Spiritual Diary* mentions on several occasions his brushes with death from illness, his return to Azpeitia for health reasons, leaving Bologna for Venice because of health,

Roser's and her nephew's retraction entered into the official record. They had accused Ignatius of seeking their fortune.

[40]Along these lines, when Ignatius wished to persuade the king to support a Jesuit college at Louvain, he did not hesitate to remind the king about his family's exploits, the rewards granted the Loyola family from the monarchy in the past, how great the Society's present reputation was, and the like.

[41]The following remarks are based on Dalmases, *Ignatius of Loyola,* pp. 40-43, 56, 77, 88, 126, 135, 139, 242-245, 251, 287-289, 293.

and his ups and downs in Rome. Moreover, an autopsy revealed that Ignatius suffered from severe gallstones that must have caused him excruciating pain for almost thirty years. Not only did Ignatius bear this pain with serenity and fortitude, but he worked almost incessantly for God's greater service. His productivity during this period was almost miraculous.

Nonetheless, Ignatius did not passively accept this ill health. Whereas suffering-servant mystics would have rejoiced in their infirmity as a way of sharing in Christ's sufferings, because of his service mysticism, Ignatius employed all human means possible to have his health restored.[42]

For example, when Ignatius' doctors told him he would go blind unless he curbed his mystical gift of tears, Ignatius did so. St. Francis of Assisi angrily rejected the same advice. Karl Rahner is undoubtedly correct, then, when he says of Ignatian indifference: "yet this indifference in its turn disguises that love for the foolishness of the Cross into daily *moderation* of a *normal style of life* marked by *good sense.*"[43] Thus, Ignatius' service mysticism required the cross-mysticism of daily life, of the middle way, of discretion.[44]

Still another way his service mysticism modified his mysticism of the cross can be seen in his attitude toward

---

[42]His *Constitutions,* for example, offer much advice on the care of the body and the preservation of health for divine service (nos. 296-306, 825-826), on the importance of selecting only those of good health for the missions and the more difficult work (no. 624b), and for temperance in spiritual and bodily labor (no. 822). Only those with good health were acceptable candidates for the Society (nos. 44, 107, 151, 159, 162, 185). Ill health could be cause for dismissal from the Society (nos. 212, 213, 216). When electing the Society's general, attention must be given to the potential candidate's health (no. 731).

[43]"The Ignatian Mysticism of Joy in the World," p. 291, Rahner's emphases.

[44]Ignatius had undoubtedly discerned in the course of his life that the severe penances and "holy follies" of his early conversion years had impeded God's greater service. In his mature years, therefore, he insisted on moderation and forbade his Jesuits to indulge in severe penances and holy follies. For a few examples, see his letters of May 27, 1547, to the Fathers and Scholastics at Coimbra (*Letters,* pp. 120-130), of February 22, 1554, to Father James Lainez (*Letters,* pp. 323-324), and of February 24, 1554, to Father Gaspar Berse (*Letters,* pp. 324-326). Again, Ignatius considered obedience, interior abnegation, and purity of intention the best ways to conquer oneself for the sake of serving God.

human means. If he placed his trust and confidence in God above all else, nonetheless he availed himself of every possible human means to serve God. Although he considered the supernatural gifts, endowments, and means the most important, he also esteemed natural gifts and means, as long as they were "exercised for the divine service alone" (*Const,* no. 814).

For Ignatius, the person who was not good for the world was not good for the Society of Jesus. Concerning those to be admitted to the Society, he said: "To speak in general of those who should be admitted, the greater the number of natural and infused gifts someone has from God our Lord which are *useful for what the Society aims at in His divine service,* and the more experience the candidate has in the use of these gifts, the more suitable will he be for reception into the Society" (*Const,* no. 147, my emphasis).

The mature Ignatius did not directly seek out pain, suffering, and the like in imitation of Christ crucified as did victim-soul mystics. Nor did his mystical life focus explicitly on passive suffering to highlight his imitation of Christ suffering. First and foremost, he sought God's will and tried to carry it out in far-ranging apostolic service. He embraced the cross of service, that is, those setbacks encountered in developing his talents for Christ, in promoting social justice, in humanizing the world, and in the worldwide work of the redemption. The Father had placed Ignatius with the *cross*-bearing Christ for their *service.*

A Sacramental Mysticism

Broadly speaking, two different approaches to the mystical life can be found in the Christian mystical tradition.[45] First, there is the apophatic way (Greek: *apophatikos*=negative), the *via negativa.* This tradition emphasizes the ever-greater God

---

[45]See my "Christian Apophatic and Kataphatic Mysticisms." *Theological Studies* 39/3 (September 1978), pp. 399-426, and my *Christian Mysticism, passim.*

so radically different from all creatures. Hence, God is best known by negation, elimination, forgetting, unknowing, without images and symbols, and in darkness. As St. John of the Cross says, "all the being of creatures compared with the infinite being of God is nothing ... Nothing which could possibly be imagined or comprehended in this life can be a proximate means of union with God."[46]

Paradoxically, the apophatic tradition asserts that God can be known only through the unknowing engendered by mystical love. God is "not this, not that." All images, thoughts, symbols, and the like—even ones about God, Christ, and the mysteries of salvation history in general—must be forgotten after a certain stage of mystical ascent. To be sure, the contemplative must have reached a definite level of spiritual maturity. Certain signs must clearly indicate a calling to place *everything* into a cloud of forgetting, for the sake of the cloud of unknowing pierced only by God-given mystical love.

On the other hand, the kataphatic way (Greek: *kataphati-kos*=affirmative), the *via affirmativa,* underscores finding God in all things. It emphasizes the similarity between God and creatures, that God can be reached by creatures, images, symbols, and the like, because he has manifested himself in creation and salvation history. The incarnational, sacramental dimension of Christianity forces the kataphatic mystic to take seriously God's self-revelation in images, symbols, and the great mysteries of salvation. These need never be forgotten.

According to the Fourth Lateran Council, "between the Creator and the creature no similarity can be expressed without including a greater dissimilarity."[47] It would seem that for psychological and theological reasons, the apophatic mystic experiences, expresses, and emphasizes more the dissimilarity; the kataphatic emphasizes the similarity. Nevertheless, both are orthodox Christian ways of reaching God,

---

[46] *The Collected Works of St. John of the Cross,* trans. K. Kavanaugh, O.C.D., and O. Rodriguez, O.C.D. (Washington, D.C.: Institute of Carmelite Studies, 1973), pp. 79, 127.

[47] Karl Rahner, S.J., ed. *The Teachings of the Catholic Church,* trans. Geoffrey Stevens (New York: Alba House, 1966), no. 156, p. 99.

and one type of mysticism always contains elements from the other.

Insofar as Christian mysticism is *mysticism,* there must be apophatic elements that unite the person to the ever-greater, incomprehensible God. But insofar as Christian mysticism is *Christian,* there must be kataphatic, incarnational, sacramental elements to mediate this union. In fact, inasmuch as any mysticism involves the relationship of human persons to what they consider absolute, all mysticism contains both apophatic and kataphatic elements.

St. Ignatius' mysticism presents itself as a paradigm of authentic sacramental, or kataphatic, mysticism. Instead of knowing by not knowing, instead of an emphasis upon forgetting all created things to dwell in a dark, "naked" love of God, Ignatius' mysticism focused upon a progressive simplification of prayer culminating in the highest levels of sacramental contemplation. Nowhere in the entire Ignatian corpus does he speak about the need to forget, to dwell in a cloud of unknowing, or to walk the path of dark faith.

In fact, his autobiography shows that soon after Ignatius' conversion he wrote things down to be *remembered* both for his spiritual profit and that of others (*Auto,* no. 11). His *Spiritual Diary* indicates that he continued and refined this process by underlining and marking out key passages that triggered his mystical *memory,* enabling him to retaste previous mystical experiences by simply recalling them to mind.[48]

The *Exercises* show clearly Ignatius' sacramental, kataphatic emphasis. Instead of calling upon the exercitant to forget everything for the sake of the naked love of God, Ignatius guides exercitants in the progressive simplification of their prayer. The *Exercises* foster an increasing *transparency* of the images, symbols, and mysteries of salvation history.

For example, the "preparatory prayer" for any exercise requires exercitants to direct themselves totally "to the service and praise of His divine Majesty" (*Ex,* no. 46). The "first prelude" usually calls upon the exercitant to create a "mental

---

[48]For specific examples of his mystical memory, see *SD,* nos. 9, 22, 44, 51, 52, 80.

image of the place" (*Ex,* no. 47) in the gospel scene, or uses some other way of directing the exercitant's imagination and fantasy to the truths of salvation history.

In the "second prelude" (*Ex,* no. 48), the exercitant asks for a specific grace, a "consolation with previous cause" (*Ex,* no. 331) consonant with the matter of the exercise, for example, joy with Christ rejoicing. The exercitants must place themselves into the mystery of salvation history as if they were actually present while it occurred (*Ex,* no. 114).

Even the more laborious "meditations" of the first week require the exercitant to seek an "interior understanding and savoring of things" (*Ex,* no. 2). The exercitant should linger with those aspects of the meditation that are satisfying (*Ex,* no. 76), never rushing from point to point, but following the consolations and the spiritual nourishment. Then, Ignatius would have the exercitant repeat previously made exercises to dwell especially upon those aspects that brought the most consolation and desolation (*Ex,* no. 62).

The "résumés" (*Ex,* no. 64) likewise recall and review intellectually what happened in the previous exercise. The Application of the Senses exercises (*Ex,* nos. 66-70) require the exercitant to see, hear, touch, taste, or smell in imagination certain aspects of a particular Christian mystery. This greatly condenses, intensifies, and transforms the prayer begun in the exercises of any particular day. Some link the Ignatian application of the senses to the deeply mystical prayer of the mystical, or spiritual, senses, in which the mystic prays with his or her senses of the soul.[49]

Each exercise ends with a "colloquy," "made properly by speaking as one friend speaks to another, or as a servant speaks to his master, now asking some favor, now accusing oneself for some wrong deed, making known his affairs to Him and seeking His advice concerning them" (*Ex,* no. 54). The colloquy actually carries forward, strengthens, and unifies the movement initiated in the exercises of any particular day.

---

[49]For an excellent discussion of the "mystical senses," see: H. Rahner, *Ignatius the Theologian,* chap. 5; K. Rahner, *TI* 16, chaps. 6, 7.

In short, instead of having exercitants forget the mysteries of salvation history, the *Exercises* aid them to experience each mystery in its totality.

Apophatic mystics sometimes recommend that a person use a meaningful word in prayer,[50] not concentrating on its meaning, but using it to control distractions while emptying the mind of all created things. For Ignatius, however, at the higher levels of mystical prayer the Christian mystery itself becomes a highly concentrated "word" with which the exercitant mystically resonates. It is a word that draws attention not to itself nor to its "letters," but to what it is in its essence: a sacrament of the healing, transforming presence of God.

The key to Ignatian mysticism, therefore, can be found in the dynamism of his *Spiritual Exercises,* which render the Christian mysteries increasingly *transparent.* Transparency, not forgetting and unknowing, underpins Ignatius' radical sacramental, or kataphatic, mysticism. In and through the increasing simplicity and transparency of the Christian mystery, the exercitant penetrates to its very depths to experience its saving power. In fact, the mystery may become so simplified and transparent that it draws the exercitant "wholly to the love of His Divine Majesty..." (*Ex,* no. 330) through "consolation without previous cause" (*Ex,* nos. 330, 336).

The *Exercises* are a paradigm, therefore, of Ignatius' sacramental, kataphatic contemplation, and may culminate in genuine sacramental mysticism. Karl Rahner writes: "the basic incarnational structure of the unconfused unity of God and his creatures gives to understand that we can apprehend God in the sign ... only if we do not cling to the sign ... as if it were the ultimate reality, God himself. The sign must be welcomed and passed by, grasped and relinquished."[51]

Hence, both the revealing and concealing fullness of the ever-greater God, found in the finite sacramental reality of the

---

[50]See, for example, *The Cloud of Unknowing and the Book of Privy Counselling,* chapters 36-40.

[51]*Visions and Prophecies,* trans. Charles Henkey and Richard Strachan (New York: Herder & Herder, 1964), p. 14, n. 12.

mysteries of salvation history, show themselves in Ignatius' gradual process of simplification and transparency. These mysteries must be welcomed, simplified, grasped, and rendered transparent if God will "one day reveal himself even to the pure mystic as the God of the transfigured earth because [the mystic] is more than pure spirit."[52]

[52]*Ibid.*

6

An Ecclesial Mysticism of Discernment, Election, and Confirmation

As we have seen, Ignatius' mysticism is trinitarian, christo-centric, mediator-centered, eucharistic, and priestly, and a service mysticism of reverential love. These aspects of his mysticism, however, are fused inextricably with his ecclesial mysticism of discernment, election, and confirmation. Precisely as a loyal son of the Church, the Body of Christ, Ignatius discerned God's will, decided accordingly, and sought to have this election confirmed by God.

Discernment and the Autobiography

The *Autobiography* attests to Ignatius' mysticism of dis-cernment, election, and confirmation. For example, while recuperating at Loyola from his serious leg injury at Pamplona, "he came to perceive the different spirits that were moving him; one coming from the devil, the other from God" (*Auto,* no. 8). In the former case his fantasies about the romantic literature he read left him dissatisfied; in the latter, thoughts triggered by reading about the lives of Christ and the saints consoled him, even after he stopped thinking about them.

Still unlettered in the things of God and of the interior life at this time, thoughts about imitating the saints in their great penances filled Ignatius with great joy. As he became more mature spiritually, Ignatius learned to mitigate these penances because they hindered his studies. Thus he discerned the role penances would assume in his life in the light of his service mysticism.

At Manresa, Ignatius discerned that the devil spoke to his soul to discourage him (*Auto,* no. 20). Severe scruples about the sins of his past life also tortured him there (*Auto,* nos. 23-25), tempting him to give up his newly converted life. "Now that he had some experience with the different spirits," however, "he began to think about the way that that spirit had come to him. Thus he decided, and with great clarity of mind, never to confess his past sins again and from that day forward he was free of his scruples..." (*Auto,* no. 25).

With the great mystical graces received at Manresa, especially those near the river Cardoner, Ignatius discerned that the serpent form with many eye-like features came from the evil spirit (*Auto,* nos. 19, 31). He also discerned "little by little" that the great consolations and spiritual lights that caused him to lose sleep or distracted him from his studies (*Auto,* nos. 26, 54-55, 82) came from the evil spirit, in an attempt to avert him from true service of God.

External circumstances often forced Ignatius to discern God's particular will for him. For example, only when the Franciscan provincial threatened to excommunicate Ignatius if he did not leave the Holy Land did he realize that it was God's will to leave (*Auto,* nos. 47-50).

Later, when the inquisitors prohibited him from speaking about spiritual things and teaching the distinction between mortal and venial sin, the door to his service mysticism seemed closed. So Ignatius decided that going to Paris to study was for God's greater service (*Auto,* nos. 62-63, 70-71). His service mysticism likewise prompted him to go to Flanders for a few months to beg for enough money to support himself for an entire year of study, instead of taking time away from his studies by begging daily (*Auto*, nos. 74-76).

Numerous visions played a part in Ignatius' mysticism of discernment, election, and confirmation (*Auto*, nos. 99-100). For example, the vision of Our Lady and the Christ child confirmed him in his new way of life and implanted the immovable resolve to go to the Holy Land to "help souls" (*Auto*, no. 10). Visions of Christ in a bright, undifferentiated bodily form, like the sun or a golden globe, deepened his resolve and *confirmed* yet more deeply his decision about going to the Holy Land (*Auto*, nos. 29, 40-42, 44-45).[1]

Ignatius' letter of June 5, 1552, to Francis Borgia offers another excellent insight into Ignatius' usual way of deciding an important matter.[2] Charles V had petitioned the Pope to make Borgia a cardinal. Because Ignatius saw good reasons for and against, he was unclear what God wanted. Hence, he ordered the priests in his community to offer Masses and the nonpriests to pray for three days "for divine guidance, to God's greater glory." During these three days, Ignatius himself prayed over the matter, reflected, and spoke with many others about it.

As Ignatius prayed, fears arose and abated, "until finally, on the third day, I made my usual prayer with a determination so final, so peaceful and free, to do all that I could with the pope and the cardinal to prevent it. I felt sure at the time, and still feel so . . . therefore I have felt, and now feel, that it is God's will that I oppose this move."[3] Borgia did not get the hat!

---

[1] In Chapter Three, "The Trinity and the Election," we noted the intimate link in the *Spiritual Diary* between Ignatius' trinitarian graces and his mysticism of discernment, decision, and confirmation. In the midst of these extraordinary mystical experiences, Ignatius never lost his focus: to seek, find, and carry out God's will with respect to certain aspects of the *Constitutions*. And he received infused loving reverence as mystical corroboration with his decision (*Auto*, nos. 99-100). In Chapter Four, "A Felt Knowledge of Jesus Christ," we explicated the christocentrism of Ignatius' mysticism of discernment, decision, and confirmation.

[2] *Letters*, pp. 257-258.

[3] *Letters*, p. 258. It is instructive to read about Ignatius instructing Borgia that others, also under God's direction, might think that he should accept. "I do not see," he wrote, "that there would be any contradiction, since the same Divine Spirit could move me to this action for certain reasons and others to the contrary for other reasons, and thus bring about the result desired by the emperor. May God our Lord

Discernment and the Spiritual Exercises

Ignatius saw his *Spiritual Exercises* as a method to free persons from inordinate attachments, so that they could more effectively seek and find God's specific will (*Ex*, no. 1).[4] They prepare the exercitant to make a decision based solely on a divine call that is "always pure and clean without any admixture of flesh or other inordinate attachments" (*Ex*, no. 172).

The matter of the election dominates the center of the *Exercises* (*Ex*, nos. 169-189). The *Directories*, that is, writings by Ignatius and the early Jesuits to answer specific questions that arose while giving the spiritual exercises, devote almost one-third of their space to the election. Thus the *Exercises* are never only a series of meditations nor are they a blueprint of the spiritual life. Rather they reveal their meaning through their *goal:* in an *election* transforming one's life, to find God's will in peace through the greatest assimilation to Christ.[5]

Ignatius had discovered the intrinsic relationship between consolation, desolation, and spiritual movements, and discernment, decision, and confirmation. These elements are essential to his service mysticism of reverential love. In other words, the *Spiritual Exercises* are "an attempt, especially in the Rules for Discernment of Spirits, to provide and give practice in a formal, systematic method of discovering this individual will of God ... [and] ... they are actually the first and so far the only detailed attempt at such a systematic method."[6]

always do what will be to His greater praise and glory." Take note, too, that he invited Borgia into the discernment process, for Ignatius' method of finding God's will often depended upon person-to-person relationships.

[4]For an excellent introduction to the nature of the *Spiritual Exercises*, see Joseph de Guibert, *Jesuits*, pp. 109-139, 527-543.

[5]See: Hugo Rahner, "Exerzitien," *Lexikon der Pädagogik* I (Freiburg i.B.: Herder, 1952), p. 1106.

[6]Karl Rahner, "Logic of Ignatius," p. 115.

A) The First Time of Election

Ignatius speaks of three occasions when a wise and good choice can be made. "The first occasion," he writes, "is when God our Lord moves and attracts the will so that the devout soul, without question and without desire to question, follows what has been manifested to it. St. Paul and St. Matthew did this when they followed Christ our Lord" (*Ex,* no. 175).

During this "first time," exercitants experience the divine call with such clarity, power, and immediacy that they respond "without question and without the desire to question." This God-initiated experience so overwhelms the exercitants that they respond to Christ with a simplicity and wholeheartedness that parallel that of St. Paul and St. Matthew.

When the Creator works directly with the person, as Ignatius clearly expects (*Ex,* no. 15), God's call indeed bears the mark of his presence. There can be "no deception in it, since it proceeds only from God our Lord" (*Ex,* no. 336). Moreover, "every divine call is always pure and clean and without any admixture of flesh or other inordinate attachments" (*Ex,* no. 172). As Ignatius taught Sister Teresa Rejadell: "For it frequently happens that our Lord moves and *urges* the soul to this or that activity ... lifting it up wholly to His divine love and ourselves to His meaning *without any possibility of resistance* on our part, even should we wish to resist."[7] Because the God component of this experience drowns out, at least temporarily, every form of dubious psychosomatic reaction, that is, every form of human echo, the human response must be "without question and without the desire to question."

Karl Rahner claims that Ignatius "regarded the first mode of Election as an extraordinary phenomenon which he mentions more out of a certain liking for system than for its practical importance."[8] But Ignatius, many first-generation Jesuits, and some who made the spiritual exercises under their direction definitely experienced this "first time" of election.[9]

---

[7]*Letters,* p. 22, my emphasis.

[8]"Logic of Ignatius," pp. 127-128, no. 25.

[9]See my *Ignatian Mystical Horizon,* pp. 134-139.

Hence, Ignatius definitely expected some who made these exercises to reach a decision according to the promptings of the "first time." The first mode of election did have "practical importance." And just as the consolation without previous cause is *the* consolation against which all other consolations must be measured, so, too, the "first time" is the norm for all other decisions.

B) The Second Time of Election

"The second occasion is present," Ignatus writes, "when one has developed a clear understanding and knowledge through the experience of consolations and desolations and the discernment of spirits" (*Ex,* no, 176). The *Spiritual Exercises* create the atmosphere for the "second occasion."

Every exercise contains a prelude in which the exercitant begs for "what I want and desire' and asks for specific consolations and interior movements. In fact, "when the one who is giving the Exercises feels that the soul of the exercitant is experiencing neither consolation nor desolation nor any other spiritual movements, or that he has not been troubled by different spirits, he should question him closely about the Exercises..." (*Ex,* no. 6).

As the Ignatian *Directory* says, the second time occurs "by proceeding in his meditations on Christ our Lord, and then observing to what God moves him when he finds himself in consolation. And the same when he finds himself in desolation."[10] Thus, the second time of election requires a long period of experimentation. Both intellectual and affective phenomena need to arise, that is, thoughts, insights, intellectual clarities, and a variety of affective stirrings. In order to perceive and understand "to some degree the different movements that are produced in the soul" (*Ex,* nos. 313, 328), the exercitant must assimilate the rules for the discernment of spirits.

In the second time, then, the exercitant actually pieces together a first time election, which was scattered into

---

[10]*Autography Directories of St. Ignatius of Loyola,* pp. 9-10.

consolations, desolations, and various movement of spirits that must be perceived and understood according to the rules for the discernment of spirits. If in the first time the exercitant experiences God's call from his or her deepest center, in the second time the exercitant becomes explicitly aware of the psychosomatic reverberations of this deepest movement throughout various levels of the psyche. Discerning during the second time is like using echoes to find the source of a sound, or tributaries to find a river's origin, or focusing a lens to concentrate many rays into a single point. Discernment during the second time seeks to put together the scattered rays of divine light and love in a way that approximates the immediacy and intensity of the first time. Hence, the second time of election has the same goal as the first: the divine call that comes from above. Discernment during the second time seeks the power and purity of the first time.

C) The Third Time of Election

Ignatius describes the third time of election as follows:

> The third occasion is in a time of tranquillity. Here one considers first for what purpose man is born, which is to praise God our Lord and to save his soul. Since he desires to attain this end, he chooses some life or state within the bounds of the church that will help him in the service of God our Lord and the salvation of his soul. I said "a time of tranquillity," when the soul is not agitated by diverse spirits, and is freely and calmly making use of its natural powers (*Ex*, no. 177).

This third occasion, then, focuses upon *tranquillity* of soul, the graces received from the Principle and Foundation exercise, and the use of one's "natural powers" for God's service and one's eternal salvation. This tranquillity also seems to be a form of consolation, that is, the "peace and quiet in Christ our Lord" (*Ex*, no. 316), or the "peace, tranquillity, and quiet" described in *Ex*, no. 333. It may be the result of the

"indifference" attained during the *Exercises*.[11]
Ignatius describes two methods for the third time of
election. The first method contains six points (*Ex*, nos. 178-
183). First, the exercitant must place before the "mind's eye the
thing on which I wish to make a choice" (*Ex*, no. 178).
Second, then, "remaining indifferent and free from inordinate
attachments" (*Ex*, no. 179), the exercitant must be ready to
follow whatever he or she *feels* is more for "the glory and
praise of God our Lord" and his or her salvation.

Third, the exercitant must beg God to move his or her will
and to reveal to the spirit what would best advance "God's
praise and service" (*Ex*, no. 179). Fourth, the matter must be
given careful rational scrutiny by weighing the advantages and
disadvantages of a certain choice.

Fifth, after examining the matter from every angle, the
person must take the "more reasonable" alternative, act "upon
the stronger judgment of reason," and decide (*Ex*, no. 182).
Sixth, "after such a choice or decision has been reached, I
should turn with great diligence to prayer in the presence of
God our Lord and offer Him this choice that His Divine
Majesty may deign to accept and confirm it, if it be to His
greater service and praise" (*Ex*, no. 183).

This method summarizes well the Ignatian method attested
to in his *Spiritual Diary*. The third time is not a purely rational
method, as some commentators have contended. The exercitant must make use of consolations, beg God for both inner
movements and clarity, weigh the pros and cons, examine the
matter, decide what is the most reasonable through a felt
knowledge of God's greater service, and have this decision
accepted and confirmed by God.[12]

---

[11]Ignatius' letters and the testimony of the early Jesuits indicate that Ignatius
expected the attitude of indifference to dominate in any discernment process. And
despite his emphasis upon obedience, if Ignatius found his men indifferent, he usually
decided in favor of their inclinations, i.e., what they preferred to do in the way of
apostolic service. If Ignatius did not have first-hand information about a geo-
graphically distant matter, he usually entrusted the decision to the person at the scene,
if he trusted the man's indifference and obedience. On this point, see *Mémorial*, no.
117, p. 112.

[12]The second method contains four main points and a note (*Ex*, nos. 184-188). The
exercitant must call to mind that "the love which moves me and causes me to make

Ignatius' own life indicates that the ideal election consists of a fusing of the three occasions discussed above.[13] His *Spiritual Exercises* show this. All three occasions require that God work directly with the person, at least at some stage. And the reasons pro and con must be considered eventually in each occasion, no matter how powerful God's felt presence.

For example, even the first time tends to flow into a "time that follows it ... Often in this latter period the soul makes various plans and resolutions which are not inspired directly by God our Lord" (*Ex*, no. 336). St. Paul felt it necessary to go up to Jerusalem to put "before them the Gospel which I preached ... lest somehow I should be running or had run in vain" (*Gal* 2:1f.). Was St. Matthew's first-time election intense enough to prevent all doubts about Jesus even after the resurrection (*Acts* 1:6f.)?

The *Spiritual Diary* indicates that despite the most exalted mystical experiences—seemingly indicative of the mood of the first time for election—Ignatius still had to discern carefully and continue to weigh the reasons for and against the election matter. Was Ignatius' error about God's will concerning a life of service in the Holy Land made because he did not attend enough to the difference between the consolation without previous cause and "this latter period" in which the soul is acting on its own?

The second time for election requires a normative consolation at some point, against which the exercitant can measure all other consolations and desolations. The exercitant in the second time seeks a consolation without previous cause, a consolation that God alone can give, a consolation, therefore, with no deception.

---

this choice should come ... from the love of God" (*Ex*, no. 184). Obviously, the third way cannot be reduced to a purely rational method. Next, Ignatius has the exercitants consider themselves on their death bed (*Ex*, no. 186), or on judgment day (*Ex*, no. 187). He requires that they ask themselves how they wish they had decided about the present matter, or, what advice they would have given to a complete stranger about the matter (*Ex*, no. 185). And in all this, they must finally turn once again to God for acceptance and confirmation of the election (*Ex*, no. 188).

[13]See my *Ignatian Mystical Horizon*, pp. 152-155.

The second time, moreover, must turn to reason and understanding. The proper discernment of God's specific will requires the exercitant to have accurate information about the election matter. For example, Ignatius sought the advice of well-informed people. He always tried to know the facts of the matter. He did not depend upon mystical affectivity alone.[14] Hence, the second time requires both the divine initiative of the first time and the accurate information and reasons of the third time.

Finally, the third time requires tranquillity, indifference, a felt knowledge of what is for God's service and praise, pondering the pros and cons, being moved from above, acting upon the stronger judgment of reason, deciding, and having this decision accepted and confirmed. In short, the third time of election contains aspects of the first two.

The three times, therefore, are not three distinct ways of finding God's will, but three aspects of one core experience, process, and election in which all three aspects *must* be present in varying degrees of intensity.[15]

D) Rules for the Discernment of Spirits

Ignatus wrote "Rules for the Discernment of Spirits" (*Ex,* nos. 313-336) on the basis of his own mystical life.[16] These

---

[14]In Ignatius' letter of March 30, 1556, to Alphonse Ramirez de Vergara (*Letters,* pp. 416-417), he insisted that *reason* often points out what is best for God's greater service and praise. Hence, continual recourse to spiritual affectivity is often unnecessary.

[15]The *Mémorial* (no. 282b, p. 205) also attests to this in Ignatius' life.

[16]See, Michael Buckley, S.J., "The Structure of the Rules for the Discernment of Spirits," *The Way. Supplement* 20 (1973), pp. 19-37; Maurizio Costa, S.J., "Spiritual Discernment," *Progressio* 48 (1979), pp. 3-12, 21-29; John Futrell, S.J., "Ignatian Discernment," *Studies in the Spirituality of Jesuits* II/2 (April 1970); Jacques Guillet, S.J., "Discernment of Spirits," *Dictionnaire de spiritualité ascétique et mystique,* III, trans. Sister Innocentia Richards. *Discernment of Spirit* (Collegeville, Minn.: Liturgical Press, 1970); Hugo Rahner, "The Discernment of Spirits," *Ignatius the Theologian,* pp. 136-180; Hugo Rahner, "Be Prudent Money-Changers: Toward the History of Ignatius' Teaching on the Discernment of Spirits," *Ignatius of Loyola. His Personality and Heritage 1556-1956,* ed. Freidrich Wulf (St. Louis: Institute of Jesuit Sources, 1977), pp. 272-279; Karl Rahner, "The Logic of Ignatius," pp. 84-170; Karl Rahner, S.J., "The Ignatian Process for Discovering the Will of God in an Existential Situation; Some Theological Problems in the Rules for Election and Discernment of

"Rules for perceiving and understanding to some degree the different movements that are produced in the soul—the good, that they may be accepted; the bad, that they may be rejected" (*Ex,* no. 313), therefore, must be read and studied carefully in the light of Ignatius' own mystical life. These rules are presented here as a paradigm of Ignatius' mysticism of discernment, decision, and confirmation.

Various "spirits" profoundly influenced Ignatius' life. He also expected exercitants to experience "spiritual movements," tides of consolation and desolation, hence to be "troubled by various spirits" (*Ex,* no. 6). So Ignatius gives fourteen rules for discernment in the first week and eight in the second. The rules for the first week are more suited to those "tempted strongly and openly" (*Ex,* no. 9); they focus more on coping with the struggles, desolation, and discouragements of following Christ's call. The rules of the second week are for those "being attacked and tempted under the appearance of good" (*Ex,* no. 10).[17] They "serve for the greater discernment of spirits" (*Ex,* no. 328), centering more on consolations and the subtle temptations encountered by those more proficient in the spiritual life.

i) Rules for the First Week

Rules one and two of the first week center upon the exercitant's existential stance. Ignatius depicts two diametrically opposed postures: one centered upon "going from mortal sin to mortal sin" (*Ex,* no. 314), the other, advancing "from good to better in the service of God our Lord" (*Ex,* no. 315). To mask the inauthenticity of the first stance, the "enemy" suggests "apparent pleasure," "sensual delights and pleasure" (*Ex,* no. 314). The "good spirit," on the other hand,

---

Spirits in St. Ignatius' *Spiritual Exercises," Ignatius of Loyola. His Personality and Heritage 1556-1956* ed. Friedrich Wulf, S.J., pp. 280-289; John Sheets, S.J., "Profile of the Spirit: A Theology of the Discernment of Spirits," *Review for Religious* 30 (1971), pp. 363-376; Jules Toner, S.J., *A Commentary on Saint Ignatius' Rules for the Discernment of Spirits* (St. Louis: Institute of Jesuit Sources, 1982).

[17]Ignatius' letter of June 18, 1536, to Sister Teresa Rejadell (*Letters,* pp. 18-24) is almost a personal summary of his rules for the discernment of spirits. See my *Ignatian Mystical Horizon,* pp. 46-51.

counters this by harassing the person's conscience "to a sense of remorse through the good judgment of reason" (*Ex*, no. 314).

The two spirits reverse their actions, however, for those zealous in God's service. The evil spirit will harass, discourage, and place obstacles in the way of those progressing in the spiritual life. On the other hand, the good spirit consoles, makes everything easy, and bestows joy, courage, and strength. In short, consolation and desolation have both a positive and a negative valence, depending upon the person's basic stance toward or away from God.

Rules three and four describe consolation and desolation, key realities in Ignatian mysticism. In terms of the two existential stances, consolation "calls and attracts to heavenly things . . . desolation . . . to low and earthly things" (*Ex*, nos. 316-317). They appear in consciousness, respectively, as inflaming love, "interior joy," "peace and quiet," or as "darkness of soul," "turmoil of the mind." They can also signify either an increase or a decrease of faith, hope, and love, depending upon the person's spiritual maturity. Moreover, Ignatius saw an explicit connection between consolations and desolations, and what God wished for God's praise and service.[18]

Rules five to nine describe the strategy to follow in times of desolation. Of major importance to Ignatius is that "in times of desolation one should never make a change, but stand firm" (*Ex*, no. 318). The exercitant should never make major decisions during this time because "in desolation the evil spirit guides and counsels" (*Ex*, no. 318). The Ignatian exercitant should not remain passive, however, but must "strive diligently against the desolation" (*Ex*, no. 321) by more prayer, penance, examinations of conscience, and patience. The person must remember, too, that "consolation will soon return" (*Ex*, no. 321).

---

[18]The *Autobiography* (no. 21) offers an excellent example of the Ignatian tides of consolation and desolation. It says: ". . . he began to feel notable changes in his soul. Sometimes he was so dejected that he found no enjoyment in the prayers he recited, not even in attending Mass, nor in any other form of prayer. Sometimes the exact opposite happened to him, and so suddenly that is seemed he had stripped away all sadness and desolation. . . ."

The exercitant may experience desolation because of personal tepidity, sloth, or negligence (*Ex*, no. 322). God may be testing the person's fidelity when the signs of the Holy Spirit's presence are not manifested. Ignatius assures the exercitant, however, that "even though he may not clearly perceive it . . . [God] . . . has nevertheless left him sufficient grace for eternal salvation" (*Ex*, no. 320). Although always to be directly countered, desolation may still be a special grace that brings "true knowledge and understanding" (*Ex*, no. 322). It teaches that consolations, progress in the mystical life, and even the desire for God itself are all "a gift and grace of God our Lord." Ignatius reminds the exercitant in desolation to find strength in God. Both consolation and desolation may effectively initiate the "flight from self-love, self-will, and self-interest" (*Ex*, no. 189) concretely seen in the exercitant's willingness to follow Christ poor, suffering, and humiliated.

Rules ten and eleven center upon the behavior suitable in periods of consolation. Perhaps these rules' brevity indicates that, for Ignatius, consolation speaks for itself because it comes from God. The key to Ignatian prayer is to follow what consolation does or where it might lead. At this point, in order to strengthen, deepen, moderate, and extend the effects of the present consolation, Ignatius has the exercitant look to the past to "recall how little he is worth in time of desolation" (*Ex*, no. 314) and to the future to "think of how he will conduct himself during the desolation that will follow" (*Ex*, no. 323).

Rules twelve to fourteen depict the devil's tactics and the exercitant's counterattacks. The enemy is symbolized as a "woman . . . weak in the presence of strength, but strong if she has her will" (*Ex*, no. 325), "a false lover who wishes to remain hidden and does not want to be revealed" (*Ex*, no. 326), and a military commander who studies and then attacks our "weakest side" (*Ex*, no. 327).

In the first case, fidelity to God's service and praise is obtained only through unwavering courage and fearless faith that "does exactly the opposite to what [the devil] suggests" (*Ex*, no. 325). Thus, one aspect of Ignatian mysticism is to face the enemy head on.

In the second case, the exercitant turns weakness into strength. He or she must rely upon another by revealing the devil's "deceitful words and depraved intentions ... to a confessor or some other spiritual person who understands the [enemy's] deceits and evil designs" (*Ex,* no. 326). In this way, Ignatius unites self-assurance with radical humility in opening up one's most secret temptations to another. Certain graces attain their fullness and certain temptations will be vanquished only after they have been revealed to another. In this matter, Ignatius underscores implicitly the social dimension of the mystical life, which must never be abolished in favor of the flight of the "alone to the Alone."

Finally, exercitants must be as shrewd as military commanders in being aware of, evaluating, and fortifying the weaknessess in their spiritual lives. Fearless confidence, a distrust of self, dependence on God and others, shrewd awareness of one's weaknesses, and constant vigilance are absolutely necessary to vanquish the enemy and to be under Christ's standard, the standard of true service and praise of God.

ii) Rules for the Second Week

The eight rules for the second week provide more refined discernment for the experienced exercitant in times of subtle temptations. The first rule describes consolation as "true happiness and spiritual joy" (*Ex,* no. 329). God's presence dispels all sadness, for in God's presence the exercitant experiences holiness and wholeness. This consolation illuminates the exercitant's real meaning, direction in life, and true self. It is no wonder, therefore, that the enemy will "fight against such joy" (*Ex,* no. 329) as deviously, subtly, and mightily as possible.

Rules two and eight focus upon "consolation without previous cause."[19] Because only God can give consolation in this specific way, it is the paradigm of all consolations. This unexpected, disproportionate consolation attracts the exerci-

[19]See my *Ignatian Mystical Horizon,* pp. 31-65, 132-156.

tant "wholly to the love of His Divine Majesty" (*Ex,* no. 330). In this consolation, therefore, the exercitant imitates Christ's total self-emptying and self-surrender to loving mystery.

Some contemporary theologians define the human person as one able to belong totally to God; this consolation perfectly actualizes this potential. It supports the thesis that anthropology in depth is really christology, that only from Christ do we know what it means to be human: perfect self-surrender to loving mystery.

Because this consolation comes entirely from God, "there is no deception in it" (*Ex,* no. 336). It is irrefutable evidence, therefore, of God's presence and a first principle against which all other consolations can be measured. Any experiences that enhance being drawn "wholly to the love of His Divine Majesty" (*Ex,* no. 330) may be accepted; experiences that diminish this should be rejected.

Even with this consolation, however, Ignatius advises caution. The exercitant "should carefully distinguish the exact time of such consolation from the time that follows it" (*Ex,* no. 336). The afterglow of this consolation may be used in subtle ways by the evil spirit against the exercitant. In the afterglow, it is also difficult to distinguish what comes from God, from the self, and from the "good spirit or the evil one." As already mentioned, this rule may have arisen from Ignatius' mistaken certitude that God wanted him to remain in the Holy Land his entire life to "help souls."

Rule three speaks of consolations with previous cause, in which "both the good angel and the evil one may console the soul but for different purposes" (*Ex,* no. 331). This rule echoes the second rule of the first week, but appeals more to intellectual than to affective criteria. Ignatius makes the invaluable distinction between consolations that nurture persons in their zeal for the praise and service of God and those consolations that only seem to do so. The former promote God's praise and service; the latter promote "the opposite."

Rule four states that "it is characteristic of the evil one to transform himself into an angel of light" (*Ex,* no. 332), an echo of 2 Corinthians 11:14. Knowing that a fervent person progressing in God's service cannot be tempted crudely, the evil one offers "good and holy thoughts" that seem congruent with the exercitant's state of faithful service, but that are really beset with "hidden deceits and perverse designs." Whereas the enemy in the first rule for the first week effectively masked his intentions by offering "apparent pleasures," he now employs intellectual camouflage, that is, "good and holy thoughts." Satan's temptation of Christ in the desert is this rule's paradigmatic dramatization.

The fifth rule is perhaps the very heart of Ignatian discernment. It complements the thirteenth rule of the first week, which would have exercitants reveal "to a confessor or some other spiritual person who understands [the devil's] deceits and evil designs... (*Ex,* no. 326) how they are being inspired or tempted. In rule five they must examine carefully both the entire scope of their thoughts and the resulting peace, quiet, and tranquillity. Both the intellectual and the affective components must be "directed to what is entirely right" (*Ex,* no. 333). "The beginning, middle, and end" of the thoughts must be "all good and directed to what is entirely right." If these thoughts propose something "less good," "distracting," or "evil," "this is a clear sign that they proceed from the evil spirit" (*Ex,* no. 333).

From the affective side, "if these thoughts weaken, disquiet, or disturb the soul by destroying the peace, tranquillity, and quiet which it had before" (*Ex,* no. 333), this, too, signifies the presence of the enemy. The new man with the new understanding of Cardoner and the man with the new heart of La Storta clearly transposed his cherubic (intellectual) and seraphic (affective) mysticism into this rule.

The fifth rule seems intimately related to the second and eighth rules. Rule eight speaks of "various plans and resolutions" that arise in the aftermath of the consolation without previous cause. These deserve careful scrutiny, for many consider the ideas that arise during religious fervor to be divinely inspired. As Ignatius says, however, they "are not inspired directly by God our Lord" (*Ex,* no. 336). Exercitants must ascertain whether the thoughts that arise in this period enhance or dilute the consolation without previous cause. On this basis they can determine their congruence or incongruence with God's will.

One would seriously misunderstand Ignatius, however, by thinking he urges the exercitant toward some abstract good. It is always a question of God's will *for the exercitant,* what is for his or her greater service and praise of God, what is better for the end for which he or she has been created. The thoughts discussed in this rule must resonate, therefore, with the exercitant's entire life and being.

The sixth rule gives instructions on how to profit from the experience of temptation. Both "his deceptions" and "the end to which he leads" (*Ex,* no. 334) eventually unmask the enemy of our human nature. By carefully examining "afterwards the course of the good thoughts that were suggested to him" (*Ex,* no. 334), the exercitant discovers the gradual ("little by little") and subtle process by which the enemy attempts to snatch away genuine consolation. Out of all this should come "experience and knowledge" by which the exercitant "may better guard himself in the future against the customary deceits of the enemy."

Rule seven proffers a more refined version of rules one and two of the first week. For those advancing in the spiritual life, "the action of the good angel is gentle, light, and sweet, as a drop of water entering a sponge. The action of the evil spirit is sharp, noisy, and disturbing, like a drop of water falling upon a rock" (*Ex,* no. 335).

For Ignatius, the most valuable consolations, those that promote the most radical progress, are usually delicate, simple, and silent. Only when the person's existential stance is in opposition to that of the "good angel" or "the enemy of our human nature" do these good and bad spirits act "with noise and disturbances that are easily preceived" (*Ex,* no. 335). If the person's and the spirit's stances are congruent, the spirit acts "silently, as one coming into his own house through an open door" (*Ex,* no. 335).

E) Intellectual and Affective Discernment

From what has already been said, it is clear that "the balanced union of the intellectual and volitional powers is perhaps the most characteristic trait in Ignatius' spiritual personality."[20] At Cardoner, Ignatius received a new understanding; at La Storta, a new heart. Both intellectual (cherubic) and affective (seraphic) experiences permeate his entire mystical life. His was not only a mysticism of moods[21] but also a mysticism of thoughts. Yet some Ignatian commentators overlook the cherubic dimension of his mysticism of discernment and emphasize its seraphic dimension.

Consolations, desolations, inner motions, and the *thoughts* that spring from these arise during the meditations and contemplations on Christ's life, death, and resurrection. "Within the stirring of spirits," one commentator writes, "rational reflection can and must develop as an indispensable element in the motion of spirits. After all, these stirrings . . . consist of thoughts, acts of knowing, perception of values, etc. They themselves contain an objective conceptual element, they can be expressed and verified."[22]

The rules for the discernment of spirits, therefore, focus not only on affectivity but also on knowledge, understanding, the unmasking of "false reasonings, seemingly serious reasons, subtleties" (*Ex.,* nos. 315, 324), and the thoughts that spring from consolation and desolation (*Ex,* no. 317). The exercitant must discern that the evil spirit *counsels* during desolation (*Ex,* no. 318); that God gives "true knowledge and understanding" (*Ex,* no. 322); that the evil one may suggest "good

---

[21]See R. González de Mendoza, *Stimmung und Transzendenz. Die Antizipation der existentialanalytischen Stimmungsproblematik bei Ignatius von Loyola* (Berlin: Dunker & Humblot, 1970). To be sure, de Mendoza uses the word "mood" (*Stimmung*) in its full Heideggerian sense, and this connotes much more than affectivity. For a brief summary of de Mendoza's position, see my *Ignatian Mystical Horizon,* pp. 27-29.

[22]Karl Rahner, "Logic of Ignatius," pp. 102-103.

and holy thoughts" (*Ex,* no. 322); and that "we must pay attention to the course of our thought" (*Ex,* nos. 333-334). Hence Ignatius learned from his own mystical life not only that some thoughts produced consolations and desolations, but also that consolations and desolations bring about certain thoughts.

Therefore, one aspect of Ignatian discernment is cherubic, or intellectual. Ignatius wished to impart through the *Spiritual Exercises* something of the "new understanding" and intellectual clarity he had received. The *Exercises* impart the ability to discern "good and holy thoughts that are in conformity with the disposition of a just soul" (*Ex,* no. 332), yet lead to "something evil ... or less good than the soul had previously proposed to do" (*Ex,* no. 333). Thus, the exercitant detects and recognizes more readily the evil one "by his deceptions and by the bad end to which he leads" (*Ex,* no. 334).

The moods of consolations and desolations caused by contemplating Christ's life also must be discerned, for they are signs of God's will. Of course, this requires affective discernment. For example, let us presuppose someone who has implicitly yet decisively chosen Christ poor, suffering, and humiliated. If consolations result from the congruence between this implicit election and the exercitant's explicit, specific election, for example, to enter religious life, these consolations may very well indicate God's will. If the specific election brought on desolations—in other words, clashed with the implicit election of the poor Christ—this would indicate an incorrect decision.

Moreover, affective discernment requires a consolation without previous cause. Only a basal, or touchstone, experience of exclusively divine origin, and thus free of all deception, can serve as the first principle of Ignatius' supernatural logic. The consolation without previous cause is the standard against which all other consolations and desolations are measured.

Exercitants must attend carefully to the emotional tone of their prayer, especially to the affectivity attached to the thoughts that arise during prayer. What emotional "echo" does the election produce in the exercitant's being? If "these thoughts weaken, disquiet, or disturb the soul by destroying the peace, tranquillity, and quiet which it had before, this is a clear sign that they proceed from the evil spirit" (*Ex,* no. 333). Also, if these thoughts suggest something "distracting," or "little by little" cause the exercitant to "fall from the state of sweetness and spiritual delight he was enjoying" (*Ex,* no. 334), they must be rejected. When the emotional tone of these thoughts enhance, strengthen, deepen, and harmonize with the exercitant's consolations without previous cause, this indicates God's specific will.[23]

Communal Discernment of Spirits

We have already seen that during the severe Roman winter of 1538-1539, Ignatius and his companions engaged in extensive corporal works of mercy. In fact, it is estimated that during this period of hardship they aided at their Frangipani house over 3,000 people in a city of approximately 40,000 inhabitants. In addition to feeding the hungry, caring for the sick, sheltering the homeless, burying the dead, and the like, they also continued their work of catechesis, preaching, administering the sacraments, and giving the spiritual exercises.

Requests for their services, however, began to pour in from cities outside Rome. The Pope had also requested that Broët

---

[23]Ignatius prohibited the reading of the works of Erasmus in the Society of Jesus. This prohibition seems to have come from his affective discernment. We read in his biography (P. Ribadeneira, *Vida de Ignacio de Loyola* [Madrid, 1868], I, c. 13): "He observed something totally new and strange: whenever he picked up and began to read a book from Erasmus, his ardour disappeared and his devotion grew cold. If he read further, this change increased, so much so, that if he had finished a certain section, it seemed to him that also his earlier fervour was lost, that his spirit became deaf and his heart exchanged for another and that he was no longer the same person he was before the reading. When he had noticed this a few times, he finally threw the book away and developed such an aversion and disgust for the book and the author's other books that he later never wanted to read them again and that he likewise did not allow them to be read in the Society of Jesus, except for a few well-chosen sections and with great caution." Ignatius' dislike of Erasmus lessened in his later years. On this point, see Leo Bakker, *Freiheit und Erfahrung. Redaktionsgeschichtliche Untersuchungen über die Unterscheidung der Geister bei Ignatius von Loyola* (Würzburg: Echter, 1970), pp. 121, 221.

and another companion go to Siena to reform a monastery of Benedictine nuns. The companions knew that the time for their dispersal was soon at hand. They needed to answer this question: when the Pope requested them for a specific mission, should they reply as independent individuals or as members of a stable group? If the latter, then should they vow obedience to one in their group as their religious superior? [24]

To answer these questions, the companions decided to deliberate in common for as long as it would take to settle the matter. This gave rise to the "deliberations of the first fathers" that lasted from March to June 24, 1539. [25]

Ignatius and his companions decided, therefore, "to get together for a good long time before our dispersal and to discuss our vocation and covenanted way of life" (no. 1,a). This international group was of "one mind and heart in seeking God's gracious and perfect will according to the scope of our vocation" (1,b). However, they held differing opinions on the best means for better apostolic service.

So, "since we did hold different judgments, we were eagerly on the watch to discover some unobstructed way along which we might advance together and all of us offer ourselves as a holocaust to our God, in whose praise, honor, and glory we would yield our all" (no. 1,c). To accomplish this, they agreed to "prayer, Masses and meditations more fervently than usual and, after doing our very best we would for the rest cast all our concerns on the Lord" (no. 1,c). In short, the procedure

[24] For this section, see: John C. Futrell, S.J., *Making an Apostolic Community of Love; idem,* "Communal Discernment," *Studies in the Spirituality of Jesuits* (November 1972), pp. 159-194; *idem,* "Ignatian Discernment," *Studies in the Spirituality of Jesuits* (April 1970), pp. 47-88; Jules J. Toner, S.J., "The Deliberations that Started the Jesuits. A Commentary of the *Deliberatio primorum Patrum.* Newly translated with a historical introduction," *Studies in the Spirituality of Jesuits* (June 1974), pp. 179-216; *idem,* "A Method of Communal Discernment of God's Will," *Studies in the Spirituality of Jesuits* (September 1971), pp. 121-152; Ladislas Orsy, S.J., "Towards a Theological Evaluation of Communal Discernment," *Studies in the Spirituality of Jesuits* (October 1973), pp. 139-188; Dalmases, *Ignatius,* pp. 164-169.

[25] The text of the "Deliberations of the First Fathers" is in *Constitutions, Monumenta Historica Societatis Jesu* I, pp. 1-7. An English translation can be found in John C. Futrell, S.J., *Making an Apostolic Community of Love,* pp. 188-194, and in Jules J. Toner, S.J., "The Deliberation That Started the Jesuits," I shall use Toner's translation.

Ignatius used and to which the *Spiritual Diary* attests was now used by the community of companions.

They likewise decided not to interrupt their apostolic works during the day, but to meet as a group in the evening to deliberate matters. This required, however, that they stay recollected throughout the day, that is, even during the day they had to "ponder and meditate on these [questions] and ... prayerfully search into them" (no. 2,d).

They had offered themselves to Christ's vicar "so that he might dispose of us and send us wherever he judged it to be more fruitful" (no. 3,e). Now they had to decide whether it would be better to remain together. They decided easily and unanimously to remain united because nothing less than divine providence united them, that is, "we ought not split apart what God has gathered and united" (no. 3,f).

The second issue centered on the desirability of vowing obedience to one of their number whom they would elect superior. After several days of deliberations without a decision, they considered whether sending all or some of them to a hermitage for about a month of prayer, fasting, and penance would help the discernment (no. 5,j). They resolved to stay put, however, to avoid giving the appearance of fleeing Rome or of not persevering in what they had begun. Also, they did not want to interrupt their apostolic work.

To resolve the impasse, they decided that "each would ready himself beforehand, would take time for prayer, Masses, and meditation in order to strive for joy and peace in the Holy Spirit regarding obedience, laboring as much as he could to have a predilection for obeying rather than commanding..." (no. 6,l). Moreover, they were not to discuss the matter with each other. Finally, "each one would think of himself as a stranger to our group who would have no expectation of joining it" (no. 6,l).[26] Uninfluenced by others, each one was to

---

[26]This, of course, echoes the advice given in the "third occasion" for making an election, that is, "The second rule is to consider some man that I have never seen or known, and in whom I wish to see complete perfection. Now I should consider what I would tell him to do and choose for the greater glory of God ... I will act in like manner myself" (*Ex,* no. 185).

find his own reasons in private prayer and recollection, and then present them at the meeting.

It is instructive that each companion was called upon first to "declare all those disadvantages which could be brought against obedience..." (no. 7,m). They came up with two disadvantages. First, "the words 'religious' or 'obedience' have unseemly connotations among Christian people" (no. 7n). Secondly, the Pope might force them "to live under some Rule already drawn up and established" (no. 7.n). This would put an end to their apostolic mobility, as they conceived it.

"On the next day," however, "we argued for the opposite side of the question, each one putting before the group all the advantages and good consequences of such obedience which he had drawn from prayer and meditation...' (no. 7,o). It is instructive that they saw no need to complete the deliberations in one day. More importantly, this method lessened arguments and made for more active and sympathetic listening. The reasons *against* the vow of obedience are presented by *all* on one day; the reasons *for* obedience are presented by *all* on another.

The companions put forth five reasons for a vow of obedience. First, obedience promotes a reasonable and practical division of labor. Second, with obedience, the group's unity would not be in jeopardy. Third, obedience provides an opportunity for a life of heroic deeds and heroic virtues. Fourth, "nothing so casts down all pride and arrogance as does obedience..." (no. 7,p). Finally, "although we have committed ourselves in particular to obey the supreme pontiff and shepherd in general and in particular, nevertheless, he could not possibly take time for the innumerable details and contingencies of our affairs; nor would it be right for him to do so even if he could" (no. 7,p).

After many days, they came to a unanimous decision: "Obedience to someone among us is highly advantagous and highly necessary in order to actualize more effectively and exactly our primary desire of fulfilling God's will in all the details of life [*per omnia*], in order to preserve the Society more assuredly, and, finally, in order to provide properly for all the detailed matters of spiritual and temporal business which arise" (no. 8,q). In a solemn ceremony at a Mass celebrated by Peter Faber, the companions signed a document after communion stating that a vow of obedience to one of their own would preserve their unity and do more for God's greater praise and service.

From May to June, they drew up the general lines of a new religious order. They would vow poverty, chastity, obedience, and obedience to be at the Pope's disposal. Each would be required to teach children catechism. All entering their group would make the spiritual exercises, go on a month's pilgrimage, and work in a hospital. The companions would be able to possess houses but without exercising the rights of ownership over them. The superior general would be elected for life and had the right to admit novices and to dismiss those unfit for the Society, after consultation with advisers.

They terminated their deliberations on the feast of John the Baptist, June 24, 1539. "On that day, but not without long vigils, much prayer, and labor of mind and body preceding deliberation and decision, all our business was completed and terminated in a spirit of gladness and harmony" (no. 9,r).

The deliberation of the first fathers in 1539 is a communal expression of Ignatius' service mysticism and discernment, election, and confirmation. The group gathered to ensure the better service of God in their new circumstances. They sought God's will through amassing evidence, considering the reasons for and against, offering their Masses, as well as through prayer, recollection, reflection, meditation, deliberations, a felt knowledge in the Lord, and having their deliberations confirmed by God "in a spirit of gladness and harmony."

This deliberation is also an expression of their desire to be with Christ to serve, but in the grace of companionship, in the intimacy of mutual love. The superior represents Christ to his companions in order to realize more effectively the scope of their vocation.[27] In short, this deliberation and its results came

[27]The *Constitutions* speak often about seeing Christ in one's superiors. See nos. 85, 284, 286, 342, 424, 434, 547-552, 618, 619, 661, 765.

from a *mystical* body, that is, a group of men already bonded together by a mystical love for Christ *and for each other,* who decided to deepen this mystical bond among them for more effective apostolic service.[28]

Finally, this deliberation expressed and made more specific their ecclesial and papal mysticism. The vow of obedience to a Jesuit superior flowed almost naturally from their vow to place themselves at the Pope's disposal. In fact, for them the superior was the Pope's vicar. In a profound sense, therefore, the papal vow preceded the vow to the superior. Ignatius' mysticism of obedience must be understood within this context.

An Ecclesial Mysticism

Because Ignatius' mysticism is expressly Christ-centered, it is also necessarily ecclesial.[29] "The Church for Ignatius," writes one Ignatian commentator, "is not just an external organization or framework within which he sets himself and his order, but primarily the visibility and embodiment of the Lord himself, to whose greater glory he offers his service in the Church."[30]

Because of his trinitarian and Christ-related mystical experiences at Manresa, Ignatius wrote that "if there were no Scriptures to teach us these matters of faith, he would still resolve to die for them on the basis of what he had seen" (*Auto,* no. 29). Moreover, his enlightenment experience on the banks of the river Cardoner brought him great clarity about "numerous spiritual things as well as matters touching on *faith* and learning..." (*Auto,* no. 30, my emphasis). Implicit in

---

[28]Part VIII of the *Constitutions* is devoted exclusively to "uniting the distant members with their head and among themselves."

[29]For this section, see Hugo Rahner, *Ignatius the Theologian,* pp. 214-238; Joseph de Guibert, *Ignatius,* pp. 593-596; Dalmases, *Ignatius,* pp. 190-204.

[30]Berkhart Schneider, S.J., "Die Kirchlichkeit des heiligen Ignatius von Loyola," in J. Daniélou, S.J. and H. Vorgrimler (eds), *Sentire Ecclesiam* (Freiburg i.Br.: Herder, 1961), p. 300.

these experiences, therefore, is the ecclesial dimension of his mysticism.

Nadal, one of the early companions who knew Ignatius' mind and heart exceptionally well, said about Manresa: "At that time Ignatius began to probe deeply into his soul and to experience the variety of spirits. And in this the Lord gave him a sublime understanding and very lively feelings in regard to the divine mysteries and the *Church*."[31] With good reason, therefore, Ignatius could write: "... we should love the whole body of the Church in her head, Jesus Christ...."[32] In short, Ignatius' *ecclesial* mysticism of discernment, election, and confirmation actually began during his Manresan period of conversion and transformation.

Another event in Ignatius' life likewise illustrates the connection he experienced mystically between church, discernment, election, and confirmation. As already noted, Ignatius was firmly convinced that God had called him to the Holy Land to serve Christ where Christ himself had lived, served, suffered, died, and rose for us. "Nothing could prevent him from carrying it out" (*Auto,* no. 46), not even the danger of being taken hostage and enslaved.

Yet when the Franciscan provincial informed Ignatius that he had the authority from the Holy See to expel and excommunicate anyone who refused to obey, Ignatius discerned that "it was not our Lord's will for him to remain in the Holy Places..." (*Auto,* no. 46). For him, therefore, the most penetrating and convincing internal mystical experiences had to be congruent with their incarnational or sacramental dimension, that is, with the Church. Even the most exalted mystical graces, as Nadal relates about Ignatius, had to be always "in harmony with holy scripture, the virtues, right reason and edification—in short, with the *church*."[33]

---

[31] *FN* I, p. 307. Quoted in Hugo Rahner, *Ignatius the Theologian*, p. 218, my emphasis.

[32] Letter of July 23 and August 7, 1553, to the whole Society, *Letters*, p. 301.

[33] *Archivum Romanum Societatis Iesu*, Opp. 30, fol. 131. Quoted in Hugo Rahner, *Ignatius the Theologian*, p. 217, my emphasis.

Another event dramatizes more positively Ignatius' ecclesial mysticism. While he and his Paris companions were studying for the priesthood with the intent of more effective apostolic service, they decided to bind themselves more closely in a fellowship of love dedicated to Christ's service. Hence, they resolved to take private vows of chastity and of poverty (to be observed once they finished their studies), and vowed to go to the Holy Land to labor for the conversion of the Turks. If unable to go or to remain in the Holy Land, "they would return to *Rome* and offer themselves to the *Vicar of Christ* so that he could use them wherever he judged it would be for the greater glory of God and the good of souls" (*Auto,* no. 85, my emphasis). And since the Venetian-Turkish wars prevented their trip to the Holy Land, they did end up going to Rome.[34]

Ignatius' mysticism was rooted solidly in a profound sense of God's immediacy, but of an immediacy incarnated sacramentally in Jesus' flesh and in the visible Church. This sacramental mysticism became highly specific and detailed during Ignatius' trip to the Holy Land. This incarnational mysticism, moreover, enabled him to shift from Jerusalem to Rome, because he would find in both a "transparency of representation" (E. Przywara); that is, because of their sacramental significance, Ignatius could find Christ with great ease either in Jerusalem or in Rome.

To be sure, Ignatius and his companions first found their Jerusalem and Rome at La Storta, where the Father placed

---

[34]Ignatius' letter of November 23, 1538, to James de Gouvea (*Letters,* pp. 35-36) indicates that this "Roman turn" was hardly a pis aller for Ignatius and his companions. He writes: "All of us who are mutually bound in this Society have given ourselves to the supreme pontiff, since he is the lord of the worldwide harvest of Christ our Lord. In thus offering ourselves we have pointed out to him that we are ready for any duty he may wish to assign us in Christ. Should he, therefore, send us where you would like to see us, we shall go gladly. *Our reason for thus placing ourselves at his disposal is that we know that he has a better knowledge of what will be profitable for the universal Church* (p. 35, my emphasis). Dominique Bertrand, S.J. ("Ignatius von Loyola," p. 267) contends that for Ignatius the Pope was a means to the end, that is, mission. True enough, yet it must also be emphasized that Ignatius' "hyperpapal" mysticism cannot be separated from his christocentric mysticism. It is precisely as *Vicar of Christ* that Ignatius viewed the Pope in relation to his desire to reform the entire world.

Ignatius with his cross-bearing Son and stamped these words in his heart: "I shall be favorable to you [plural] *in Rome.*" The confirmation of Ignatius' trinitarian mysticism of service under the banner of Christ likewise confirmed his "Roman" and "hyperpapal" mysticism.[35]

Hence, "the ideal was henceforth to be at the service of Christ in the person of His Vicar, first of all at Rome and then in any place where this Vicar might request service."[36] Moreover, Ignatius was motivated to take a vow of special obedience to the Pope because of the mystical realization that in this way Ignatius could be *more certain* of the *Holy Spirit's guidance.*[37]

The mystical graces of La Storta had placed Ignatius with Christ to serve, but in a service under the direction of Christ's visible representatives on earth. Ignatius' attitude of being totally at the Pope's disposal, therefore, mystically flowed from that same unreserved attitude toward Christ. The generous, ardent, reverential, loving service of Christ necessarily included everything that was an intimate part of Christ, that is, his Mother (her flesh is in that of her Son), his Church (his very Body), and his vicar on earth.[38] Thus mystical experiences united him not only with the triune God and Christ, but also with the "true Spouse of Christ our Lord, our Holy Mother, the hierarchical Church" (*Ex,* no. 353). The full sacramental expression of Ignatius' felt knowledge (*sentir*) of Christ is his "Rules for Thinking and Feeling with and in the Church" (*Ex,* nos. 352-370).

These rules stress a mystical felt knowledge of and being at home in the visible, tangible, historical community of Jesus

---

[35]Hugo Rahner, *Ignatius the Theologian,* p. 234.

[36]Joseph de Guibert, *Jesuits,* p. 593.

[37]*Monumenta Ignatiana,* III, 1, p. 337. See Hugo Rahner, *Ignatius the Theologian,* p. 222.

[38]For a longer exposition of Ignatius' Roman and papal mysticism, see his letter of February 23, 1555, to Claude, Emperor of Abyssinia (*Letters,* pp. 367-372). It is instructive, however, that Ignatius' Roman and papal mysticism was counterbalanced by an excellent *missionary* discretion and prudence, even an implicit appreciation for "inculturation." On this point, see his letter of February 20, 1555, to Father John Nunez Barreto (*Letters,* pp. 381-390).

Christ, not the purely invisible Church of some reformers. Ignatius' felt knowledge, therefore, is neither a subjective, pious sense of an invisible Church nor an extrinsic, voluntaristic attachment to an ecclesiastical bureaucracy. It is the genuine Christian experience in the mystical, or spiritual, senses of full union with every dimension of a Church that is inseparable from the incarnate Christ.

The following mystical insight from the *Exercises* expresses this well: "between the Bridegroom, Christ our Lord, and the Bride, His Church, there is but one spirit, which governs and directs us for the salvation of our souls, for the same Spirit and Lord who gave us the Ten Commandments, guides and governs our Holy Mother Church" (*Ex,* no. 365). This quotation also points out that his ecclesial mysticism resulted not only from his Christ-centered mysticism, but also from his Spirit mysticism.

Genuine Spirit and incarnational mysticism results inevitably in ecclesial mysticism. The deepest, most interior movements in the soul must not only become incarnate, but these incarnations must also be congruent with the mystical Body of Christ, the Church in all its dimensions.

As a result of his own mystical life, Ignatius realized that the discernment of spirits must embody itself in a concrete decision, the election. This election, moreover, had to be congruent with the "hierarchical Church" (*Ex,* no. 170) and "within the bounds of the church" (*Ex,* no. 177). Hence, Ignatius is "Roman" and "papal" because of his mysticism of discernment, election, and confirmation.

In fact, the Church, with the Pope as its visible head, offered Ignatius the supreme form of visibility, or sacramentality, that was both an essential mark of the Church and a necessary norm for discerning interior mystical motions. Ignatius' mysticism refused resolutely to dichotomize mystical interiority, the "sacramentalization" of this interiority in concrete decisions, and the visible, historical Church.

Inner mystical experiences proved their authenticity for Ignatius if they did not hesitate to become visible, that is, by revealing themselves to the light of a living community of faith

(*Ex*, no. 326). For him, mystical graces must always be in harmony with "our holy mother the Church, her rulers and teachers."[39]

Of course, these rules must be evaluated in their historical context, for some contain an antiquated anti-Protestant tinge. Although they have an anti-Reformation tone, it is understandable why Ignatius' rules counsel obedience to the hierarchical Church; respect for the Church's sacramental, religious, and liturgical life; respect for Church laws, customs, and precepts; and care in preaching about predestination, free will, faith, and good works. Some rules may be antiquated, but not the authentic pneumatic, incarnational, and ecclesial mysticism that grounds them. In fact, Ignatius' loyalty to Church authority, doctrines, teachings, practices, and customs is an essential feature of all genuine Christian mysticism.

For Ignatius, the Church could be an immediate and positive source of mystical inspiration, an ultimate and negative boundary, or anything in between.[40] For example, his *Spiritual Exercises* state: "I will believe that the white that I see is black, if the hierarchical Church so defines it" (*Ex*, no. 365). But this must be tempered with the statement that: "Although the men of the Society are papists, they are this only when they absolutely have to be and in nothing more; and even then, only with an eye to the glory of God and the general good."[41]

Hence, Ignatius was convinced that what the Pope asked him to do in most cases was a clear sign of God's will. His and his companions' vow of obedience to the Pope put them

---

[39]Ignatius' letter of September 20, 1548, to Francis Borgia (*Letters*, p. 181). In his letter of June 18, 1536, to Sister Teresa Rejadell (*Letters*, p. 22), he insisted that even the most profound mystical inspiration must "of necessity [be] in conformity with the commandments, the precepts of the Church, and obedience to our superiors." Or as Hugo Rahner says, "...a spiritual movement is always to be measured up against what might be described as the 'extreme' visibility of the Church in the Pope of Rome" (*Ignatius the Theologian*, p. 220).

[40]See Raymond Schwager, S.J., *Das dramatische Kirchenverständnis bei Ignatius von Loyola* (Zürich-Einsiedeln-Köln: Benziger, 1970), p. 152.

[41]*MNad* II, p. 263. Quoted in Hugo Rahner, *Ignatius the Theologian*, p. 237.

unconditionally and totally at the Pope's disposal for any pontifical mission. The vow of obedience to the Pope, moreover, preceded the vow of the companions to one in their group.

Nonetheless in some cases, Ignatius' dealings with the Pope indicate that he reserved to himself the *next* to the last word, and adamantly so, especially on issues he was convinced concerned God's will. His dealing with Popes Paul III, Julius III, and Paul IV indicate clearly that his obedience was not automatic, and that he even forced them on occasion to come around to his way of thinking.[42] For example, Ignatius firmly closed the doors to any and all ecclesiastical dignities for himself and his men, despite urgings to the contrary from the hierarchy.[43] Thus with all his might he opposed the elevation of Laínez to the cardinalate, and of Canisius, Le Jay, and Juan de Arteagu to the episcopacy. Nonetheless, he allowed his men to become bishops in mission countries, because there they would suffer much for the faith. Hence, John Futrell is correct—as far as he goes—when he writes: "The norm of discernment for all things, therefore—even the wisdom of a papal command—was the apostolic end of the Company, the 'scope of our vocation.' " [44]

Ignatius' great concern to preserve the "apostolic end of the Company, the 'scope' of our vocation,' " probably explains why the usually imperturable Ignatius "showed a notable change and disturbance in his countenance and, as I came to know later . . . all his bones were shaken within him," [45] when he learned that Cardinal Caraffa was elected Pope. This long-time enemy desired to make substantial changes in the Society, although as Pope Paul IV, he eventually became one of its great benefactors.

[42]Raymond Schwager, S.J., *Das dramatische Kirchenverständnis*, pp. 136-152.

[43]On this point, see Dalmases, *Ignatius*, pp. 193, 223, 229, 236, 245 and *Const*, nos. 817, 819.

[44] *Making an Apostolic Community of Love*, p. 32. I would stress, however, that for Ignatius the "scope of our vocation" *included* "the wisdom of a papal command." Ignatius' *service* mysticism cannot be dissociated from its *ecclesial* and *papal* components.

[45] *Mémorial*, no. 93, pp. 98-99. Quoted in Dalmases, *Ignatius*, p. 286.

Ignatius viewed the entire world in terms of believers and unbelievers and desired to bring it totally into the visible Church of Christ. Hence, Ignatius conceived the mission of the Society of Jesus as nothing less than working for the reform of all believers and the incorporation of all unbelievers into the Church. Everything else he considered means to that end. In fact, one never finds Ignatius doubting or wavering about these goals. This single-minded missionary attitude suffused his social-political wisdom, which enable him to discern the appropriate means to attain his goals.

Moreover, Ignatius was convinced that nothing was more beneficial to the universal Church than the reform of the *Roman* Church. Hence, although he was a loyal son of the hierarchical Church, he was also a master of ecclesiastical diplomacy and political maneuvering.[46]

A Mysticism of Divine Providence

Divine providence also molded Ignatius' ecclesial mysticism of discernment, election, and confirmation. God taught Ignatius to seek God's hand in what happened to him, and also to discover what he must do for God in the future.

Only God's providence ultimately explains why a French cannonball led to Ignatius' long convalescence during which he read the only two books available at Loyola, one on the life of Christ and the other on the lives of the saints. During this period, God opened Ignatius' eyes to his mysterious ways, for at Loyola he received an introductory course on the discernment of spirits.

The political situation in the Holy Land at the time of Ignatius' pilgrimage made it dangerous for Christians to remain there. Hence, the Franciscan provincial, who possessed the authority to excommunicate, indirectly forced Ignatius to discern that God did not want him to remain there. Upon

---

[46]On this point, see the monumental work of Dominique Bertrand, *La politique de saint Ignace de Loyola,* (Paris: Les Éditions du Cerf, 1985), *passim.*

returning from his pilgrimage, he further discerned the need to study for God's greater service and praise.

The inquisitors at Barcelona, Alcalá, and Salamanca were also indirectly responsible for Ignatius' rethinking of his apostolic situation. Because of them he discerned the need to study *in Paris* for the priesthood. And the very person who passionately wanted to go to the Holy Land *alone,* "for his only desire was to have only God as his refuge" (*Auto,* no. 35), eventually came to discern the need to be with Christ to serve *in a companionship of mutual love.*

Even as late as 1537, Ignatius and his companions had no intention of establishing a religious order. They desired to go to the Holy Land to serve Christ and to die among unbelievers. But the Venetian-Turkish war prevented this. Hence, they discerned and elected to place themselves at the Pope's disposal for God's greater service. And because of events in Rome, they were forced to deliberate in common about the question of a vow of obedience to one of their own, again for the sake of God's greater service.

Even after Ignatius became superior general, a mysticism of divine providence forced him to discern and decide what he and his companions should do for God's service. Although he had the authority from the Pope to decide where to place his companions, usually appeals from cardinals, heads of state, benefactors, and the like determined where and how Ignatius used his men. In fact, it was precisely the reputation of the Society of Jesus that generated these appeals.

To put it in yet another way, Ignatius' mysticism of divine providence and discernment accounts for his "reentry" into the social structures of his day. When Ignatius left for Jerusalem in 1521, he had essentially broken his ties with family, money, power, prestige, and culture, withdrawing from the society of his day to become a wandering pilgrim for Christ. The Jerusalem-bound Ignatius of 1521 was unkempt, begged daily for his meals, undertook great penances, worked in hospitals, took no interest in learning, and enjoyed being accounted a fool.

His decision to study in order to serve Christ better,

however, forced him to mitigate his life as a wandering pilgrim. For example, instead of begging daily and losing precious study time, his mysticism of discernment sent him to Flanders to obtain money from rich merchants to sustain him throughout the academic year. The Montmartre vow of poverty, too, was conditional, that is, it went into effect after studies. Even a cursory glance at his writings indicates that he learned to deal with the rich, the powerful, the urbane, and the educated, for the sake of the apostolate.

His mysticism of divine providence and discernment changed him from Christ's vagabond to the immobile missionary in Rome, knee-deep in administrative detail. He who had broken with money, property, and security now wrote thousands of letters that often dealt with inheritances, finances, stable revenues to found colleges, and the like. Divine providence and discernment taught Ignatius that the true missionary is indifferent to all except God's will.

Events, situations, circumstances, successes, and failures, moreover, often determined which ministries the first Jesuits undertook. Why did Xavier go to the Indies? Because Bobadilla, who had been first appointed, got sick. Why were Laínez and Salmeron sent to the Council of Trent? Because of their previous contacts with bishops and princes. How did the Jesuit mission in Sicily begin? Because of the urging of Cardinal Carpi, one of the Society's great benefactors.

This is not to imply that Ignatius waited passively for things to happen. Neither does it deny that Ignatius preferred to send his men to places of acute spiritual and human misery. Nor does it deny that when Ignatius made up his mind for or against a project, he would follow through *totally* on his decision, even if that meant opposing the Pope himself. It was often said of Ignatius, especially even in very high places, "the saint has driven the nail," meaning, do not even try to get him to change his mind.

But it does negate the false impression that Ignatius was a master planner and grand strategist who had a detailed and meticulously worked out master plan for the Society's development: which works it would undertake, into which countries he would send his men, and the like. The irony is that the projects most dear to Ignatius' own heart either failed, were put off for a long time, or succeeded only after his death. For example, Ignatius' dream about the Holy Land never came into being. His desire to establish a college in Paris was realized only after his death. How long did it take for the Society to establish itself in England? Nonetheless, once Ignatius discerned God's will and had his election confirmed, he pursued his goal with all the means at his disposal, even if human wisdom seemed to doom the mission from the outset. In short, a mysticism of divine providence, a mysticism that learns in and through experience, a mysticism that seeks, finds, and executes God's will—no matter what the circumstances—is an integral part of his ecclesial mysticism of service, discernment, decision, and confirmation.

7

A Mysticism of
Extraordinary Experiences

Thus far this book has focused upon Ignatius' mysticism as a way of life initiated by God's living flame of love, which purified, illuminated, and transformed him for total union with God. It has emphasized his mysticism as one of direct and conscious union with God, whom he found in all things. In addition to being explicitly trinitarian, christocentric, mediator-centered, eucharistic, and priestly, Ignatius' mysticism is also reverential, ecclesial, and service-oriented. Finally, it is one of discernment, decision, and confirmation.

It is evident, moreover, that Ignatius underwent many extraordinary experiences during his mystical pilgrimage.[1] The Christian mystical tradition attests that unusual mystical experiences often occur with the primary phenomenon of *infused contemplation,* or the mystic's experience of God's

---

[1]For an overall view of extraordinary mystical phenomena, see my *Christian Mysticism,* pp. 303-359; Joseph de Guibert, S.J., *The Theology of the Spiritual Life,* trans. Paul Barrett, O.F.M. Cap. (New York: Sheed and Ward, 1953), pp. 305-339, 353-357; A. Poulain, S.J., *The Graces of Interior Prayer,* trans. Leonora L. Yorke Smith (Westminster, Vt.: Celtic Cross, 1949); Evelyn Underhill, *Mysticism* (New York: E.P. Dutton, 1961), pp. 266-297, 358-379.

loving self-communication.[2] If past studies tended to over-emphasize these extraordinary experiences at the expense of the essential mystical phenomenon of infused contemplation, contemporary studies seem to dissociate them too sharply.[3] In Ignatius' case, for example, infused contemplation often cannot be distinguished clearly from the extraordinary mystical phenomena he received. The phenomena were the way he both received and expressed God's loving self-communication, that is, infused contemplation. In fact, his overall mystical life cannot be understood without comprehending the tremendous influence these unusual phenomena had in his overall mystical life. One finds the ordinariness of the extraordinary throughout most of his mystical life.

Of course, Ignatius recognized the ambiguous nature of these experiences. Because they can originate from God, the devil, or the self, he subjected them to meticulous mystical discernment. And because extraordinary mystical experiences can either promote or hinder genuine union with God, it was absolutely essential for Ignatius to discern their source.

Some of these phenomena have already been mentioned in connection with other aspects of Ignatius' life and mysticism. For teaching purposes, however, it seems best to treat them here in a more orderly fashion.

---

[2]Joseph de Guibert (*Jesuits,* pp. 44-45) describes the distinctive traits of infused contemplation as "an experience of God as being present under a form of knowledge which is simultaneously general and obscure yet rich and satisfying; an experience of love penetrating and dominating the soul in its innermost depths, in a manner connected with passivity; the mystic's experiencing this passivity while he is under the all powerful control of God; his complete impotence to awaken, prolong, or renew these experiences, or even to foresee their approach or their end; also his inability to translate what he has experienced into forms of current language or, above all, to give an idea of them which is fairly clear to one who has never experienced anything similar."

[3]On this point, see Karl Rahner, "The Ignatian Mysticism of Joy in the World," p. 279.

Visions

Both the *Autobiography* and the *Spiritual Diary* reveal clearly that the divine communication Ignatius received frequently came in the form of visions. In fact, Ignatius received so many visions that he often noted them in his diary simply with shorthand symbols.

Ignatius' mystical life, in the strict sense, began with a vision, a clear likeness (*imagen*) of Our Lady and the Christ child that profoundly consoled him and cauterized his memory with respect to thoughts about his past life (*Auto,* no. 10). This vision likewise brought with it a God-given, or infused, chastity that empowered him not to consent to the least desire of the flesh for the rest of his life. Because this vision confirmed Ignatius in his holy desires and transformed him both internally and externally, he concluded that it must have come from God.

During his stay at the hospital in Manresa, Ignatius began to have a type of vision that would occur often in his life (*Auto,* nos. 19, 31). In broad daylight, he saw in the air a serpent-like form that shone brightly with many eye-like things. This vision brought much consolation, yet because it lost color in the light of the cross before which Ignatius knelt, he concluded that it came from the devil. Although he drove it away with his pilgrim's staff, the vision continued to appear to him. It is remarkable that among all the visions Ignatius had, this is the only one he discerned as demonic and rejected.

Ignatius had decided not to eat meat with such a firm resolve that "for nothing would he think of changing it" (*Auto,* no. 27). Yet "some meat appeared before him" at Manresa one morning "just as if he saw it with his body's eyes, though he had no prior craving for it." One commentator reduces this vision to something "natural enough,"[4] but much more seems to be going on. While the vision was taking place, "a powerful inclination of will came over him henceforth to eat meat." Despite his former resolve, the cautionary advice of his

[4]Hugo Rahner, *The Vision of La Storta,* p. 102.

confessor, and his careful discernment of what might be only a temptation, "he did not hesitate to decide that he ought to eat meat." Further, to doubt would offend the "Divine Majesty."

Hence, this was not merely a "natural" vision flowing from Ignatius' unconscious desire to eat meat, but a vision to be understood in the context of his service mysticism. Ignatius spoke of the "firm will that God Himself had implanted in him to *serve* Him." Ignatius could not doubt the authenticity of this vision because it contained elements from both the "first time" to make a good election (*Ex,* no, 175) and from the consolation without previous cause (*Ex,* nos. 330, 336).

As indicated above, in the first time to make a good election, "God our Lord moves and attracts the will so that the devout soul, without question and without desire to question, follows what has been manifested to it." And *only* God can give a person consolation without previous cause, a consolation that contains no deception because it comes solely from God.[5]

Despite his firm resolve to abstain from meat, the meat vision brought with it an unshakeably "firm will" to eat meat. God's service now demanded that he mitigate his severe penances to conserve his strength for future apostolic work. Moreover, if genuine God-given mystical experiences provide the mystic with energy, clarity, and courage during crucial periods, then one must not too readily dismiss Ignatius' meat-vision as only "natural."

At Manresa Ignatius' "understanding was raised on high" (*Auto,* no. 28) to such an extent that he saw the Trinity represented like "three keys on a musical instrument." So powerful was this experience that it produced powerful bodily reactions: uncontrollable tears and sobs. More importantly, this experience proved ineradicable, grounding his lifelong trinitarian mysticism.

These visions occurred once again at Venice and Vicenza (*Auto,* no. 95) and also during his work on the *Constitutions* (*Auto,* no. 100). Trinitarian visions, of course, permeate the *Spiritual Diary.* He *saw* or *felt* the Father as a person, how the

---

[5]On this point, see my *Ignatian Mystical Horizon,* pp. 136-138.

other persons are in the Father, the Most Holy Trinity, and the Father, Son, and Holy Spirit proceeding from the divine essence.[6] He likewise saw clearly the very being or essence of God, the divine being presenting itself in lucid color, or like a sphere or a large spark.[7] Visions of the Father's being and of the close "proximity" of the Father to the divine essence also occurred.[8] Ignatius even saw or felt, in a way pregnant with meaning, the Holy Spirit "in a dense brightness, or in the color of a flame of fire..." (*SD*, nos. 14, 18).

During his stay at Manresa, Ignatius received an understanding of how God created the world, seeing a "white object with rays stemming from it, from which God made light" (*Auto*, no. 29). Moreover, with "inner eyes," he saw white rays coming from Christ's body during the elevation and understood how Christ was present in the Eucharist. On other occasions, he saw—again with his "inner eyes"—Christ's humanity in a white, undifferentiated form, or as a round gold object, or as the sun.[9] Of course, he also saw Mary with his inner eyes, as a white form "without differentiation of members" (*Auto*, no. 29).

Ignatius "saw or felt" not only Jesus in his humanity, but also how Jesus was his God (*SD*, no. 87). Experiences of feeling or seeing disclosed Jesus at the feet of the Trinity (*SD*, no. 88), the person of the Son in the person of the Father (*SD*, no. 89), Jesus as the means of union with the eternal Father (*SD*, no. 83), and the manifold ways in which Jesus mediated between Ignatius and the Trinity or the eternal Father.[10] Moreover, mystical experiences of seeing or feeling terminated not only in Jesus, but also in Mary[11] and in the saints (*SD*, no. 27).

---

[6]See *SD*, nos. 63, 83, 85, 123. It must be emphasized that Ignatius' visions usually occurred "more by *feeling* and *seeing* than by understanding" (*SD*, no. 54, my emphasis).

[7]See *SD*, nos. 99, 121, 123-125, 136, 180.

[8]See *SD*, nos. 142, 143, 153, 172.

[9]See *Auto*, nos. 29, 41, 44, 52, 99; *SD*, no. 87.

[10]For examples, see *SD*, nos. 4, 6, 12, 63, 67, 70, 75, 77, 101.

[11]For examples, see *SD*, nos. 4, 6, 12, 24, 25, 29, 30, 31.

Cherubic Experiences

On the banks of the river Cardoner, God opened the eyes of Ignatius' understanding. He was transformed into a new man with a new understanding who saw everything in a new light from that time on. This was the greatest grace of Ignatius' life (*Auto,* no. 30). Through this architectonic, synthetic, and holistic experience, he grasped how everything held together and also the particulars of many things pertaining to faith and learning.

Deeper than a vision, this foundational experience imprinted itself on his soul, endowing him with radical intellectual clarity. This "cherubic," or intellectual, experience transformed Ignatius' spiritual horizon, that is, the way he knew and would know. It was a fundamental shift in Ignatius' intellectual horizon, and resulted immediately in Ignatius' discernment of the serpent-like vision as coming from the evil spirit. It may also account for Ignatius' emphasis upon the need to discern *thoughts* very carefully in one's spiritual life.

To be sure, the *Spiritual Diary* attests to a great variety of cherubic experiences. "Thoughts" concerning the Trinity, Christ, mediators, loving reverence, matters related to the election, and the like, often penetrated to the core of Ignatius' soul and drew him to greater devotion.[12]

His understanding was often drawn with great clarity "beyond the heavens" to behold the Trinity, various aspects of the inner trinitarian life, Christ, and the like.[13] "Understandings," "elevation of the mind," "spiritual lights," "illuminations," and "transparent clarities" about the Trinity, the inner trinitarian life, Christ, Ignatius' mediators, the matter of the election, and so on, often occurred and bestowed deep devotion and delight.[14]

---

[12]See *SD,* nos. 5, 70, 156.

[13]For examples, see *SD,* nos. 70, 87, 89, 122, 136, 140.

[14]For examples, see *SD,* nos. 15, 21, 22, 26, 27, 33, 52, 54, 58, 62, 64, 65, 82, 89, 92, 111.

On occasion, he received "representations" and "advertences" of the Trinity and Christ that he distinguished from visions (*Auto,* no. 52; *SD,* nos. 74, 101). Then, too, when Diego de Hoces died, the first person to die in the Society of Jesus, Ignatius had such a clear vision of him entering heaven that it brought him great consolation and conviction about the matter (*Auto,* no. 98).

These cherubic phenomena imparted to Ignatius in one stroke more than an entire lifetime of study (*SD,* no. 52), and aided him to reason more securely in matters relating to the election (*SD,* no. 12). Even the thought of death flooded his soul with joy and consolation (*Auto,* no. 33). When certain graces took place without these intellectual lights, Ignatius considered it significant enough to note their absence (*SD,* nos. 39-40, 56). Finally, certain thoughts disturbed him, and some spiritual illuminations robbed him of the little time he had given to sleep. He rejected such thoughts and illuminations as temptations from the evil spirit (*Auto,* nos. 20, 26, 54).

Seraphic Experiences

From its effects on his life, Ignatius' La Storta experience was second in importance only to Manresa. As already mentioned, at La Storta Ignatius received a vision of the Father and of the cross-bearing Christ (*SD,* no. 67; *Auto,* no. 96). From the very depths of his soul, Ignatius heard the Father say to Christ: "I want you to take this man as your servant." Then Christ infused these words into Ignatius' heart, "I want you to serve us." Finally, the Father burned these words into Ignatius' soul: "I shall be favorable to you [plural] at Rome."

This mystical vision containing mystical words confirmed Ignatius' mysticism of service under the banner of the cross-bearing Christ. The Father infused Jesus' name into Ignatius' heart with firmness and certitude. Just as Cardoner had transformed his intellect, La Storta transformed his heart and will.[15] In short, the La Storta experience is "seraphic," an experience in which God's gifts affect primarily the mystic's will and heart. It stands out as a paradigm of Ignatius' mysticism of confirmation. This mystical event confirmed Ignatius' ever-growing desire to be placed with Christ crucified to serve.

Earlier in his life, Ignatius had experienced firmness and certitude of soul that God would bring him to the Holy Land (*Auto,* nos. 40, 42). He valued the various visions he had received, not so much in themselves, but for the specific ways in which they transformed him for God's service or confirmed a particular course of action in that service.[16] His *Spiritual Diary,* too, indicates the importance he placed upon confirmation.[17]

It is in the context of Ignatius' mysticism of confirmation that one should understand his instructions in the *Spiritual Exercises:* "After such a choice or decision has been reached I should turn with great diligence to prayer in the presence of God our Lord and offer Him this choice that His Divine Majesty may deign to *accept and confirm* it, if it be to His greater service and praise" (*Ex,* no. 183, my emphasis). The election must be understood, then, in the context of Ignatius' mysticism of service and discernment. If exercitants make the spiritual exercises well, they can and should expect God's confirmation of their decision.

Ignatius' many and varied God-given cherubic visions and mystical experiences contained a highly significant seraphic component. Furthermore, even a cursory reading of the *Spiritual Diary* discloses a wide variety of affective, or seraphic, phenomena. Ignatius spoke of "impulses," "inner movements," "inner motions," "inner visitations," "deep inner touches," "varied spiritual movements," and of being drawn, carried away, or inwardly embraced.[18] These experiences

[15]H. Rahner, *The Vision of La Storta,* pp. 64, 125.

[16]For a few examples, see *Auto,* nos. 10, 28-31, 100.

[17]For a few examples, see *SD,* nos. 6, 48, 53, 69, 70, 71, 73, 146.

[18]For examples, see *SD,* nos. 6, 8, 11, 17, 22, 26, 31, 34, 36, 43, 47, 63, 66, 69, 107-110, 153, 160.

almost always terminated in the Trinity, one specific person in the Trinity, Christ, Mary, or the saints. At times they impelled Ignatius to a practical course of action.

Experiences of "intense love," "intense feeling," "greater flavor in spiritual things," "intense affection," deep "consolations," "strength," and "surrender and reverential love" also fill the *Spiritual Diary.*[19] Numerous visions or inner impulses trigger consolation without previous cause, that is, a consolation that *only* God can give, that contains no deception, and that draws the entire person totally into the love of the Trinity, one specific person in the Trinity, Christ, Mary, or the saints.[20]

The word "devotion" occurs with great frequency in the Ignatian corpus. Broadly speaking, devotion is ease in finding God (*Auto,* no. 99), but Ignatius also used the word to connote his attitude of surrender, reverential love, and service to the ever-greater God. It also referred to his experiential affection for God manifested by the prompt and alert love by which he sought, found, and carried out God's will. Because of the ease with which he found God in all things, Ignatius' mystical devotion sought out, served, and worshipped God in all things. Because of his familiarity and union with God, devotion grounded his mysticism of discernment, decision, confirmation, service, and reverential love.

Obviously Ignatius received frequent mystical consolations, that is, graces that inspired him "with peace and quiet in Christ our Lord" (*Ex,* no. 316). The *Spiritual Diary* abounds with talk about "interior peace," "quiet of soul," a "remarkable tranquillity" of spirit, "satisfaction," "interior gentle graces," or a "great flavor in divine things."[21] Ignatius' pilgrimage to the Holy Land also brought him a joy that seemed to transcend the natural (*Auto,* no. 45). Finally, he received numerous "spiritual gifts" (*SD,* nos 36-38), but without specifying their exact nature.

---

[19]See *SD,* nos. 22, 37-38, 40, 47, 51, 63, 70, 73, 82, 83, 128, 156, 163-171.

[20]See *SD,* nos. 85, 113, 115-116, 121, 129-130, 137, 140.

[21]See *SD,* nos. 9, 11, 13, 40, 65.

One notices in the *Diary* how carefully Ignatius noted the psychosomatic reverberations accompanying the graces he received. For example, many of God's gifts produced a delightful inner and outer warmth.[22] These mystical graces seemed to radiate warmth from the very depths of his soul outward to his body. Other divine visitations caused his hair to stand on end (*SD*, no. 8) or made his veins and bodily members "sensibly felt" (*SD*, no. 47). In fact, one of his early companions recorded that he often found Ignatius after Mass with his face all aglow, "something clearly heavenly and very extraordinary."[23]

Tears

Mystical tears accompanied the trinitarian graces Ignatius received at Manresa. These graces arrived "with so many tears and sobbings that he could not control himself" (*Auto*, no. 28). From that time on, infused tears became increasingly significant for his mystical life. In fact, one commentator has noted that "it seems to me that no other saint . . . has in practice given to these tears a place equal with that of St. Ignatius."[24]

His early companions testified that unless Ignatius shed tears three times during Mass, he felt deprived of consolation.[25] Eventually his doctor forbade him to surrender to tears because it was destroying his eyesight and his overall health. As was his wont, he obeyed his doctors and received even more consolation, albeit without tears.[26]

Throughout the forty-day election recorded in the *Spiritual Diary*, Ignatius said "Mass every day with daily tears" (*Auto*,

[22]See *SD*, nos. 6, 8, 11, 22, 36, 39-40, 49, 111, 197.

[23]*Mémorial*, no. 179, p. 149.

[24]Joseph de Guibert, *Jesuits*, pp. 62-63.

[25]*Mémorial*, no. 183, p. 151.

[26]*Ibid.*

no. 100).[27] Indeed, the first part of the *Diary* mentions tears about 175 times; in the second part, every single entry mentions tears. Furthermore, sobs often accompanied these tears, with an intensity that frequently prevented him from speaking.

The *Spiritual Diary* indicates, moreover, that Ignatius experienced a great variety of tears. Some seemed to overflow from the very center of his soul into his eyes; others were not so profound. Some infused tears actually resulted from other mystical graces that opened the soul "wide" to tears (*SD,* no. 64). Other infused tears terminated in mystical experiences of the Trinity, a specific person in the Trinity, his mediators, and the like.

The *Diary* reveals that Ignatius eventually grew indifferent toward tears. Nonetheless, God instructed him for a long time to seek them for their spiritual benefits. Tears were often both the result of and the cause of a great variety of mystical gifts. It seems reasonable to assume, therefore, that the frequent references to tears in the *Diary* were in part Ignatius' shorthand way of remembering the occasion, the nature, and the circumstances of other mystical graces.

Thus it is understandable why the *Spiritual Exercises* frequently mention tears.[28] One must ask for tears because of one's sins or to commiserate with Christ suffering. So important are tears that Ignatius even suggests creating a climate conducive to them by rejecting joyful thoughts and darkening one's room. In fact, tears are specifically mentioned in Ignatius' definition of consolation: "It is likewise consolation when one sheds tears inspired by love of the Lord, whether it be sorrow for sins or because of the Passion of Christ our Lord, or for any other reason that is directly connected to His service and praise" (*Ex,* no. 316).

---

[27] In his July 1549 letter to Francis Borgia, Ignatius chided Fr. Onfroy for saying that the Society "is not well instituted." Ignatius points out that the *Constitutions* "are only partly drawn up, some parts of them being still under discussion, and even in the bulls some points are being revised, after recommending the whole matter to God our Lord with many Masses, prayers, and *tears*" (*Letters,* pp. 205-206, my emphasis).

[28] See *Ex,* nos. 48, 56, 78, 86, 195, 199, 203.

Ignatius' emphasis on consolation, desolation, and other spiritual movements during the *Exercises* (*Ex,* no. 6) also highlights the importance of tears. In fact, Ignatius linked tears to his mysticism of service, that is, consolation in the form of tears for a "reason that is directly connected to His *service* and praise."[29]

Ignatius' letter of September 20, 1548, chided Francis Borgia for his penitential excesses, especially for penances that drew blood.[30] "[I]nstead of trying to draw blood," Ignatius wrote, "seek more immediately the Lord of all, or what comes to the same thing, seek his most holy gifts such as the gift of *tears*" (p. 181, my emphasis). This letter also taught that tears may come from pondering one's sins or those of others; from contemplating Christ's life, death, and resurrection; or from a loving contemplation of the Trinity. Ignatius reminded Borgia that the higher the mind is elevated, the more worthy the thoughts. He nevertheless wrote, "But for a given person that level will be much better on which our Lord communicates more of Himself in His holy graces and spiritual gifts..." (p. 181). Hence, Ignatius intimately linked tears with nothing less than God's very own *self*-communication.

In his letter of November 22, 1553, to Father Nicholas Gaudano, however, Ignatius contended that the gift of tears should not be asked for unconditionally and that it is not a good gift for everyone.[31] If a person has true compassion for his or her neighbor and seeks actively to relieve that neighbor's miseries, tears are not really necessary. In fact, Ignatius pointedly wrote: "Even if it were in my power to allow this gift of tears to some, I would not give it, because it would be no help to their charity, and would harm their heads and their

[29]The May 22 entry of the *Diary* (no. 234) expresses the fear that the sweetness and relish from another mystical gift, that is, *loquela,* may come from the devil. Hence, paying too much attention to *loquela* may cause "the ceasing of the spiritual consolation of tears." Ignatius feared the cessation of tears because of their significance to his mysticism of discernment and service. As he said, "I then felt many tears, thinking that I *was being taught how to proceed, with the hope of always finding further instruction as time went on.*"

[30]*Letters,* pp. 179-182.

[31]*Letters,* pp. 311-312.

health and consequently stand in the way of every act of charity" (p. 312).

Thus, Ignatius assumed implicitly the same attitude toward tears as the great Eastern Fathers, especially John Cassian, John Climacus, Isaac the Syrian, and Symeon the New Theologian. For them, prayer was both "the mother and the daughter of tears." Tears signified the presence of the Holy Spirit, washed away the sins committed after baptism, and consumed spiritual and bodily impurities.

One could also shed penitential tears, tears from contemplating the hardheartedness of others, tears of fear from meditating upon judgment and hell, or tears from mystically tasting and desiring God. Forced tears or demonic tears that fed a person's vainglory and pride, however, were sinful.

Loquela

The May 11 to May 28 entries in the *Spiritual Diary* speak of the mystical gift of *loquela,* that is, "voices," "speech," "language," or "discourse."[32] Ignatius, moreover, always mentions them in conjunction with the presence or absence of tears. Two entries seem especially significant. The May 11 entry says:

> In the same way, in all the Masses of the week, although I was not granted tears, I felt greater peace and contentment throughout the whole Mass because of the relish of the *loquelas,* together with inner devotion. Those of today seemed to be much, much different from those of former days, as they came more slowly, more interiorly, gently, without noise, or notable movements, coming apparently from so deep within, my not knowing how to explain them. During the interior and exterior *loquela* everything moves me to divine love and to the gift of the *loquela* divinely bestowed. I felt so much harmony in the interior *loquela* that I cannot explain it (*SD,* no. 222).

[32]See *SD,* nos. 221-240.

The May 22 entry says:

> During the greater part of the Mass, no tears, but much
> *loquela.* I felt some doubt about the relish and sweetness of
> the *loquela* for fear it might be from the evil spirit, thus
> causing the ceasing of the spiritual consolation of tears.
> Going on a little further, I thought that I took too much
> delight in the tone of the *loquela,* attending to the sound,
> without paying so much attention to the meaning (*signifi-
> cación*) of the words (*palabras*) and of the *loquela.* I then
> felt many tears, thinking that I was being taught how to
> proceed..." (*SD,* no. 234).

Ignatius wrote of both internal and external *loquela.* He
considered them a "divinely bestowed" gift for which he
prayed (*SD,* nos. 221, 222). Some *loquela* came slowly, gently,
silently, ineffably, perhaps even "miraculously" (*SD,* no.
224), from Ignatius' deepest core in a manner reminiscent of
consolation initiated by the good spirit. That is, "In those who
are making spiritual progress, the action of the good angel is
gentle, light, and sweet, as a drop of water entering a sponge"
(*Ex,* no. 335). Other loquela, however, came more quickly,
more brusquely, with "notable movements," and from the
surface levels of the psyche.

Both the interior and the exterior *loquela* brought about
devotion, great relish, and delight. When present, everything
moved Ignatius to divine love. The interior *loquela* produce
ineffable interior harmony. It would seem, therefore, that they
either initiated or were a form of consolation without previous
cause, a consolation that God alone can give. Furthermore,
these *loquela* seem to be connected with "heavenly *loquela* or
music" (*SD,* no. 224), tones, words, and meanings.

Therefore, *loquela* seem to be mystical music, unusually
lovely in tonality, pregnant with meaning and often
accompanied by significant words. Ignatius chided himself
for being less attentive to the meaning of the *loquela* and the
accompanying words. Nevertheless, he never questioned
their divine origin. Rather, he examined their "relish" and
the "sweetness" for possible signs of the evil spirit. One

should note that he did this for fear the gift of tears would cease, and tears often "taught [him] how to proceed" (*SD*, no. 234) in the election process.

To be sure, Ignatius had experienced various types of mystical words long before he experienced *loquela*. At La Storta, from the depths of his spirit, he heard the Father and Christ speak to him in a way that transformed his heart. In his June 18, 1536, letter to Sister Teresa Rejadell, he wrote: "For it frequently happens that our Lord moves and urges the soul to this or that activity. He begins by enlightening the soul; that is to say, by *speaking interiorly* to it *without the din of words* (*voces*), lifting it up wholly to His divine love and ourselves to His meaning (*sentido*)...."[33] He also cautioned her, as he cautions in the *Spiritual Exercises* (*Ex*, no. 336), to be aware that in the aftermath of such great experiences, in which God has consoled and inspired the soul, the devil may add to or subtract from God's message. In fact, at Manresa Ignatius discerned the devil attempting to turn him away from God's service by speaking discouraging words to his soul.[34]

Nonetheless, during *loquela*, music rather than words seems to predominate. Ignatius' love of music must be kept in mind. He once saw the Trinity represented by three keys on a musical instrument. Sacred music enraptured him and nourished him both spiritually and physically.[35] Thus Ignatius is in the company of the music-loving mystics. Francis of Assisi, Catherine of Siena, Hildegard of Bingen, Richard Rolle, and Suso, to name but a few, sometimes experienced the divine harmony as heavenly song. Some even wrote music to express their mystical experiences. Mystical poetry and the dialogue nature of much mystical writing seem to indicate that God's self-communication

---

[33] *Letters*, p. 22.

[34] "It was like someone speaking within his soul" (*Auto*, no. 20), Ignatius recounted.

[35] Ignatius relates that at Manresa "he daily attended High Mass as well as Vespers and Compline, which were *always sung*, and from which he derived great consolation" (*Auto*, no. 20, my emphasis). Also see, *Mémorial*, nos. 177-178, pp. 148-149.

must be expressed in rhythmical language because of the spiritual and psychosomatic rhythm this self-communication produces.

This gift remains obscure and defies the classification of interior locutions given by St. John of the Cross. Nonetheless by way of the mystical senses, Ignatius seems to have experienced God's self-communicaton under the modality of music, rhythm, tone, and words—all pregnant with meaning. Perhaps one can even connect Ignatian *loquela* with today's charismatic phenomenon of sung glossolalia or with a meditation mantra, that is, a word selected more for its psychosomatic rhythm than for its meaning.

Concluding Reflections

Christian mystics agree that mystical visions, locutions, touches, tastes, and scents that occur at the soul's very core, that is, purely spiritual experiences, are linked intrinsically with God's self-communication.[36] Neither the devil nor the self can counterfeit them. These purely spiritual mystical experiences must be distinguished carefully from the psychosomatic shocks they cause outside the core. Yet can these core experiences themselves ever take place in a pure state? Do they not almost always produce aftereffects or concomitant effects from which they must be discerned carefully?

It appears that God's loving influx refracts itself throughout the entire body-person. Therefore other mystical experiences must be considered as the echoes, reverberations, radiations, shocks, and percolations of God's self-communication from the core into the total body-person. Through these phemonena, the mystic's psychosomatic structure assimilates and adjusts God's self-communication to his or her deepest core.

[36]Mystical theologians commonly speak of corporeal, "imaginary," and spiritual, mystical experiences. The first affect the bodily senses; the second, the inner senses; and the third, the spiritual or mystical senses, that is, the very core.

By means of these mystical, psychosomatic experiences, God purifies, illuminates, transforms, and reintegrates the entire body-person. These psychosomatic manifestations are the enfleshment of infused contemplation, showing grace's incarnational dimension. Both the devil and the self can counterfeit these manifestations, but only to a certain degree.

These extraordinary mystical experiences reveal God's intimate presence, but using the language of the mystic's psychosomatic structure. If the scriptures are God's word in human words, genuine psychosomatic, mystical phenomena express God's self-communication, or infused contemplation, in psychosomatic language.

Hence, God's pure light, voice, touch, odor, and food refract themselves into the prism of the full body-person. They reveal two things. First, they express symbolically the way the mystic's inner mystical life reaches the surface mind, and so represent both God and the mystic. Thus they should be compared to the work of a great artist. Second, they reveal something more intimate and deeper, namely, infused contemplation.

Ignatius often experienced God's loving influx primarily in the form of visions at the core of his being. Although highly deficient in imagery and symbols, they both transformed him and enlightened him about a wide range of matters. For example, Ignatius saw the Trinity represented by three keys on a musical instrument; Christ and Our Lady as a white, undifferentiated body (or in the form of the sun); the divine essence in the form of a sphere or a large spark in lucid color; the Holy Spirit in dense brightness or in the color of a flame of fire; and unspecified trinitarian experiences in light and color.

Two things must be emphasized about these experiences. First, they transformed Ignatius into another man, gave him a certainty about the faith for which he was willing to die, and confirmed his mysticism of service and discernment. Without a doubt, they are specific ways in which God communicated God's self to Ignatius.

Second, the experiences suffer from a poverty of images and symbols. God's self-communication to his spirit's very center radiated outward into cherubic, or intellectual, experiences. These spiritual insights and understandings contained only shards of psychosomatic phenomena. As one commentator has correctly noted: "For his imagination, indeed, was as weak in creating images in the symbolic order as it was strong in picturing the concrete scenes of life."[37]

Moreover, Ignatius said that most of his visions were more by feeling and seeing than by understanding, that is, they took place *ineffably,* beyond understanding, at his spirit's very apex. The clear image of Our Lady with the Christ child is an exception. The vision was produced by infused contemplation in the deepest center of his spirit, but revealed itself psychosomatically, that is, in imagery in the more superficial levels of his being. In such "imaginary visions," God's self-communication discloses itself by way of the interior senses, as noted above. Yet because of this vision's transforming effects, especially of infused chastity, it indisputably had its deepest roots in infused contemplation. This is likewise true of the La Storta visions and words, of the meat vision, and of his various mystical "representations" and "advertances."

It would seem, then, that Ignatius' "external" *loquela* are the "imaginary" aspect of the "internal" *loquela.* He experienced these musical tones, words, and meanings neither with his bodily senses nor with his spiritual senses, but with his inner senses. That is, he experienced these *loquela* from deeply within his person, but not from his inner core.

This is also true of Ignatius' seraphic, or affective, experiences. In these cases, God's self-communication to his deepest core manifested itself primarily in the will, that is, in consolations without previous cause, devotion, touches, visitations, inner tears, and the like. These began at his spirit's center, but revealed their presence a little beyond the

---

[37]Joseph de Guibert, *Jesuits,* p. 61.

point where spirit divides into intellect and will. Both the *Autobiography* and the *Spiritual Diary* are replete with examples of how these spiritual, seraphic experiences overflowed into accompanying psychosomatic ones.[38]

St. John of the Cross taught emphatically that one should never seek extraordinary mystical experiences, but instead reject everything except what God had imprinted upon the soul. In contrast to John, Ignatius said nothing about rejecting or dismissing extraordinary mystical experiences. To be sure, he carefully discerned whatever happened to him. Yet he actively sought and prized a whole variety of unusual phenomena, neither for themselves or out of spiritual gluttony, but for what they taught him about God's will.

For example, the eagerness for consolations and his slight impatience with the Trinity and Christ when they did not confirm his election, as related in the *Spiritual Diary*, were not symptoms of spiritual greed. Ignatius grew impatient because he so eagerly wanted to know and put into execution God's will. He realized mystically that it was God's will to seek God's confirmation and corroboration through mystical experiences.

These extraordinary experiences are an intrinsic part of Ignatius' mysticism of discernment, decision, and confirmation, as well as his service mysticism. They occurred at critical times in his life, bringing him peace, strength, perseverance, and discernment for and in God's service. He prized them for transforming and helping him seek, find, and carry out God's will. Thus, his mysticism of extraordinary experiences cannot be separated from other aspects of his mysticism.

It can be argued that Ignatius' dark night—when he experienced intense self-hatred, a burning desire for great penances, profound dejection, ennui, dryness, apathy, and scruples so severe that he was brought to the brink of

---

[38]Ignatius was also aware that one could dispose one's psychosomatic structure to receive God's graces. For example, he advises the exercitant to make use of light and darkness or the weather, to experiment with fasting and sleeping, and to control the imagination in conjunction with the matter to be meditated upon or contemplated. See *Ex,* nos. 79, 89, 206, 229.

suicide—was actually the reverse, or dark, side of infused contemplation. His dark night was really God's self-communication purging him of sinfulness and expanding his capacity to receive more of God's self-communication. As Ignatius' union with the Trinity and Christ intensified through frequent extraordinary mystical experiences, he likewise became more one with himself, that is, integral and whole.[39] These extraordinary mystical experiences were the means God used to transform Ignatius into a new man with a new understanding and a new heart. Eventually he was purged of all inordinate attachments, and his powers of self-reflection and self-control increased dramatically. The *Spiritual Diary* indeed shows the intensity of his recollection, his custody of the heart, and his alert sensitivity to the slightest deviation in seeking, finding, and executing God's will.

Ignatius' own unaided efforts, however, did not bring about his incredible self-control, self-mastery, and acute sensitivity to the least sign of God's will. No spiritual martinet or willful disciplinarian brought this about. Nothing less than God-given graces working in, with, and through his unique personality caused his extraordinary integrity.

Unusual mystical experiences integrated him. Hence, his mysticism is one of integration and personal wholeness. One with God and Christ, he became totally one with himself. Numerous mystical graces effected a balanced union and harmonious interaction of all his volitional, intellectual, psychological, and emotional powers.

These experiences purified, integrated, and transformed his imagination, memory, and fantasy. They christified his emotional spontaneity, his innate courage, and his generosity. God purified his will and gave him well-ordered desires, as well as an architectonic, intellectual clarity. Ignatius balanced and harmonized within himself, then, enthusiasm and reason, wholesome self-mastery, and loving integrity for God's service. As one commentator correctly notes, "Ignatius possessed an

---

[39]For the rest of this section, see Joseph de Guibert, *Jesuits*, pp. 66-67, 174-181; Harvey D. Egan, *Christian Mysticism*, pp. 44-51.

imaginative and emotional temperament joined to an outstanding power of reflection and self-analysis, and—what is
more surprising—joined above all to a will of iron."[40]

By way of extraordinary mystical experience, Ignatius
became emotionally and psychosomatically whole, as well as
reasonable, incisive, decisive, accurate in judgment, and strong
of will. Initially impulsive and impetuous, he was infused by
God with clarity of reason, prudence, and discreet love. His
powers of concentration, moreover, allowed him never to lose
sight of the essentials, to perceive accurately the exact relationship of the means to the desired end, and to pass beyond
appearances to the heart of the matter. In short, his mysticism
is one of discreet, prudential, and wise love.

The force of his character often astonished his first
companions. For example, he could make them quake, if that
were necessary for God's greater service.[41] But he likewise
awed them with his kindness, fidelity, generosity, and love.
Both strength of character and genuine love for others
attracted them to him.

His companions likewise marveled at his meticulous planning, his clear-sightedness, his calmness, and his impertur-
bability. Once he had decided what God wanted him to do, he
remained calm and immovable in the face of all opposition,
pursuing his goal steadfastly. He blended cold realism,
genuine mystical logic, and a passionate love of the Christ he
served with his entire being. In brief, Ignatius' mystical gifts
resulted in a mysticism of service that united his "passionate,
enthusiastic, and devoted love for Christ with the prudent
reflections of a firm and positive reasoning power."[42]

---

[40]Joseph de Guibert, *Jesuits,* p. 70.

[41]For this and for what follows, see *Mémorial,* nos. 26, 207, 250, pp. 62-63, 163, 185.

[42]Joseph de Guibert, *Jesuits,* p. 595. For an exposition of how Ignatius transposed
this mysticism of integration into a spirituality of integration in the *Spiritual
Exercises,* see my *Ignatian Mystical Horizon* pp. 66-85.

8

A Genuine Portrait of St. Ignatius

In his *Constitutions,* Ignatius sketched his ideal superior general.[1] Many have long considered it to be a genuine *self-*portrait. Father Louis Goncalves da Câmara wrote: "How often I have observed that in his whole manner of proceeding, the Father observes with exactitude all the rules of the Exercises. Thus he appears to have planted these rules in his own soul and then to have drawn them from his own interior acts.... The same thing is true of the Constitutions, *especially of the chapter in which he portrays the general,* in whose case he *seems to have portrayed his own self.*"[2]

This chapter will attend to this self-portrait, and so correct the skewed portrait of St. Ignatius delineated in Chapter One and summarize the various aspects of his mysticism.

The first quality required of the general of the Society of Jesus is that "he should be closely united with God our Lord and intimate with Him in prayer and all his actions, that from God, the fountain of all good, the general may so much the better obtain for the whole body of the Society a large share of

---

[1] See part IX, chapter 2, nos. 723-734.

[2] *Mémorial,* no. 226, p. 171, my emphasis. Quoted by Ganss in *Const,* p. 309, n. 1.

His gifts and graces, and also great power and efficacy for all the means which will be used for the help of souls" (*Const,* no. 723).

We have already seen that Ignatius' trinitarian mysticism rendered him intimate with each trinitarian person and plunged him into the Trinity's very heart, that is, into the divine essence. Moreover, his Christ-centered, Marian, eucharistic, and priestly mysticism, as well as his service mysticism in general, are all facets of Ignatius' radical intimacy with God.

Furthermore, his mysticism of reverential love, of divine providence, and of discernment, decision, and confirmation indicate clearly how much Ignatius looked to God as the "fountain of all good." Because his mystical union with the triune God and Christ was spiritually fecund, it overflowed into and incarnated itself in a mysticism of apostolic service "for the help of souls." It must be emphasized that Ignatius' apostolic service mysticism resulted from his trinitarian and christocentric intimacy. The latter sanctions the former.

Second, the general must possess and practice all the virtues in a way that edifies the other members (*Const,* no. 725). Ignatius served explicitly as a paradigm of Jesuit virtues for the first generation of Jesuits, as da Câmara attests.[3] These Jesuits considered it a great grace merely to be in Ignatius' presence. In fact, those sent on delicate or dangerous missions profited greatly by spending some time with him at the Roman House of Our Lady of the Way. Ignatius' sanctity not only made him holy; it extended to the entire Society. No greater compliment could be given to any first-generation Jesuit than to say he had Ignatius' mind, heart, and manner of proceeding.

The *Constitutions* go on to say that "charity should be especially resplendent in him, toward all his fellowmen and above all towards the members of the Society; and genuine humility too should shine forth, that these characteristics may make him highly lovable to God our Lord and to men" (*Const,* no. 725).

---

[3] *Mémorial,* no. 3, p. 50.

The early Jesuits often spoke of Ignatius' great love for them and of their love for him. As da Câmara wrote, Ignatius had a great penchant to love, was himself loved by all, possessed great affability, and concerned himself with everyone's well-being, especially the sick.[4] His many letters also witness to his universal charity. For example, even a man like Xavier read Ignatius' letters kneeling and in tears. What the author of the *Cloud of Unknowing* says about contemplatives, therefore, indeed applies to Ignatius: "No man is a stranger to him because he looks on each one as his brother. And none is his enemy. All are his friends."[5]

Indeed, Ignatius founded an apostolic community of love, a community held together by a mystical love of Christ and of each other to help souls—in fact, an apostolic mystical body that formed one body, heart, and spirit, obeyed one superior, and experienced Christ as their head. His was a mysticism of companionship for more effective apostolic service.

Ignatius also loved and valued humility. As already noted, he feared nothing more than vainglory. Only at his confessor's urgings did he allow himself to be elected general. Moreover, he expressly said that because the Jesuit vocation was to help souls *through humility*, Jesuits should not do the work of the Inquisition or accept ecclesiastical honors.[6]

The superior general of the Society of Jesus must also "be independent of all passions, by his keeping them controlled and mortified, so that in his interior they may not disturb the judgment of his intellect, and in his exterior he may be so

---

[4] *Mémorial*, nos. 86, 89, 104, 106, 160, 285, 332, pp. 96-97, 103-104, 139, 206-207, 227. It must be emphasized, however, that Xavier, Nadal, Hoces, and others were not immediately attracted to Ignatius. A person of such self-control, force of will, and clarity of goal is simultaneously both attractive and repellent.

[5] Chapter 24, pp. 80-81. Aelred of Rievaulx (*Spiritual Friendship,* trans. Mary E. Laker, SSND [Washington, D.C.: Cistercian Publications, 1974], p. 112) writes: "In that multitude of brethren I found no one whom I did not love, and no one by whom, I felt sure, I was not loved. I was filled with such joy that it surpassed all the delights of this world. I felt, indeed, my spirit transfused into all and the affection of all to have passed into me . . . ." Ignatius both fostered and experienced this in his own apostolic community of love.

[6] *Mémorial*, nos. 368, 382, pp. 241, 245.

composed, particularly so self-controlled when speaking, that no one, whether a member of the Society who should regard him as a mirror and model, or an extern, may observe in him any thing or word which does not edify him" (*Const*, no. 726). We have already spoken of Ignatius' long-continued ascetical practice, his frequent examinations of conscience, his total self-mastery, and his mystical integrity. Ignatius had long discovered the ascetical dimension of mysticism and the mystical dimension of asceticism.

Da Câmara gives numerous examples of Ignatius' circumspection both in speaking and in writing, his delicacy in both, and the emphasis he placed on tasteful and tactful conversations, especially with those in power, for attaining apostolic goals.[7] Ignatius blended in his person incredible self-control and recollection, as well as compassion for others and tact in dealing with them.

Even his much-maligned rules of "religious modesty" must be understood in this context. They are actually "rules of conversation and courtesy" ordered to promote personal relationships, to deepen community life, and to aid Jesuits to promote their apostolic goals, especially when dealing with persons of importance in delicate matters.

Of course, the general must also "know how to mingle rectitude and necessary severity with kindness and gentleness to such an extent that he neither allows himself to swerve from what he judges to be more pleasing to God our Lord nor ceases to have proper sympathy for his sons" (*Const*, no. 727).

The first Jesuits attest that Ignatius was often harsh with his stronger men, but easy with others, the better to develop their spiritual and apostolic potential.[8] He imposed penances, but never publicly, on those who committed faults. With those showing signs of repentance, moreover, he often immediately lessened or dropped the penances.

According to the author of the *Cloud of Unknowing,* the genuine contemplative "will even be able to discern the

---

[7] *Mémorial,* nos. 15, 88, 102-104, 145-148, 153, 192, 199, 202, 227, 236b, 238, 379.

[8] *Mémorial,* nos. 86-87, 90, pp. 96-97.

character and temperament of others when necessary. He will know how to accommodate himself to everyone...."[9] There is no doubt that Ignatius possessed this gift of discerning the "character and temperament" both of his men and of others with whom he came into contact.[10] This gift flowed not only from his mystical powers of discernment, but also from and into his service mysticism.

Moreover, "magnanimity and fortitude of soul are likewise highly necessary for him to bear the weaknesses of many, to initiate greater undertakings in the service of God our Lord, and to persevere in them with constancy when it is called for, without losing courage in the face of the contradictions (even though they come from persons of high rank and power) and without allowing himself to be moved by their entreaties or threats from what reason and the divine service require. He should be superior to all eventualities, without letting himself be exalted by those which succeed or depressed by those which go poorly, being altogether ready to receive death, if necessary, for the good of the Society in the service of Jesus Christ, God and our Lord" (*Const.* no. 728).

From what we have already seen, Ignatius' life was definitely a paradigm of magnanimity, courage, fortitude, and tenacity in searching for, finding, and carrying out God's will in service to Christ's vicar, the Pope. His intellectual and affective mystical experiences anchored him so firmly to God's will that neither persons nor any other obstacles could discourage him.

For example, he claimed that even if God destroyed the Society, it would take him only a few minutes of prayer to be fully reconciled and at peace with this will. And he was willing to die, if necessary, for God's greater praise and service.

The next quality is "that he ought to be endowed with great understanding and judgment, in order that this talent may not fail him either in the speculative or the practical matters which may arise. And although learning is highly necessary for one who will have so many learned men in his charge, still more

---

[9] Chapter 54, p. 117.

[10] *Mémorial,* no. 199, pp. 159-160.

necessary is prudence along with experience in spiritual and interior matters, that he may be able to discern the various spirits and to give counsel and remedies to so many who will have spiritual necessities.

"He also needs discretion in exterior matters and a manner of handling such diverse affairs as well as of conversing with such various persons from within and without the Society" (*Const,* no. 729).

Ignatius, of course, embodied these ideals. Cardoner had given him a new understanding, and further cherubic and seraphic graces deepened his mystical prudence, discretion, discernment, and ability to guide others. His approach to education and learning may have been pragmatic, but he earned nevertheless higher degrees as part of his ecclesial mysticism of apostolic service. He also respected both "positive and scholastic theology" (*Ex,* no. 363), underscoring the affective side of the former and the intellectual side of the latter. And his service mysticism of discreet love deeply and effectively involved him in the social and political realms of his day.

The general's next quality, "one highly necessary for the execution of business, is that he should be vigilant and solicitous to undertake enterprises as well as energetic in carrying them through to their completion and perfection, rather than careless and remiss in such a way that he leaves them begun but not finished" (*Const,* no. 730).

What we have already said about Ignatius speaks for itself. Promptness, exactitude, thoroughness, painstaking discernment, meticulous planning, and unwavering perseverance resulted from Ignatius' ecclesial mysticism of service, discernment, decision, and confirmation.

The fifth quality "has reference to the body. In regard to health, appearance, and age, on the one hand, account should be taken of propriety and prestige, and on the other hand, of the physical energies which his charge requires, that in it he may be able to fulfull his office to the glory of God our Lord" (*Const.* no. 731).

Ignatius suffered much from the ill health brought on by the cannonball leg injuries, the successive operations, butcheries, excessive penances, and gallstones. Still, this never prevented him from carrying out his office with incredible energy and zeal. The Christian mystical tradition confirms that the mystical life of itself often brings with it extraordinary physical and psychological stamina. This was obviously true in St. Ignatius' life. Moreover, the mystical life normally graces a person with wisdom and poise, making them attractive to others both in spirit and body. Clearly, Ignatius attracted people through his spiritual and even physical bearing.

The sixth quality the ideal general should possess "pertains to extrinsic endowments. Among these, preference ought to be given to those which help more toward edification and the service of God in such a charge. Examples are generally found in reputation, high esteem, and whatever else aids toward prestige with those within and without" (*Const,* no. 733).

This exemplifies, of course, Ignatius' penchant to use all human means for God's greater praise and service. We have already seen that Ignatius labored zealously to preserve both his reputation and that of the Society, and that to offset attacks upon the Society he used letters of recommendation from those who have seen the Society's good works firsthand. It must be emphasized, however, that his concern for reputation, high esteem and prestige can only be understood correctly in the context of his service mysticism.

Also, the general "ought to be one of those who are most outstanding in every virtue, most deserving in the Society, and known as such for a considerable time. If any of the aforementioned qualities should be wanting, there should at least be no lack of great probity and of love for the Society, nor of good judgment accompanied by sound learning" (*Const,* no. 735).

To be sure, Ignatius had attained the heights of virtue in and through his extraordinary mystical experiences and mystical life. These likewise endowed him with integrity, uprightness, circumspection, and prudence. Although never an intellectual, his service mysticism taught him the value of solid and sound learning.

Ignatius' mysticism, moreover, cannot be understood without the "explicit vow to the sovereign pontiff as the present or future vicar of Christ our Lord. This is a vow to go anywhere His Holiness will order, whether among the faithful or the infidels, without pleading an excuse and without requesting any expenses for the journey, for the sake of matters pertaining to the worship of God and the welfare of the Christian religion" (*Const.* no. 7). As we have emphasized, his Christ-centered service mysticism was incarnated and sacramentalized in an ecclesial mysticism, a mysticism both Roman and papal.

It is clear, therefore, that the ideal superior general finds its full realization in Ignatius because he unconsciously projected himself into the portrait of the ideal superior general. Ignatius remains the paradigm of every Jesuit superior general, in fact, of every Jesuit and all whose spirituality is Ignatian. And it is precisely because of his mysticism that he was and is this paradigm.

Saints, even religious founders, can be ephemeral. Their person, mysticism, spirituality, and the like may have value for only their region or for only a particular period of time. How many saints and mystics have had the privilege to leave behind a lasting patrimony, a universal message, and be a source for the mysticism and spirituality of the ages that follow?[11] St. Ignatius of Loyola is such a mystic. He is a "creative prototype" whose person, writings, and heritage can and should form the subject of today and tomorrow's mysticism, spirituality, and theological reflection.[12] His explicitly trinitarian, christocentric, eucharistic, mediator, Marian, service, ecclesial, reverential love, and discernment mysticism significantly shaped Catholic spirituality after the sixteenth century. This mysticism and its derivative spirituality, moreover, have fed the spiritual lives of countless Jesuits, religious orders of men and women whose spirituality is Ignatian, and

[11] For an excellent introduction to Ignatius' heritage, see J.F. Broderick, S.J., "Jesuits," *New Catholic Encyclopedia* 7 (New York: McGraw Hill, 1967), pp. 899-909.

[12] Karl Rahner ("Logic of Ignatius," pp. 85-87) says this about Ignatius' *Spiritual Exercises*.

numerous others who for various reasons came into contact with this radical form of spirituality.

Out of Ignatius' mysticism came a religious order that gave the Church a multitude of saints and blesseds. This order sent missionaries to all parts of the world to preach the gospel and to establish or reform the Church. Jesuits have been scholars in just about every field. One might even argue that the Jesuits have produced a unique theological tradition.[13] Also, the Jesuit *Ratio Studiorum,* or method of study issued in 1599, was responsible for the often-astonishing success of Jesuit secondary education from the sixteenth century to the present day.

Jesuits were also confessors to the heads of state and to those of power in the Church. The history of the Society of Jesus glows, then, with men of incredible talent and ability, but also with men of lesser talent whose silent and efficient service for Christ got the job done.

In every age, through periods of social and political calm or upheaval, Jesuits have done the one thing necessary in a more or a less glamorous way: they have loved God with their whole heart and soul and their neighbors as themselves. Regardless of the country, the situation in the country and the Church, Jesuits have been intimate with God, living in apostolic communities of often banal, humdrum, daily love and serving in a variety of ways. Because of their mysticism of involvement, the Jesuits were controversial and hated enough to be suppressed in 1773, but nonetheless controversial and loved enough to be restored in 1814. Much to Ignatius' credit, Jesuits in the twentieth century are still controversial, still loved and hated.

Ignatius' secret is his mysticism and spirituality. These are acutely sensitive to the call of grace at the heart of individuals, groups, institutions, and social movements. Call it contemplation in action, seeking and finding God's will in all things,

---

[13]See Avery Dulles, S.J., "Saint Ignatius and the Jesuit Theological Tradition," *Studies in the Spirituality of Jesuits* XIV/2 (March 1982) (St. Louis: Institute of Jesuit Sources, 1982), pp. 1-21.

familiarity with God that demands "helping souls" by radical social and political involvement, God's greater praise and service, the third degree of humility, *magis,* a mysticism of joy in the world—nonetheless, Ignatius' mysticism and spirituality is one of unrestricted love of God, as well as discreet love and service of the world.

Ignatius lived and harmonized the tension of mystical familiarity with God and pragmatic service. His mysticism is radically humanistic because it is christocentric. And his humanism is radically theocentric because it resulted from his experience of God's triune and Christ's divine-human unity. It is a mysticism of social and political involvement because of the ever-greater God who poured himself out for love of the world.

St. Ignatius, the mystic, is especially important today because his mysticism has been and can still be decanted into a spirituality that purifies and transforms the universal, human, threefold religious sense. Every human being has an immense longing for transcendence, for belonging totally to the world, and for radical interiority. This threefold religious sense finds its fulfillment only in a genuine trinitarian spirituality centered on the all-transcendent Father, on the Son as God in the world, and on the Holy Spirit who is true interiority.

Ignatius' Father-centered mysticism fulfills the need of an ecstatic, vertical experience of the all-transcendent Father, the ever-greater God, that is, God-*above*-us.

His Son-centered mysticism fulfills the human need for God-*with*-us, that is, for life's horizontal, earthly meaning to be fulfilled. Imbedded in Ignatius' christocentric mysticism is a mysticism of apostolic service that comprehends implicitly how love of neighbor *is* actually love of God. A Son-centered spirituality is one that loves the earth, sees everything as a sacrament of the divine presence, and contemplates the resurrection as the pledge of a yet to be fulfilled earth and new humanity.

Ignatius likewise awakens us to God-*in*-us, to an *en*static experience of God's gift of self to our deepest interiority, making us connatural with the Father and Son of Love.

Finally, the experiences of the triune God—the divine community united in ineffable oneness who loves the world to the point of the Son's having died on the cross and risen—underpins Ignatius' mysticism of being with the triune Christ to serve apostolically in a community of love.

Selected Bibliography

(Focusing Especially on Works in English.)

Bibliographical Works

Guilmont, Jean Francois, S.J. and Daman, Paul, S.J. *Bibliographie Ignatienne* (1948-1957). Museum Lessianum, section historique, no 17. Paris and Louvain: Desclée de Brower, 1958.

Iparraguirre, Ignacio, S.J. *Oreintaciones bibliográficas sobre san Ignacio de Loyola.* Subsida ad historiam Societatis Iesu, no. 1, 2nd. ed., rev. Rome: Institutum Historicum S.I., 1965.

Polgár, László, S.J. *Bibliographie sur l'historie de la Companie de Jesus,* 1901-1980. I. *Toute la Companie.* Rome: Institutum Historicum S.I., 1981. This work contains extensive entries of publications on St. Ignatius, his life, his works, his mysticism, his spirituality, and the like, which have appeared from 1901 to 1980.

Ruiz, Jurado, Manuel, S.J. *Oreintaciones bibliográficas sobre san Ignacio de Loyola,* Vol. II (1956-1976). Subsida ad historiam Societatis Iesu, no. 8. Rome: Institute Historicum S.I., 1977.

Sources

(The abbreviations are those of the Institute of Jesuit Sources.)

MHSJ—MONUMENTA HISTORICA SOCIETATIS JESU: The historical sources or records of the Society of Jesus in critically edited texts. This scholarly series now contains 124 volumes. It was begun in Madrid in 1894 and transferred to Rome in 1929. Most of the manuscripts on which these volumes are based are in the archives of the Society of Jesus in Rome. The series is being continued by its publisher, the *Institutum Historicum Societatis Iesu,* Via dei Penitenzieri 20, 00193 Rome.

MI—MONUMENTA IGNATIANA: a section of MHSJ that contains the writings of St. Ignatius and of his contemporaries.

SERIES I

EppIgn—S. Ignatii...Epistolae et Instructiones. Edd. M. Lecina, V. Augustí. F. Cervós, D. Restrepo. 12 vols., Madrid, 1903-1911. The letters and instructions of St. Ignatius.

SERIES II

*SpEX*MHSJ—*Exercitia Spiritualia S. Ignatii...et eorum Directoria.* Ed. A. Codina. 1 vol. Madrid, 1919. The critical text of the *Spiritual Exercises* and of the *Directories* for conducting them. For an English translation, see *Autograph Directories of Saint Ignatius of Loyola.* Trans. by Bernard Bush, S.J., Jersey City, Program to Adapt the Spiritual Exercises. For an English translation of the *Official Directory of 1599,* which certainly has its root in St. Ignatius himself, see: *The Spiritual Exercises of St. Ignatius of Loyola,* trans. W.H. Longridge. London, 1919.

NEW SERIES II. A REVISION

*Sp Ex*MHSJTe—Vo. I. *Sti. Ignatii de Loyola Exercitia Spiritualia. Textuum antiquissimorum nova editio. Lexicon textus hispani.* Edd. J. Calveras and C. de Dalmases. Rome, 1969. A revision of *SpExMHSJ.*

DirSpEx—Vo. II. *Directoria Exercitiorum Spiritualium* (1540-1599). Ed. I. Iparraguirre. 1 vol. Rome, 1955. This is a more ample edition of the *Directories* than the earlier one of 1919 in *SpExMHSJ.*

SERIES III

ConsMHSJ—*Constitutiones et Regulae Societatis Iesu.* 4 vols. The critically edited texts of the *Constitutions* and *Rules* of the Society of Jesus, along with copious introductions and notes.

ConsMHSJ, I—Vol. I. *Monumenta Constitutionum praevia.* Ed. A. Codina. Rome, 1934. Sources and records previous to the texts of the *Constitutions.* Historical introductions.

ConsMHSJ, II—Vol. II. *Textus hispanus.* Ed. A. Codina. Rome, 1936. Critical texts of the four chief and successive texts of the Spanish original.

ConsMHSJ, III—Vol. III. *Textus latinus.* Ed. A. Codina. Rome, 1938. The critical text of the Latin translation that was approved by the first general congregation of the Society in 1558.

ConsMHSJ, IV—Vol. IV. *Regulae Societatis Jesu.* Ed. D.F. Zapico. Rome, 1948. Ancient drafts of rules or directives.

SERIES IV

SdeSI—*Scripta de Sancto Ignatio.* Edd. L.M. Ortiz, V. Augustí, M. Lecina, A. Macia, A. Codina, D. Fernández, D. Restrepo. 2 vols. Madrid, 1904, 1918. Writings about St. Ignatius by his contemporaries.

SERIES IV. A REVISION

FN—Fontes narrativi de S. Ignatio de Loyola et de Societatis Iesu initiis. Edd. D. Fernández Zapico, C. de Dalmases, P. Leturia. 4 vols. Rome, 1943-1960. Vol. I—1523-1556. Vol. II—1557-1574. Vol. III—1574-1599. Vol. IV—Ribadeneira's *Vita Ignatii Loyolae* (1572). Narrative sources, that is, writings about Ignatius by his contemporaries. An enlarged edition of the documents contained in *SdeSI.*

FD—Fontes Documentales. Ed. C. de Dalmases, S.J., 1977. On his family, country, youth, and acquaintances.

St. Ignatius' Works

Obras completas de San Ignacio de Loyola. Introductions and notes by Ignacio Iparraguirre, S.J., and Cándido de Dalmases, S.J. 4th ed., rev. Biblioteca de Autores Cristianos, no. 86. Madrid: La Editorial Católica, 1982. This volume contains the Spanish critical texts of all St. Ignatius' major works, except his letters. There is, however, a good selection of his letters.

Nicolas, de T. Antonio, *Powers of Imagining. Ignatius of Loyola. A Philosophical Hermeneutic of Imagining through the Collected Works of Ignatius de Loyola with a Translation of These Works,* Albany: S.U.N.Y, 1986. After a long introductory essay, this book contains English translations of Ignatius' *Spiritual Exercises, Spiritual Diary, Autobiography,* and some of his letters. Many of the footnotes are based on the *Obras completas* text. Be careful of the typos.

Autobiography

St. Ignatius' Own Story as Told to Luis González da Câmara. Translated by William J. Young. Chicago, 1956; Loyola University Press reprint, 1968.

The Autobiography of St. Ignatius of Loyola, with Related Documents. Edited with introduction and notes by John C. Olin. Trans. by Joseph F. O'Callahan. Harper Torchbooks. New York: Harper and Row, 1974.

A Pilgrim's Journey: The Autobiography of Ignatius of Loyola. Introduction, translation, and commentary by Joseph N. Tylenda, S.J. Wilmington, Del.: Michael Glazier 1985.

A Pilgrim's Testament: The Memoirs of St. Ignatius of Loyola, as faithfully transcribed by Luis Goncalves da Câmara and newly translated into English by Parmananda R. Divarkar. Rome: Gregorian University Press, 1983.

The Constitutions

The Constitutions of the Society of Jesus. Translated, with an introduction and a commentary, by George E. Ganss, S.J. St. Louis: Institute of Jesuit Sources, 1970.

Letters

Letters of St. Ignatius of Loyola. Selected and translated by William J. Young, S.J. Chicago: Loyola University Press, 1958.

Saint Ignatius Loyola, Letters to Women, by Hugo Rahner. Trans. Kathleen Pond and S.A.H. Weetman. New York: Herder and Herder, 1960.

Spiritual Diary

The Spiritual Journal of St. Ignatius of Loyola, February 2, 1544 to February 27, 1545. Trans. William J. Young, S.J. *Woodstock Letters* 87 (1958), 195-267.

Counsel for Jesuits. Selected Letters and Instructions of Saint Ignatius of Loyola. Ed. Joseph N. Tylenda, S.J. Chicago: Loyola University Press, 1985.

Commentaries on the Letters and Spiritual Diary of St. Ignatius of Loyola, Plus the Autograph Text of the

Spiritual Diary by Simon Decloux, S.J. Rome: Centrum Ignatianum Spiritualitatis, 1980.

Spiritual Exercises

The Spiritual Exercises of St. Ignatius. A new translation based on studies on the language of the *Autograph,* by Louis J. Puhl, S.J. Westminster, Md., 1951. Reprinted Chicago: Loyola University Press, 1968.

The Spiritual Exercises of St. Ignatius. Trans. Anthony Mottola, with an introduction by Robert W. Gleason, S.J. Garden City, N.Y.: Doubleday, 1964.

Selected Lives

Broderick, James, S.J. *St. Ignatius of Loyola. The Pilgrim Years.* London, 1956.

Dalmases, Cándido de, S.J. *Ignatius of Loyola. Founder of the Jesuits.* Trans. Jerome Aixalá, S.J. St. Louis: Institute of Jesuit Sources, 1985.

Dudon, Paul, S.J. *St. Ignatius of Loyola.* Trans. W.J. Young, S.J. Milwaukee, 1949.

Leturia, Pedro de. *Inigo de Loyola.* Trans. Aloysius J. Owen. Syracuse, N.Y.: LeMoyne College Press, 1949.

Purcell, Mary. *The First Jesuit, St. Ignatius of Loyola.* Dublin and Westminster, Md., 1956, 2nd ed., rev. Chicago: Loyola University Press, 1981.

Ribadeneira, Pedro de. S.J. *The Life of Blessed Father Ignatius of Loyola.* London: Scholar Press. This is the first biography of Ignatius, and from someone who knew him well.

Particular Aspects

Bangert, William V., S.J. *A History of the Society of Jesus.* St. Louis: Institute of Jesuit Sources, 1962.

Bertrand, Dominique. *La politique de S. Ignace de Loyola: Analyse Sociale.* Paris: Les Éditions du Cerf, 1985.

Câmara, Louis Goncalves da, S.J. *Mémorial.* Traduit Roger Tandonnet, S.J. Paris: Desclée de Brouwer, 1966. An excellent French translation of the remembrances of the Jesuit to whom Ignatius dictated his *Autobiography.*

Clancy, Thomas, S.J., *The Conversational Word of God. A Commentary on the Doctrine of St. Ignatius of Loyola Concerning Spiritual Conversation, With Four Early Jesuit Texts.* St. Louis: Institute of Jesuit Sources. 1978.

Egan, Harvey D., S.J. *The Spiritual Exercises and the Ignatian Mystical Horizon.* St. Louis: Institute of Jesuit Sources, 1976.

Futrell, John C., S.J. *Making an Apostolic Community of Love. The Role of the Superior according to St. Ignatius of Loyola.* St. Louis: Institute of Jesuit Sources, 1970.

Guibert, Joseph, de S.J. *The Jesuits: Their Spiritual Doctrine and Practice. A Historical Study.* Trans. W.J. Young, S.J. Chicago, 1964. Reprinted St. Louis: Institute of Jesuit Sources, 1972. One of the best overall books on Ignatius and history of the Society of Jesus available.

_____, *St. Ignace mystique d'aprés son Journal Spirituel.* Toulouse, 1938.

Haas, Adolf, S.J. "The Mysticism of St. Ignatius according to His *Spiritual Diary,*" *Ignatius of Loyola. His Personality and Spiritual Heritage.* Ed. Friedrich Wulf, S.J. (St. Louis: Institute of Jesuit Sources, 1977), 164-199.

König-Nordhoff, Ursula. *Ignatius von Loyola: Studien zur Entwicklung einer neuen Heiligen-Ikonographie im Rahmen einer Kanonisationskampagne um 1600.* Berlin: Gebr. Mann Verlag, 1982. This volume contains almost 550 photos of the sacred art focused on Ignatius that began around 1600.

Rahner, Hugo, S.J., *The Vision of St. Ignatius in the Chapel of La Storta*. Trans. Robert O. Brennan, S.J. Rome: Centrum Ignatianum Spiritualitatis, 1979.

_____, *Ignatius the Theologian*. Trans. by Michael Barry. London and New York: Herder and Herder, 1968.

_____, *Ignatius the Man and the Priest*. Rome: Centrum Ignatianum Spiritualitatis, 1977.

Rahner, Karl. S.J. *Ignatius of Loyola*. With an historical introduction by Paul Imhof, S.J. Color photographs by H.N. Loose. Trans. Rosaleend Ockenden. London and Cleveland: Collins, 1979. This volume contains Rahner's well-known article, "Ignatius of Loyola Speaks to a Modern Jesuit," 9-38.

_____, *Spiritual Exercises*. Trans. Kenneth Baker, S.J. New York: Herder and Herder, 1965.

Ravier, André, S.J. *Ignace fonde la Companie*. Paris: Bellarmin-Desclée, 1974.

Saldarriaga, Rodrigo Mejia, S.J. *La Dinámica de la Integratión Espiritual*. Rome: Centrum Ignatianum Spiritualitatis, 1980.

Toner, Jules, A., S.J. *A Commentary on Saint Ignatius' Rules for the Discernment of Spirits*. St. Louis: Institute of Jesuit Sources, 1982.

Wulf, Friedrich, S.J., ed. *Ignatius of Loyola: His Personality and Spiritual Heritage 1556-1956*. St. Louis: Institute of Jesuit Sources, 1977. This volume contains important articles on Ignatius' personality, spirituality, mysticism, and the like.

Important Articles

Bertrand, Dominique, S.J., "Ignatius von Loyola und die gesellschaftliche Dynamik seines Lebensprogramms," *Geist und Leben* 4 (1986), 261-269.

Broderick, J.F., S.J. "Jesuits," *New Catholic Encyclopedia* 7.

Dalmases, Cándido de, S.J. "Ignatius of Loyola," *New Cathoic Encyclopedia* 7, 354-356.

Buckley, Michael, S.J. "The Structure of the Rules for the Discernment of Spirits," *The Way. Supplement* 20 (1973), 19-37.

Costa, Maurizio, S.J. "Spiritual Discernment," *Progressio* 48 (1979), 3-12, 21-29.

Dulles, Avery, S.J. "Saint Ignatius and the Jesuit Theological Tradition," *Studies in the Spirituality of Jesuits* XIV/2 (March 1982). St. Louis: Institute of Jesuit Sources, 1982, 1-21.

Egan, Harvey D., S.J. "Christian Apophatic and Kataphatic Mysticisms," *Theological Studies* 39/3 (September 1978), 399-426.

Futrell, John C., S.J. "Communal Discernment," *Studies in the Spirituality of Jesuits* (November 1972), 159-194.

_____, "Ignatian Discernment," *Studies in the Spirituality of Jesuits* (April 1970), 47-88;

Guibert, Joseph de, S.J. "Mystique ignatienne,'" *Revue d'ascétique et de mystique* 19 (1938), 3-22; 113-140.

Guillet, Jacques, S.J. "Discernment of Spirits," *Dictionnaire de spiritualité ascétique et mystique,* III. Trans. Sister Innocentia Richards. *Discernment of Spirits.* Collegeville, Minn.: Liturgical Press, 1970.

Mollat, Donatian, S.J. "Le Christ dans l'expérience spirituelle de saint Ignace," *Christus* 1 (1954) 23-47.

Olphe-Galliard, M., S.J. "Contemplation ignatienne," *Dictionnarie de spiritualité et mystique* III, 2023-2029.

O'Malley, John W., S.J. "The Fourth Vow in its Ignatian Context," *Studies in the Spirituality of Jesuits* 15/1 (January 1983), 36-37.

Orsy, Ladislas, S. J. "Towards a Theological Evaluation of Communal Discernment," *Studies in the Spirituality of Jesuits* (October 1973), 139-188.

Rahner, Karl, S.J. "The 'Spiritual Senses' according to Origen," and "The Doctrine of the 'Spiritual Senses' in the Middle Ages," *Theological Investigations* 16, 81-103, 104-134.

──────────, "The Logic of Concrete Individual Knowledge in Ignatius Loyola," *The Dynamic Element in the Church.* Trans. W.J. O'Hara. New York: Herder and Herder, 1964, 86-87.

──────────, "The Ignatian Mysticism of Joy in the World," *Theological Investigations* III. Trans. Karl-H. and Boniface Kruger (Baltimore: Helicon, 1967), 277-293.

Sheets, John, S.J., "Profile of the Spirit: A Theology of the Discernment of Spirits," *Review for Religious* 30 (1971), 363-376.

Stierli, Josef, S. J., "Ignatian Prayer: Seeking God in All Things," *Ignatius of Loyola,* ed. Friedrich Wulf, 135-163.

Toner, Jules J., S.J. "The Deliberations that Started the Jesuits. A Commentary of the *Deliberatio primorum Patrum.* Newly translated with a Historical Introduction," *Studies in the Spirituality of Jesuits* (June 1974), 179-216.

──────────, "A Method of Communal Discernment of God's Will," *Studies in the Spirituality of Jesuits* (September 1971), 121-152.

Truhlar, K., S.J. "La découverte de Dieu chez saint Ignace de Loyola pendant les derniéres années de sa vie," *Revue ascetique et mystique* 24 (1948), 313-337.

Veale, Joseph, S.J. "Ignatian Prayer or Jesuit Spirituality," *The Way. Supplement* 27 (1976), 11.

Vercruysse, O., S.J. "Our Creator and Lord," *Ignatiana* Ranchi, 1956, 244-249.

General Works on Christian Mysticism

The Collected Works of St. John of the Cross. Trans. K. Kavanaugh, O.C.D. and O. Rodriguez, O.C.D. Washington, D.C.: Institute of Carmelite Studies, 1973.

Egan, Harvey D., S.J. *Christian Mysticism. The Future of a Tradition.* New York: Pueblo, 1984.

——————, *What Are They Saying About Mysticism?* Ramsey, N.J.: Paulist, 1982.

Guibert, Joseph de, S.J. *The Theology of the Spiritual Life.* Trans. Paul Barrett, O.F.M.Cap. New York: Sheed and Ward, 1953.

Otto, Rudolf. *The Idea of the Holy.* Trans. John W. Harvey. New York: Oxford University Press, 1958.

Poulain, August, S.J. *The Graces of Interior Prayer.* Trans. Leonora L. Yorke Smit. Westminster, Vt.: Celtic Cross Books. 1978.

Rahner, Karl, S.J. *Visions and Prophecies.* Trans. Charles Henkey and Richard Strachan. New York: Herder and Herder, 1964.

Saudreau A., S.J. *The Degrees of the Spiritual Life.* Trans. Bede Camm, O.S.B. London, 1926.

Underhill, Evelyn, *Mysticism.* New York: E.P. Dutton, 1961.

Studies in the Spirituality of Jesuits (St. Louis: Institute of Jesuit Sources) has been publishing important fascicles since 1969 on a variety of Ignatian topics.

Index

Index

About the Author

Harvey D. Egan, S.J., having completed philosophical and theological studies at Woodstock and Boston College, went on to recieve his doctorate of Theology from Westfälische Wilhelms-Universität, West Germany in 1973. He later served as an Associate Professor at Boston College and recently earned the title of Bannan Distinguished Professor of Religious Studies at Santa Clara University. His previous books include *The Spiritual Exercises and the Ignatian Mystical Horizon, What Are They Saying About Mysticism?* and *Christian Mysticism: The Future of a Tradition.* He is also widely known for his articles and book reviews which have appeared in *Theological Studies, The National Catholic Reporter* and others.